MOTIVATION AND EMOTION
IN SPORT

Motivation and Emotion
in Sport
Reversal Theory

John H. Kerr

Institute of Health & Sports Sciences
University of Tsukuba
Tsukuba, Ibaraki 305, Japan
kerr@taiiku.tsukuba.ac.jp

Published in 1997 by Psychology Press Ltd
27 Church Road, Hove, East Sussex, BN3 2FA, UK

http://www.psypress.co.uk

Reprinted 2002

Psychology Press Ltd, Publishers
27 Church Road, Hove
East Sussex, BN3 2FA, UK

Psychology Press is part of the Taylor & Francis Group

© 1997 by Psychology Press Ltd

British Library Cataloguing in Publication Data
A catalogue record for this book is available from the British Library

ISBN 0-86377-499-7 (hbk)
ISBN 0-86377-500-4 (pbk)

Typeset by Gilbert Composing Services, Leighton Buzzard, Beds.
Printed and bound in the UK by TJ International Ltd, Padstow, Cornwall

This book is dedicated to my father, John Kerr,
the most courageous man I have ever known.

Contents

Preface

In September 1974, aged 19, I arrived at what was then Loughborough College of Education in England, along with more than a hundred other freshers. We came supposedly to spend three or four years learning how to teach Physical Education, but the truth was that many of us just wanted to play sport. The group comprised enthusiastic and extremely fit and talented young sportsmen from almost every sport imaginable. Some were already performing successfully at international level, many had been schoolboy internationals, and almost all had been the best sportsmen and something of heroes in their respective schools. Little did we know it at the time, but we had willingly stepped into a melting pot that would test our motivation, competitiveness, and dedication to the limit.

My sport was rugby union and it wasn't long before the full realisation of the journey I had embarked on hit home. Arriving in September meant that time for training and team practices was short. Sessions had to be highly intense prior to Loughborough's first match of the season. I well remember wandering over to my first training session at the running track, something I had not associated with rugby training before. There I met those players who had returned from the previous year, a few other newcomers who had been invited to attend, and the coach, Scotsman Jim Greenwood. We put in a hefty session of track work in which, even though it was new to me, I was keen to keep up with the other players. I should say at this point that, as a 6ft 5in and 16 stone second row player, I found that doing interval sprint work against much lighter and faster flankers and threequarters on the track was tough work, to say the least.

The sprint training ended and I thought that my first training session was over. I was privately congratulating myself on doing reasonably well when Jim ordered us over to a plateau in the middle of a short but steep hill close to the track. There we pulled on our boots and paired off for one-on-one scrummaging work. I was paired with another fresher, Fran Cotton. Fran, who was three years older and heavier than I, would shortly be selected to play prop for the full England team; later he would be a mainstay of the British Lions in New Zealand and South Africa. Anyone who knows anything about rugby knows that a second row has little chance against a prop when it comes to one on one scrummaging, let alone someone of Fran's calibre. Needless to say, for the next 30 minutes or so, I was crucified. After the scrummaging, again to my surprise, the training session still wasn't finished. Jim, the coach, paired us off again and, exhorting us to greater efforts in a way that only he could, announced that we would finish off with a series of sprints up the nearby hill.

Somehow I managed to complete the hill work and, completely exhausted, I walked slowly back to my room in the halls of residence. There I filled one of the old-fashioned deep baths with hot water and, with the water up to my chin, lay there for well over an hour, soaking out the aches and pains and realising that rugby at Loughborough would be the biggest challenge I had yet faced. There was no let-up in the training, but ten days later I was selected to play my first match for the Loughborough 1st XV, this time fortunately packing down behind Fran in the scrum. The match was against Staffordshire and my immediate opponent was Mike Davies, an England International. I had always enjoyed playing in important games and against tough opponents and this game was no exception. I enjoyed it thoroughly. All the tough training and aches and pains had been worthwhile.

Although I was not particularly interested in sport psychology at the time (that would come later), in these first months at Loughborough I probably learned more about myself and psychology than at any other time in my life. Many of the topics addressed in this book, such as coping with potentially stressful situations, enjoying the thrills of playing sport at a high level, being aggressive and on occasion violent, and experiencing the emotions associated with winning and losing, were brought home to me on a decidedly personal level. Yet, that first year at Loughborough was one of my most successful because, as well as Fran and myself, the team also included Steve Smith, Clive Rees, Louis Dick, Dick Cowman, and John Gray, all of whom would become top international players, and my second-row partner, Maurice Trapp, who would later gain fame as a very successful Auckland coach. It was a tremendous team and I consider myself very privileged to have been able to play with them.

Some ten years later, having completed my degree at Loughborough and a part-time Masters degree in Educational Psychology, I found myself in the position of teaching physical education students at the University of Ulster, where my responsibilities included teaching sport psychology and bio-mechanics. Eventually, as these subjects became more and more specialised, I was able to leave aside biomechanics and concentrate on my real interest, sport psychology. At that time (around 1980), sport psychology in the UK was still somewhat of a fledgling subject, received with a certain scepticism amongst sports people and without much respect from psychologists working in the more traditional areas of psychology. Psychology textbooks rarely mentioned sport and few research studies were sports-based. Partly as a response to this lack of interest in sport, but also as part of my own career development, I was determined to obtain a PhD from a psychology department.

I was fortunate to be able to enrol (again part-time) at the University of Nottingham under Tom Cox's supervision. Tom proved to be an outstanding supervisor and soon I was carrying out experiments, analysing data, and trying to write up research papers. My particular interest was focused on the relationship between arousal and performance and, as part of the research process, I undertook a literature search. The available theoretical work on the effects of arousal on performance in sport was largely limited to so-called drive theory and inverted-U hypothesis explanations. However, on a personal level, these explanations just did not fit my own and what I observed of my team mates' experience in rugby (I was still playing for the Irish club, Ballymena at the time), nor did they fit with what I knew of the performances of participants in other sports. Tom Cox and his colleagues in work psychology had developed one model and, after considerable searching, I discovered another approach, known as reversal theory, which seemed to offer more valid explanations of the psychological processes taking place in sport. I was more than willing to incorporate these approaches into my doctoral work and subsequently to concentrate my academic work firmly on reversal theory.

Reversal theory had appealed to me right from my first contact with its concepts and ideas. Not only did Mike Apter, in his book *The experience of motivation* use frequent examples from sport, but his arguments fitted in well with my own experience. I am pleased to be able to say that research on sport has become a major focus of my work in the Reversal Theory Society and sports-based research is currently being carried out in the US and Canada, the UK and Europe, Japan and Australia. In addition, the reversal theory approach has generated interest and gained a degree of credibility amongst sport psychologists. Virtually all new sport psychology textbooks now include a description of reversal theory.

Tremendous interest in the theory has also been shown by students and this book is directed to them. There is now a critical mass of reversal theory sports-based research material which warrants the writing of this book. It will not be possible, nor do I wish to review all possible studies or previous work carried out on topics in sport psychology like motivation or personality. There are a variety of other texts where such reviews can be read. The intention here is to highlight reversal theory work, so that only other work that links in with reversal theory or, in some cases, presents an important rival approach, is referred to.

In fact, there has been a plethora of sport psychology books of late. Few say anything different and most appear to provide more of the same. Reversal theory *is* different and this book *does* say something different. In addition, it attempts to make what it says accessible to students and others keen to learn about the potential of reversal theory for extending their understanding of motivation and emotion in sport.

Taking a longer-term perspective, although considerable progress has been made in reversal theory sports research, the programme is still in its infancy. This book is offered in the hope that it will add to applications of reversal theory in sport psychology by sparking new discussion and argument and generating new lines of inquiry.

In closing, my thanks are due to all those sports people who have helped to organise or volunteered to take part themselves as subjects in reversal theory research studies. Reversal theory work could certainly not have been developed to the extent it has without their assistance. I would also like to thank my colleagues amongst the dedicated group of reversal theory researchers across the world who comprise the Reversal Theory Society. We have had tremendous fun together over the last few years. The central figure within this group is, of course, Mike Apter, and I would like to thank him for his continuing support and, in particular, his reading of, and comments on, the drafts of this book. In this regard, I am also indebted to Mieke Mitchell who remains, at one and the same time, my greatest critic and strongest supporter. Thanks are also due to Iain Brown, Jonathan Males, Aidan Moran, and Dierdre Scully for their helpful comments, and suggestions on earlier drafts of this book. Finally, I would like to thank Comfort Jegede for taking on this book project, and Michael Forster, Sonia Sharma and Rachel Windwood at Psychology Press for their professional approach in seeing it through to publication.

ACKNOWLEDGEMENTS

The author is grateful to Taylor & Francis for permission to reproduce Figures 4.2, 4.3 and 4.4, George Wilson for permission to reproduce Figures 5.3a, b, c, Academic Press for permission to reproduce Figure 6.1, the National Coaching Foundation (England) for permission to reproduce Figure 6.2, Mike Apter for permission to reproduce Figure 9.1, and John Wiley & Sons for permission to reproduce Table 10.1. Thanks are also due to Mike Apter, Mark McDermott and Mike Apter, and Sven Svebak who gave their permission for the reproduction of Telic Dominance Scale, the Negativism Dominance Scale and the Tension and Effort Stress Inventory, respectively.

1

Introduction

The sports pages of Saturday newspapers are often mundane. Most of the week-end sport is about to happen. Sports editors generally fill these pages with articles that either review what has happened in the previous week or speculate on the outcome of the coming weekend's sports events. On Saturday 2 July 1994, the back page of one newspaper was far from mundane. It ran four major stories. One was based on rumours about the future plans of a world sports figure; a second concerned the expulsion of a star performer from a world sports competition; another concerned a lifetime ban for yet another top sports person; and a fourth focused on the climax of an outstanding career in sport. Two were stories of tremendous success, about performers in their prime, and the other two were sad stories of personal failure, which brought disgrace to the stars concerned.

The newspaper concerned happened to be *The Japan Times*, an English-language newspaper, which includes syndicated stories from other newspapers and press agencies in the US, Europe, and other parts of the world. It may just have been an editing coincidence that all four appeared on the same sports page, but these were four of the hottest sports stories in 1994. The contents of the stories contrasted sharply with each other and each raised different questions about the motivation of the top athletes concerned. To anyone interested in what motivates people in sport, that atypical back page and those four articles were especially fascinating.

The events reported in the newspaper and the questions they raise are worth examining. By doing so, the observer can begin to gain some insight into the complex and intriguing nature of the motivational processes involved in sports. Probably the best place to start is with the lead story on that Saturday in July.

1

MARADONA GETS BOOT FROM CUP

In June, the World Soccer Cup being played in the US was to be the scene of the downfall of one of the game's stars. In an early Cup match Argentina were playing Nigeria. The star, Maradona of Argentina, had an exceptional game. The weather was hot and humid yet the 33-year-old Argentinian captain was still running and chasing around the field when other, younger players were showing the effects of fatigue. Argentina won the match 2–1. Five days later the story of the biggest scandal in World Cup history broke.

At a press conference it was announced that "Diego Maradona has violated the provisions of doping control regulations". In spite of his denial, he was withdrawn from the Argentinian team and sent home.

Maradona had been one of two players chosen at random for a post-game urine sample. The procedure was that the sample was divided in two and the second sample was analysed only if the first proved to be positive for banned drugs. It later transpired that analysis of both the first and second samples indicated the presence of five illegal substances, including ephedrine, phenyl-propanolamine, pseudo-ephedrine, non-pseudo-ephedrine, and methylephe-drine. In *The Japan Times* (2/7/94, p.22) a member of FIFA's executive committee, Michel d'Hooghe, a medical doctor, said:

> Maradona must have taken a cocktail of drugs because the five identified substances are not found in any one medicine . . . It is absolutely scientifically proved that these products have a positive action on the central nervous system, increasing the player's ability and physical action. That is absolutely certain.

Maradona spoke with Argentinian television in tears, telling, the viewers, "I did not take drugs and above all I did not let down those who love me". He also told the Brazilian team doctor that, to counteract an allergy, he had taken Decidex and Naftizol, two medicines he bought in Argentina. However, according to the doctor, their effect would have been minimal.

People in Argentina were devastated. Their hero, whose name they had chanted after the victory over Nigeria, had disgraced the whole nation. Now, instead of playing in his twenty-second game in the World Cup finals, which would have been a new record, he was suspended and sent home, the villain of the piece. Argentina reached the last 16, but were eliminated from the World Cup by Romania. Later in August, Maradona was banned for 15 months and fined 20,000 Swiss francs by FIFA officials in Switzerland.

Maradona had first played for Argentina as a 16-year-old in 1977; he led them to World Cup victory in 1986 and in 1990 captained the team that lost in the final to West Germany. He had broken the world record in transfer fees three times. Maradona had been in trouble with the soccer authorities before for using cocaine. He tested positive after a game for Naples where he played from 1984–1991 and received a 15-month ban.

What could have caused Maradona to take such a huge risk? He must have known that players in the World Cup were being given random doping checks. Was it perhaps that he realised that his phenomenal skill, speed, and control, his complete mastery over both soccer ball and opponents, was not what it had been in previous World Cup competitions? Was this just an extension of his previous drug abuse? Someone who had been banned for cocaine use might, in circumstances of high pressure and national expectation, see the solution to his diminishing ability in taking stimulants. For one who had been at the pinnacle of soccer when he led his team to victory in 1986, was this the only means open to him for achieving his previous level of success?

JORDAN MUM ON RUMOUR HE'LL QUIT BASEBALL, RETURN TO BULLS

Imagine you are at the height of your career as a professional sportsman and have led your team to three consecutive national championships. A fellow professional has described you as the most exciting, awesome player in the game today and a journalist has said you are the best and most influential player in the history of your sport. You make over $40 million a year and you can command more or less any salary you ask for from your sport. Just when it seems that absolutely everything is going for you, you decide to retire from the sport that has made you famous throughout the world to take up a sport you have not played since your high-school days. Impossible? Crazy irrational behaviour? Not at all. This story is true. The sportsman in question is Michael Jordan, star of the Chicago Bulls professional basketball team.

The previous summer he had made the decision to stop playing basketball and to start playing baseball. By the summer of 1994, Jordan had made remarkable progress and was playing baseball for the Birmingham Barons in the US, AA Southern League. There were frequent speculations during the summer of 1994 about his possible return from baseball to basketball. The reports all proved to be based on unsubstantiated rumours. Michael Jordan confirmed his departure from basketball with a last farewell exhibition game in Chicago on 9 September. The game was a sell-out, attracting more than 18,600 fans to Chicago stadium. Playing against other top basketball players and three of his former team mates in the game, Jordan's team won by 187–150 points and he personally was successful with 24 out of 46 shots, scoring 52 points. In spite of being out of basketball for a year, Jordan showed all of his skill and ability, using his full range of reverse dribbles, drives and dunks, and layups. Jordan had proved that he could still perform at the top level[1]. What

[1]Michael Jordan did, of course, return to the game of basketball and the Chicago Bulls in the spring of 1995 with devastating effect. Within a few games of his comeback he was playing as well as ever, scoring 55 points in a 113–111 victory against the New York Knicks. It seemed that the short period he had spent playing baseball was enough to whet his appetite again for basketball.

commonsense explanation or theory of motivation could account for him giving up all his success? Why had his strong intrinsic motivation (see e.g. Vancil, 1994) and the enormous extrinsic rewards not served to keep him playing basketball for longer?

Some of his post-game quotes (*The Japan Times*, 11/9/94, p.22) provide a clue as to why he may have made the decision:

> It meant a lot to me. It's given me a lot, and I think I've given it a lot. It's mutual love and understanding. It's time to move on.

> I can still do this . . . I just don't have to do it in front of 18,676. I can do it in any gym with any people I want. That's a rare freedom.

> The game of basketball has always been a part of me . . . I never said I'd stop playing the game, I just said I wouldn't play organized basketball.

It seems that, in spite of still having a tremendous feeling for the game, Jordan felt somehow restricted by the constraints of organised basketball and all that that entails in contemporary professional sport. He talked about enjoying the freedom of playing when, where, and with whom he liked. In addition, he said, "It is time to move on". As a player, he was recognised as being the best in basketball, but he had achieved everything there was to achieve, he needed a new challenge and that challenge was to be found in baseball (Vancil, 1994, p.84):

> One thing I would like to do, either when I'm through playing or one of these summers when I do have free time, is play baseball. I haven't totally dismissed that yet. I'd really like to go to a training camp, which I can't do because it's in the middle of our season, and give it a shot. I wouldn't have to stay there long, but I'd really like to see if I could do it. I'm serious. I'd love to try. It's an unfulfilled part of my life because I was never able to do what I wanted in college.

HARDING STRIPPED OF U.S. TITLE, BANNED FOR LIFE BY SKATE BODY

In July, a five-member disciplinary panel of the US Figure Skating Association took the US championship away from Tanya Harding and banned her from the association for life. It was a severe punishment for her part in the attack on her rival Nancy Kerrigan, which the disciplinary panel stated "evidence a clear disregard for fairness, good sportsmanship and ethical behavior". In an attempt to make it easier for Harding to become US champion and qualify for the US Olympic team, her ex-husband and three accomplices plotted the attack on Kerrigan, the defending women's champion.

On 6 January, a single assailant used a short black weapon to strike Kerrigan a savage blow to her right knee as she left the ice after practice at Detroit's Cobo Arena. If the blow had been slightly lower it might have shattered her kneecap and put her future in skating in jeopardy. As a result of the injury, 24-year-old Kerrigan was forced to withdraw from the national championships which the US Figure Skating Association was using as trials for the Winter Olympics in Lillehammer, Norway, and Harding became national champion for a second time.

Harding's attorney denied that she had any prior knowledge of the assault, but there was evidence enough to indicate to the panel that she not only had prior knowledge, but was also involved prior to the incident. Two of the attackers testified that Harding was in on the plot and she was named as an unindicted co-conspirator by a grand jury in Portland. Other evidence included bank and phone records, video evidence, and statements by two witnesses. In addition, Harding had previously admitted that she had conspired to hinder the prosecution of the attackers. The ban will prevent Harding from competing or coaching in any skating events authorised by the association. In effect, the career of a top-rank skater was finished.

It could have been that, even though Harding was skating better than she had for some time, she may have been aware that her closest rival was also performing extremely well. Kerrigan had won two competitions, the Piruetten in Norway and the AT&T Pro Am in Philadelphia, prior to the US champion-ships. Could it have been fear of failure, fear of not qualifying for the Olympics and missing a chance of a medal, fear of being displaced by Kerrigan from the top of her sport, that drove Harding to such a desperate means of trying to eliminate her rival?

NAVRATILOVA ONE WIN SHY OF 10TH CROWN

In the world of women's tennis, few players have come close to the achievements of Martina Navratilova since her career began in 1974. In a career with a record 165 doubles titles and 167 singles titles, she had already won nine Wimbledon Championships; in July 1994 she was battling to win her tenth. She progressed steadily through the draw until she played Gigi Fernandez in the semi-final. Fernandez, Navratilova's friend and practice partner, known for her doubles play, has not been so successful in singles games. Nevertheless, tennis buffs were treated to an exciting and thrilling match, one of the best women's games at Wimbledon for years. Navratilova won and went on to meet Conchita Martinez in the final. She told *The Japan Times* (2/7/94, p.22):

> This is what I dreamed about. This is what I wanted—to go out in style. Win or lose, I'll be going out in style. I'm going to enjoy the moment.

In the final, another game full of tension and emotion, she lost in three sets. Martinez became 1994 Wimbledon women's champion. Martina Navratilova's dream had not quite been fulfilled. A few months later she would play her last singles match at the Virginia Slims Championships at Madison Square Garden in New York. There she would bid farewell to singles tennis after a career spanning 22 years. After the game, in an emotional farewell, she was presented with a Harley-Davidson motorcycle and a banner, the first for a woman, was raised to hang in the Garden in her honour. It seems unlikely that her achievements will ever be surpassed. When asked what she thought her legacy to sport would be and what she would miss most (*The Japan Times*, 17/11/94, p.22), she said that she considered herself:

> a consummate professional, giving it everything I had on court and off court, and striving for excellence.

> Playing against the best, playing against champions, that's the treat.

Navratilova is a very determined woman, but how was she able to keep performing well at the top level in tennis for so long? Was it the challenge of professional tennis, which she clearly enjoyed? Was there something special about her psychological hardiness and mental toughness that enabled her in tense matches to come through as the winner, outlasting opponents who often cracked under the pressure? How was she able to mobilise her enormous resources of stamina, strength and endurance as the challenge became even greater in the latter years of her career when she was up against younger and possibly fitter and stronger opponents?

CONCLUDING COMMENTS

This was easily the most interesting sports page reported in the newspaper during the summer of 1994. A summary of these articles is included here because they provide a useful introduction to some of the important aspects of human motivation in sport. These four articles help to illustrate the point that, when the motivation of individual sports participants is examined, it is likely to have a widely diverse and unique character.

As the book progresses, the motivation and emotional experience of sports performers will be explored in much greater detail. To carry out this task in an effective manner, the arguments and explanations presented will be set within a relevant theoretical framework. Such a framework must be comprehensive and sufficiently refined to be easily and directly applicable to the sports context in the broadest way. Few, if any of the theories currently on offer in the sport psychology literature can meet these criteria.

In this book, the underlying framework is provided by reversal theory (Apter, 1982), the key elements of which are presented in the next chapter.

NOTE

The factual information and the quotations from athletes, included above, were primarily obtained from newspaper articles which are listed below in date order.

REFERENCES

Apter, M.J. (1982). *The experience of motivation: The theory of psychological reversals.* London: Academic Press.

Jordan mum on rumour he'll quit baseball, return to Bulls. (1994, 2 July). *The Japan Times*, pp.21–22.

Harding stripped of U.S. title, banned for life by skate body. (1994, 2 July). *The Japan Times*, p.22.

Maradona gets boot from Cup. (1994, 2 July). *The Japan Times*, p.22.

Argentina's reaction swift, harsh for fallen idol. (1994, 2 July). *The Japan Times*, p.20.

Navratilova one win shy of 10th crown. (1994, 2 July). *The Japan Times*, p.22.

Maradona gets 15-month ban. (1994, 25 August). *The Japan Times*, p.20.

Maradona doubts he will play again; blames FIFA for making life miserable. (1994, 4 September). *The Japan Times*, pp.19–20.

His airness makes court appearance. (1994, 11 September). *The Japan Times*, pp.21–22.

Sabatini victory spoils Navratilova's farewell. (1994, 17 November). *The Japan Times*, p.24.

Tennis all-time winner wraps up on losing note. (1994, 19 November). *The Japan Times*, p.22.

Jordan is highest paid athlete. (1994, 6 December). *The Japan Times*, pp.19–20.

Vancil, M. (1994). *Rare air.* San Francisco: Collins Publishers.

2 Key Elements in Reversal Theory

Reversal theory (Apter, 1982) is a theory of personality and motivation which has a number of unique and innovative features. Summarising these features, reversal theory (a) is a *general theory* applicable to diverse areas of psychological investigation; (b) is a *phenomenologically based* theory concerned with subjective processes, cognition and affect, and the experience of one's own motivation; (c) is *structural* in the sense that phenomenological experience is thought to be influenced by certain structures and patterns; (d) posits that human beings are *inherently inconsistent* in their behaviour; and (e) argues that alternating or *reversing* between paired *metamotivational states* forms the basis of human personality and motivation.

These points are some of the important basic elements of reversal theory (see Fig. 2.1). The following sections in this chapter will expand on these points, so that the reader has a clear idea of the key elements of the theory and how they might relate to sport.

METAMOTIVATIONAL STATES AND REVERSALS

Perhaps the two most important concepts in reversal theory are the concepts of metamotivational states and the reversals that are thought to take place between these states. Metamotivational states are *frames of mind* to do with the way a person interprets his or her motives at any given time. These states do not determine motives, or necessarily affect behaviour directly, but they are concerned with how people experience their motives. In this sense, these states are considered to be *meta* or higher-order states. Reversal theorists have hypothe-

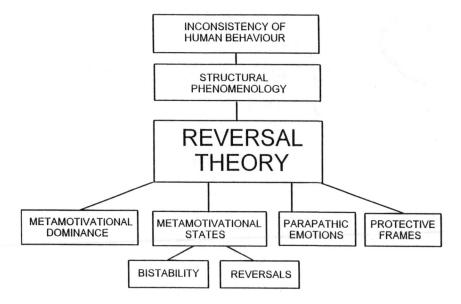

FIG. 2.1.   The main concepts in reversal theory (from Kerr, 1994).

sised that there are four different pairs of metamotivational states at work in the individual's motivational processes. These are the *telic–paratelic, negativistic–conformist, mastery–sympathy*, and *autic–alloic* pairs (see later).

Pairs of alternative metamotivational states are thought to co-exist separately within what are known in cybernetics as *bistable systems*. A simple example of a bistable system is provided by switching an electrical appliance on or off, where either of the two states (on or off) represents an alternative stable position. A system exhibits bistability if it tends to maintain a specified variable, despite external disturbance, within one or another of two ranges of values of the variable concerned. Bistable systems form the basis of the reversal experience. Reversals are the switches that take place between operative metamotivational states in any one metamotivational pair.

Incidentally, the four pairs of metamotivational states interact together within a multistable system—a more complex version of the bistable system that operates between individual pairs of states. Metamotivational state combinations and their interactive relationship will be examined later in this chapter, where it will be shown that reversal theory is a multistable theory of motivation.

One way of explaining the relationship that exists between the two metamotivational states in any pair is to make an analogy. Consider, for example, two people playing musical instruments together. Both people are playing stringed instruments, one a harp and the other a guitar. Imagine a musical arrangement that includes both instruments, but allows only one, either the harp or the guitar, to be played at any one time. Each instrument makes a contribution to the musical piece, playing in sequence with frequent changes and irregular periods of play. In this analogy the harp might, for example, represent the telic metamotivational state and the guitar its opposite, the paratelic metamotivational state.

Under normal circumstances, individuals reverse between these states frequently, but each individual will vary in the amount of time spent in the telic or paratelic state. People are thought to alternate or reverse between each stable state in the same way that either the harp or guitar is played in the musical composition. The switches or reversals back and forth in the music are similar to the way that reversals take place in everyday life.

METAMOTIVATIONAL STATE CHARACTERISTICS

A person's behaviour in the telic state (from the ancient Greek *telos* meaning "goal" or "end") is typically serious and goal-oriented. It tends to involve planning ahead and is future-related, as in many work or study situations. In this state people generally have a preference for experiencing low levels of *felt arousal* (the degree to which a person feels him or herself to be worked up). In the paratelic state, (from the ancient Greek *para* meaning "beside" or "alongside") a person's behaviour is spontaneous, impulsive and sensation-oriented, with a preference for high levels of felt arousal. In this state goals, rather than being serious in a long-term perspective, can be used to import more pleasure to a situation. Consequently, the enjoyment of present experiences, for example when surfing or skiing, has priority and people will try to prolong them as long as possible.

If the negativistic state is operative people tend to be rebellious, stubborn, and defiant. They feel a strong need to break rules or react against any outside imposition, for example, skipping training or breaking a coach's curfew. Conversely, people in the conformist state are generally agreeable and cooperative and easily comply with rules or requirements. The rules of many sports, including rules about behaviour, dress, and etiquette, mean that participants will often be in the conformist state when taking part. Combinations of these two pairs of states give rise to what are known in reversal theory as somatic emotions (see later).

As the name suggests, in the mastery state people are concerned with being masterful. Their present situation will be perceived as some kind of competition or struggle in which they are tough and strong in an attempt to gain control over, for example, an opponent. In this pair, the opposite sympathy state is about empathy with others, for example, the feelings of harmony or unity common among the members of a sports team.

The fourth and final pair of metamotivational states also focus on interactions with other people or objects. In the autic state (from the ancient

Greek *auto* meaning "self"), people are concerned with themselves and gain satisfaction from the outcome of any interaction in terms of what happens to themselves. In American football a specialist field-goal kicker may be more concerned with his personal success rate than the actual outcome of the game for his team. When the alloic state (from the ancient Greek *allo* meaning "other") is operative in any interaction, people are focused on what happens to other people or things. Pleasure and satisfaction are gained from a successful outcome in terms of what happens to the other party. A fan or spectator attending a sports event in which his or her team is playing may empathise closely with the team and individual team members, revelling in their successes and feeling dejected and depressed by their failure. In this context, the fan may well have the alloic state operative.

Combinations of mastery–sympathy and autic–alloic states give rise to what are known in reversal theory as transactional emotions (see later). In the same way that felt arousal is an important aspect of hedonic tone in the first two pairs of states, *felt transactional outcome* (the degree to which a person feels him or herself to have gained or lost in an interaction) is the key variable with respect to experience within the mastery–sympathy and autic–alloic states. However, in terms of the mastery–sympathy states, *felt toughness* (the degree to which a person feels him or herself to be tough, strong, or in control at a given time) and *felt tenderness* (the degree to which a person feels him or herself to be tender, sensitive, or caring at a given time) also play a crucial role.

The characteristics of the four pairs of metamotivational states are shown in Fig. 2.2.

THE MECHANISMS OF REVERSAL

Of course, people in sport or even daily life do not reverse according to something equivalent to a musical score. A better analogy might be the sort of jazz or blues music that occurs during jam sessions where there is no set music and musicians play off the cuff and improvise. This may be similar to the involuntary, often unexpected nature of reversals and the inherently inconsistent ways that individuals behave.

Reversals between metamotivational states are likely to be triggered in one of three ways (see Fig. 2.3). First, a reversal may be sparked by some form of environmental stimulus (see e.g. Svebak, Storfjell, & Dalen, 1982). This type of inducing agent may be referred to as *contingent*. For example, consider a female recreational sailor sailing a dinghy across open water in good weather and sailing conditions. She may be in the paratelic state, enjoying the experience of the feeling of speed and the spray from the water as the dinghy flies along. However, in trying to come about and sail back in the opposite direction she makes a mistake while manoeuvring and the boat capsizes. This type of contingent factor may spark a reversal from the paratelic to telic state. The sailor, now in the cold water struggling with a capsized dinghy, must

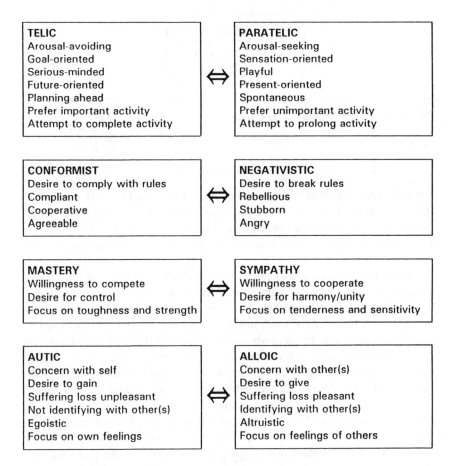

FIG. 2.2.   Characteristics of the four pairs of metamotivational states.

attempt to right the boat and get underway again. Her state of mind has changed from being relatively playful and spontaneous, and has become very purposeful and serious.

However, for another female sailor taking part in a competitive race, the same contingent factor, a capsize, might prompt a reversal in the opposite direction. In terms of the race, suppose that this sailor is up with the leaders and uppermost in her mind is the need to reach the next buoy before her co-contestants. She is in the telic state. Constant checks are made on the wind direction, the speed of the dinghy, and the best approach to make to the buoy. When the capsize occurs she finds herself in the cold water, but realises that there is no chance now of finishing in a good position in the race. A reversal takes place (prompted by the capsize, a sudden environmental event) to the paratelic state and the sailor, released from the demands of competition and

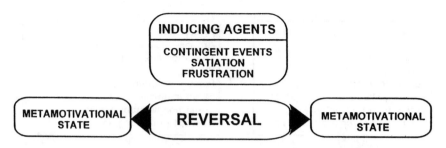

FIG. 2.3.   The reversal process with inducing agents (from Kerr, 1994).

seeing the humorous side of the situation, somewhat more playfully attempts to right the dinghy. Thus, the same contingent factor could, depending on the operative state of the sailor concerned and the circumstances pertaining at the time, spark a reversal from the paratelic to telic metamotivational state or vice-versa.

Second, reversals may take place as a result of conditions of *frustration*, through not being able to obtain satisfaction in the operative state (see e.g. Barr, McDermott, & Evans, 1990). For example, a male tennis player is taking part in a competitive tennis match in the national championships. The player is a good all-round player but depends heavily on a powerful service and resultant weak returns from opponents to set up point-winning chances using volley shots. Typically, the tennis player has the conformist state operative when playing, sticking to the rules of the game and following the code of etiquette. In this particular match his service is working well and he wins the first set easily. During the second set his opponent adopts a more attacking approach to returning serve. This works and, after a struggle, his opponent wins the second set. The player tries harder in the third set, but finds that his powerful first service will not go in. He adjusts his stance and technique slightly, without success. He loses the third set. By now his opponent is becoming more and more confident and returning serve easily. In this fourth set the tennis player tries harder and harder but nothing seems to work. On top of this the umpire calls a couple of serves out that he was sure were in. He asks the umpire about the calls but the decisions are upheld. His serve is now becoming more and more erratic and at a crucial point in the fifth game he serves two double faults. Out of sheer frustration, as he sees the second serve enter the net, he slams his racquet into the ground and swears loudly, kicking the racquet to the back of the court. He receives a warning from the umpire and now, feeling angry, he is verbally abusive to the umpire. He receives a penalty, which makes it even easier for his opponent to win the set and the match. In this example, the tennis player, frustrated by his own poor performance and inability to lift his game, reversed from the conformist to the negativistic state. His emotional reaction to frustration and disappointment led to unacceptable behaviour on court.

Finally, where a person has been in one metamotivational state for some time, the likelihood of a reversal taking place is increased as a result of *satiation* (see e.g. Lafreniere, Cowles, & Apter, 1988). Think, for example, of two male work colleagues out for a lunchtime run in a city park. Their run, which follows a trail around the park perimeter, will take just under forty minutes. The runners are of similar but not quite equal ability. For much of the run the superior runner, in the sympathy state, is happy to run at his partner's pace which is a little slow for him. As the run goes on, the less able runner begins to flag. The more able runner, still in the sympathy state slows slightly and encourages his partner to keep going. During their run this happens a couple of times. Towards the end of the run, about half a mile from home the superior runner, having been in the sympathy state for most of the run, suddenly experiences a reversal from sympathy to mastery state. He increases his pace and says to his partner, "Let's stretch it out to the finish". The less able runner, accepting the challenge, finds some extra energy and stays with him most of the way. However, the more able runner, with the mastery state operative, is determined to beat his partner and increases the pace yet again, this time leaving his partner behind and reaching the finishing point first.

As mentioned earlier, reversals are thought to be involuntary (Apter, 1982, p.42), but as Potocky and Murgatroyd (1993, p.18) state:

> ... people may place themselves in circumstances that will increase the possibility of reversals occurring. For example, after a stressful day at work in the telic state, people may intentionally go to a bar where the music, the ambiance, other's laughter and alcohol are all external contingencies that increase the likelihood of a reversal to the paratelic state.

METAMOTIVATIONAL DOMINANCE

Some individuals have a tendency or predisposition to spend more time in one or other of a metamotivational pair of states. These individuals are said to be, for example, *mastery dominant* or *sympathy dominant*. People who are mastery dominant spend a good deal of their time in the mastery state, while those who are sympathy dominant spend most of their time in the sympathy state. Although people may be mastery or sympathy dominant, they do reverse. It is not the case that they never spend time in the opposite metamotivational state. Several psychometric reversal theory instruments have been developed to measure the various forms of metamotivational dominance. These include the Telic Dominance Scale (TDS; Murgatroyd, Rushton, Apter, & Ray, 1978; see Appendix D); the Paratelic Dominance Scale (PDS; Cook & Gerkovich, 1990); the Negativism Dominance Scale (NDS; McDermott & Apter, 1988; see Appendix E); and the Motivational Style Profile (MSP (formerly known as the Personal Orientation Profile); Apter, Mallows, & Williams, 1995).

Metamotivational dominance has been shown to be important in the sports context. Telic or paratelic dominance plays a crucial role in the way that athletes experience stress (Summers & Stewart, 1993) and is a factor in people's preference for and participation in certain types of sport. *Explosive* sports (e.g. baseball, cricket) and *endurance* sports (e.g. long distance running and hiking; Svebak & Kerr, 1989) have been found to be associated with telic dominance and paratelic dominance, respectively, and dangerous sports (e.g. parachuting and motorcycle racing; Kerr, 1991) have been found to be associated with aspects of paratelic dominance. Negativism dominance has been linked to talented teenage performers of sports such as sprinting, jumping events, slalom skiing, and racquet sports (Braathen & Svebak, 1992) and the sports-related activity of soccer hooliganism (Kerr, 1994).

The findings of several of these research examples have shown that, in many sports, the role of the individual's bias or tendency towards avoiding or seeking arousal is of special importance. Apart from *dominance aspects* of arousal seeking and avoiding (explored further in Chapter 3), in any situation, the experience of arousal within, for example, the telic and paratelic states is strikingly different. This difference is outlined in the next section.

THE EXPERIENCE OF AROUSAL

Over the years, the concept of arousal, or activation as it is sometimes termed, has been one of the most enduring in psychology. Other theories in psychology have generally conceived arousal as a unitary variable representing an individual's level of motivation at any given time. For example, optimal arousal theory (Fiske & Maddi, 1961; Hebb, 1955), essentially a homeostatic theory, argues that a person's preferred level of arousal will be in the moderate range, where positive hedonic tone and performance are optimal. This is not the stance taken by reversal theory. The bistable arrangement between meta-motivational states in reversal theory gives it considerable advantage over homeostatic theories concerning the experience of arousal which, for a number of reasons, have been found to be inadequate (see e.g. Kerr, 1985, 1989).

In reversal theory, arousal is linked to two different metamotivational systems and the relationship between arousal and hedonic tone (experienced pleasure) is bistable rather than homeostatic. Amongst several definite characteristics associated with the telic and paratelic states, shown in Fig. 2.4, is a preference for a different level of arousal in each state. Typically, for the telic–paratelic pair of states the preference is for low and high felt arousal respectively, and positive hedonic tone and feelings of (telic) relaxation and (paratelic) excitement result. Conversely, high levels of arousal in the telic state and low levels of arousal in the paratelic state are associated with negative hedonic tone, and feelings of (telic) anxiety or (paratelic) boredom result (see Fig. 2.4). Reversals can, for example, result in pleasant feelings of excitement, emanating from high arousal in the paratelic state, being experienced as

	Telic state	Paratelic state
High arousal	Unpleasant (anxiety)	Pleasant (excitement)
Low arousal	Pleasant (relaxation)	Unpleasant (boredom)

FIG. 2.4. Relationship between telic or paratelic state, hedonic tone, and level of arousal.

unpleasant feelings of anxiety in the telic state. Or pleasant relaxation, emanating from low arousal in the telic state, may become paratelic boredom, perhaps as a result of a reversal due to satiation. Generally speaking, mismatches or discrepancies between preferred arousal and felt arousal are thought to provoke stress in the individual (see Chapter 9). Note however, that the relationship between the telic–paratelic pair and arousal takes the form of a *preference* and that, under certain conditions, high levels of felt arousal in the telic state or low levels in the paratelic state may well be tolerated.

As space in this chapter is somewhat limited, the intention here has merely been to underline the importance of arousal as a key element of reversal theory. The way that arousal in a whole range of sports is interpreted is so crucial to understanding the performers' sports experience that the topic will be returned to again and again later in this book.

METAMOTIVATIONAL STATE COMBINATIONS

To illustrate the concept of metamotivational state combinations, the musical analogy described earlier can be extended to make a foursome by including two woodwind instruments, such as the clarinet and the flute. The same conditions need to apply as with the harp and the guitar. A new composition has been written in such a way that only one of each pair of instruments can be played at one time. In other words, there are four possible instrument combinations; harp and clarinet, harp and flute, guitar and clarinet, guitar and flute. A new musical composition requires that each combination of stringed and woodwind instruments makes an unequal and different contribution to the music. For example, the woodwind instruments, clarinet and flute, represent the negativistic and conformist metamotivational states respectively. In this case, the various musical combinations represent possible metamotivational combinations of the four states (telic negativistic, telic conformist, paratelic negativistic, paratelic conformist). How might these different metamotivational state combinations work in sports?

For example, when players, in dispute with team owners or managers, walk out of training or go on strike, they are likely to have the telic–negativistic state combination operative (e.g. the conflict between US baseball players and management in 1994; the "walkout" by Dutch soccer player Edgar Davids after being dropped from the team by the manager during the Euro '96 tournament; the conflict between rugby union players and the rugby authorities in England in 1996).

There are many aspects of judo that appear to suit the characteristics usually associated with the telic and conformist states. For example, in judo there is a goal-oriented pyramidal system of coloured belts for various levels of achievement. Judo players must also conform to a dress "code" and are often asked by officials during competition to replace clothing that has been pulled loose during combat. At the beginning and end of competitive bouts, antagonists must complete the traditional formal bow towards an opponent. Actually on the mat, contestants are very much focused on the goal of throwing their opponent but, of course, in judo strict controls exist, and that may only be done by means of the accepted techniques for throwing opponents. All of this points to the likelihood that judo contestants are in the telic conformist state when competing.

A person playing recreational beach volleyball, soccer, or cricket may well have the paratelic and conformist metamotivational states operating in tandem. The rules of the game, at least in some simple form, have to be conformed to, but at the same time a person can enjoy all the fun and excitement of the paratelic-oriented game in which winning does not really matter.

Examples where the paratelic and negativistic states might be operating together would include rebellious negativistic sporting activities like climbing up or abseiling down a tall building just for the hell of it. These types of activities are often banned by the authorities and those who try them are often arrested for their efforts, a development that of course adds to feelings of excitement, especially if the people concerned can avoid being apprehended. So-called "extreme sports", such as skiing down Everest or canoeing down near-vertical rapids, may also be carried out by people with the paratelic and negativistic states operative.

Eight emotions (termed *somatic emotions* in reversal theory) result from the various metamotivational state combinations just described. They are relaxation, anxiety, placidity, anger, excitement, boredom, provocativeness, and sullenness, and are all linked closely to levels of felt arousal pertaining in the individual at any time (see Fig. 2.5).

Returning again to the musical analogy, suppose that a another foursome has been set up in parallel to the first one, which involves four more instruments, two percussion instruments (the side drum and the piano), and two brass instruments (the saxophone and the French horn). Here the side drum and piano are representative of the autic and alloic states and the saxophone and French horn the mastery and sympathy states respectively. Again the musical composition being played only allows for combinations of instruments to occur between the two separate sets of instruments (i.e. percussion and brass). Hence, the side drum can play in combination independently with the saxophone and

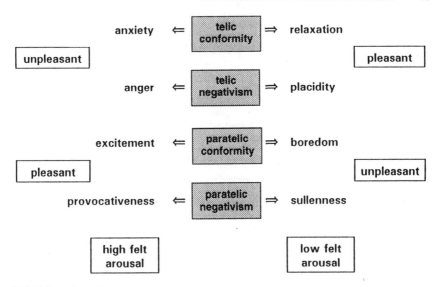

FIG. 2.5.   The eight somatic emotions generated by possible combinations of the telic–paratelic and negativism–conformity pairs of states (from Kerr, 1994).

the French horn and the piano independently with the saxophone and the French horn. These musical instrument combinations can also be likened to a number of different metamotivational combinations (autic mastery, autic sympathy, alloic mastery, alloic sympathy). How might these combinations, in turn, be applied to a sports situation?

A competent cyclist or rower is likely to have the autic–mastery states operating in tandem when he or she propels a racing cycle or single sculls along at a fast pace. The cyclist or rower feels in control, having mastered the skills and coordination necessary to work the pedals or oars smoothly and rhyth- mically. As they exert mastery over their bodies' movements and the cycle or single sculls, they are primarily concerned with what happens to themselves. Team sports like basketball and volleyball, as well a number of physical attributes, require good communication and cooperation between team mem- bers. It seems unlikely that teams could be successful if the players are not predominantly in the alloic and sympathy states. Certainly team cohesion would not be facilitated by players being firmly in the autic state. Where a desire exists for a team to be successful and gain in any competitive trans- action, the alloic and sympathy states are likely to be operative. However, reversals to the mastery state during competition may be frequent, where feel- ings of mastery over opponents also come into play.

Autic–sympathy is the state combination likely to be operative in an athlete who has been injured during play and is self-indulgently making the most of the treatment received both during and after the competition. Alloic sympathy

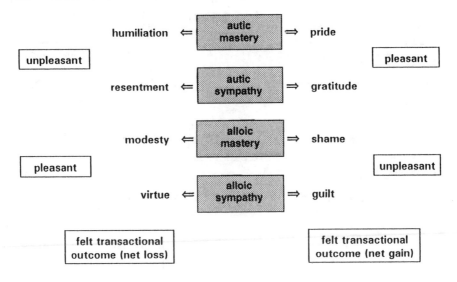

FIG. 2.6. The eight transactional emotions generated by possible combinations of the autic–alloic and mastery–sympathy pairs of states (from Kerr, 1994).

might be felt by someone for an injured team mate. Eight emotions (termed *transactional emotions* in reversal theory) emanate from the metamotivational state combinations just described. They are pride, humiliation, gratitude, resentment, modesty, shame, virtue, and guilt, and are all linked closely to levels of felt transactional outcome, pertaining in the individual at any time (see Fig. 2.6).

Referring to the musical analogy again, imagine that yet another musical composition has been written for an octet, which combines both quartets from the previous examples so that this time all eight instruments are included. The music again requires that only one instrument from each division (strings, woodwind, percussion, and brass) be played at one time, but it also incorporates an increased number of possible combinations of the four different instruments. For example, guitar, side drum, and saxophone, or harp, flute, piano, and French horn, or guitar, clarinet, flute, piano, and saxophone can be played together. These particular instrument combinations represent particular metamotivational state combinations of paratelic–negativistic–autic–mastery, telic–conformist–alloic–sympathy, and paratelic–conformist–alloic–mastery respectively. There are, of course other possible combinations, both musical and metamotivational. The style of the music in the composition is such that again there are irregular periods of play and frequent and sudden changes of instrument groupings. Also, now with four possible combinations, there is an apparently more random organisation to the input from each combination of instruments. This is the way that metamotivational state combinations also function in practice. Relatively frequent and sudden changes in metamotivational combinations and reversals between individual metamotivational pairs are thought to occur unconsciously throughout daily life.

It is possible that the musical analogy used here has been oversimplified. Readers who are musicians or music lovers may well be horrified by what I have outlined. In principle, however, the various combinations of instruments, played together in the manner described, should be possible, but whether a suitable musical score could be written to fit these combinations and whether the resulting piece might sound at all like music is certainly open to question. The analogy is used merely to try to disentangle some of the intricacies of the notion of metamotivational state combinations in reversal theory in a way that those unfamiliar with the theory can grasp more easily.

An example from equestrian sport may help to illustrate how metamotivational state combinations and reversals between particular pairs of states are thought to work in practice. In an equestrian competition, such as dressage or show jumping, it is likely that over time a person will be in an variety of metamotivational states and state combinations. For example, when preparing the horse for riding in the competition and attending to its needs a person is likely to be in the telic and conformist states. There are certain things that have to be done correctly; cleaning hooves and brushing the horse, checking equipment like bridles, reins, and saddles, and placing them correctly on the horse. There are a number of well established conventions, such as working from the left side of the horse or picking its hooves up in the correct way, which the groom or rider concerned conforms to when preparing the horse. In addition, because they are working with, and taking care of an animal they are also likely to be in the alloic and sympathy states.

The overall state combination is likely to be one of telic–conformist–alloic–sympathy. However, reversals might well take place. If, for example, the horse was not cooperating and being difficult, a reversal to the mastery state might well occur, or a rider might reverse from the telic to paratelic state during preparation in anticipation of the riding competition ahead.

In an actual equestrian event, the metamotivational state combination may well be somewhat different. In a dressage event, the rider is required to perform various compulsory movements which show the horse's complete obedience to the rider. As a result, a rider will almost definitely be in the mastery state combined with telic, conformist, and alloic states as horse and rider conform to the serious requirements of the event. If these requirements are not completed correctly, a rider's score is reduced accordingly.

In contrast, show jumping competitions are often decided by a jump-off against the clock. These are usually the finale to a jumping competition and provide great excitement for spectators and the riders concerned. In this case, it seems probable that a rider would be in a paratelic–conformist–autic–mastery state combination. He or she is likely to be caught up in the excitement of the occasion but must follow the correct course over the jumps. In addition, the rider is largely concerned with the outcome in terms of him or herself and must control the horse extremely well to, for example, cut corners and save time.

The probable state combinations just mentioned are generalisations, and the likelihood of reversals taking place in one or more states during an event is, according to reversal theory, always a possibility. For example, a refusal by a horse at a jump is the kind of contingent factor that might spark a reversal, perhaps from paratelic to telic. Or, in another type of equestrian jumping event, the cross-country event, the sympathy state may come more to the fore but alternate with the mastery state. In this type of competition, a rider must be very much aware of the strengths and capabilities of his or her mount, pacing it over the course and guiding it over the jumps and obstacles. However, at the jumps the rider should be in complete control, keeping the horse on an appropriate line, and at that time a sympathy to mastery state reversal might well occur. If a rider is not in the sympathy state, it is possible that the horse may be driven too hard in the early stages and either "blow up" or make mistakes, perhaps becoming injured later in the event.

INTENSITY OF EMOTIONS

Reversal theory claims that, at any one time, the intensity of the emotions experienced by a person will vary with the level of felt arousal (somatic emotions) and felt transactional outcome (transactional emotions) being experienced. To return to the musical analogy, the intensity of an emotion might be likened to the loudness of the music. Music can be played softly or loudly, pianissimo or fortissimo and this can be seen as similar to the way that emotions vary in intensity. For example, in soccer a goalkeeper who has conceded a soft goal might feel guilty if it was as a result of goalkeeping error. However, if the soft goal is conceded in a relatively unimportant match, the feeling of guilt is likely to be less than if it happened in a penalty shoot-out at the end of an undecided World Cup Final. In a World Cup Final penalty shoot-out, a goalkeeper is likely to feel much more aroused than in a game of lesser importance, hence the goalkeeper's feelings of guilt will be intensified in the World Cup context. The difference is the role of felt transactional outcome (and felt arousal) in each case and its effect on the emotion (guilt) being experienced. In the World Cup example, the outcome was very intense unpleasant feelings of guilt. Equally though, in other circumstances, levels of felt transactional outcome and felt arousal can work together to enhance or intensify pleasant emotions such as pride, virtue, or gratitude.

EXPERIENCING PARAPATHIC EMOTIONS

Reversal theorists argue that some negative or unpleasant emotions can actually be experienced as pleasant within a phenomenological *protective frame.* These are known in the theory as *parapathic emotions.* In other words, unpleasant anger, for instance, (which occurs when telic and negativistic states operate in tandem) can be experienced in a pleasant form if experienced within a paratelic protective frame. For example, as Coulson (1991) pointed out, those of us who watch televised news programmes, which often contain anxiety-provoking or threatening reports of war atrocities, terrorist attacks, and violent crime, can usually only do so by means of a protective frame. Coulson (1991, p.81) draws attention to a quotation from Root (1986, p.84) which helps to illustrate the point:

> Reporters may sweat, look worried and duck bullets 'out there', but inside the studio all is calm. Implicitly, newsreaders offer the possibility of a safe resolution to the moment of tension and disaster they tell us about. They have a reassuring presence suggesting that while chaotic scenes may happen elsewhere, life "at home" goes on as normal.

The safe context of the television studio becomes extended to the television room at home, helping to provide the viewer with a protective frame where the risky content can then be viewed in apparent safety. The otherwise highly un-pleasant material can then experienced as a form of entertainment. *The dangerous edge* (Apter, 1992) examines in detail the concept of protective frames and how people engage in an almost endless list of activities which can only be undertaken with some kind of phenomenological protective frame operative. Such activities include engaging in certain forms of sex, committing crimes, gambling, and other forms of risk taking and excitement seeking, not to mention taking part in dangerous sports. In Chapter 4, the discussion will focus on participation in dangerous and risky sports, and a more specific examination of the concept of protective frames in relation to dangerous or risky sports will be undertaken.

CONCLUDING COMMENTS

In Chapter 1 it was suggested that reversal theory could provide the sort of widely applicable, comprehensive theory of motivation and emotion that is currently missing from the sport psychology literature. In this chapter, the theory has been briefly outlined to allow uninitiated readers to familiarise themselves with the basic concepts and, perhaps, to act as a refresher for those who already have some knowledge of reversal theory. It is now time to move on and apply reversal theory to a detailed examination of aspects of motivation and emotion in sport. In Chapter 3, the gauntlet of a long-running debate in sport psychology about the relationship between components of personality and sports participation and performance is picked up.

FURTHER READING

1. Apter, M.J. (1989). *Reversal theory: Motivation, emotion and personality.* London: Routledge. Chapters 1–3, 6–7.
2. Potocky, M., & Murgatroyd, S. (1993). What is reversal theory? In J.H. Kerr, S. Murgatroyd, & M.J. Apter (Eds.), *Advances in reversal theory* (pp. 13–26). Amsterdam: Swets & Zeitlinger.
3. Apter, M.J. (1982). *The experience of motivation: The theory of psychological reversals.* London: Academic Press. Chapters 1–5.

REFERENCES

Apter, M.J. (1982). *The experience of motivation: The theory of psychological reversals.* London: Academic Press.

Apter, M.J. (1992). *The dangerous edge.* New York: Free Press.

Apter, M.J., Mallows, R.D.R., & Williams, S. (1995, July). *The development of the Motivational Style Profile.* Paper presented at the 7th International Conference on Reversal Theory, Melbourne, Australia.

Barr, S.A., McDermott, M.R., & Evans, P. (1990). Predicting persistence: A study of telic and paratelic frustration. In J.H. Kerr, S. Murgatroyd, & M.J. Apter (Eds.), *Advances in reversal theory* (pp.123–136). Amsterdam: Swets & Zeitlinger.

Braathen, E.T., & Svebak, S. (1992). Motivational differences among talented teenage athletes: The significance of gender, type of sport and level of excellence. *Scandinavian Journal of Medicine and Science in Sports, 2,* 153–159.

Cook, M.R., & Gerkovich, M.M. (1990). *Reliability and validity of the Paratelic Dominance Scale.* In J.H. Kerr, S. Murgatroyd, & M.J. Apter (Eds.), *Advances in reversal theory* (pp.177–188). Amsterdam: Swets & Zeitlinger.

Coulson, A.S. (1991). Cognitive synergy in televised entertainment. In J.H. Kerr & M.J. Apter (Eds.), *Adult play: A reversal theory approach* (pp.71–85). Amsterdam: Swets & Zeitlinger.

Fiske, D.W., & Maddi, S.R. (1961). A conceptual framework. In D.W. Fiske & S.R. Maddi (Eds.), *Functions of varied experience* (pp.11–56). Illinois: Dorsey, Homewood.

Hebb, D.O. (1955). Drives and the CNS (Conceptual Nervous System). *Psychological Review, 62,* 243–254.

Kerr, J.H. (1985). The experience of arousal: A new basis for studying arousal effects in sports. *Journal of Sports Sciences, 3,* 169–179.

Kerr, J.H. (1989). Anxiety, arousal and sport performance: An application of reversal theory. In D. Hackfort & C.D. Spielberger (Eds.), *Anxiety in sports: An international perspective* (pp. 137–151). New York: Hemisphere Publishing.

Kerr, J.H. (1991). Arousal-seeking in risk sport participants. *Personality and Individual Differences, 12*(6), 613–616.

Kerr, J.H. (1994). *Understanding soccer hooliganism.* Milton Keynes, UK: Open University Press.

Lafreniere, K., Cowles, M.P., & Apter, M.J. (1988). The reversal phenomenon: Reflections on a laboratory study. In M.J. Apter, J.H. Kerr, & M.P. Cowles (Eds.), *Progress in reversal theory* (pp.257–266). Amsterdam: North-Holland/Elsevier.

McDermott, M.R., & Apter, M.J. (1988). The Negativism Dominance Scale. In M.J. Apter, J.H. Kerr, & M.P. Cowles (Eds.), *Progress in reversal theory* (pp.373–376). Amsterdam: North-Holland/Elsevier.

Murgatroyd, S., Rushton, C., Apter, M.J., & Ray, C. (1978). The development of the Telic Dominance Scale. *Journal of Personality Assessment, 42,* 519–528.

Potocky, M., & Murgatroyd, S. (1993). What is reversal theory? In J.H. Kerr, S. Murgatroyd, & M.J. Apter (Eds), *Advances in reversal theory* (pp.13–26). Amsterdam: Swets & Zeitlinger.

Root, J. (1986). *Open the box*. London: Comedia.

Summers, J., & Stewart, E. (1993). The arousal performance relationship: Examining different conceptions. In S. Serpa, J. Alves, V. Ferriera, & A. Paula-Brito (Eds.), *Proceedings of the VIII World Congress of Sport Psychology* (pp.229–232). Lisbon, Portugal: International Society of Sport Psychology.

Svebak, S., & Kerr, J.H. (1989). The role of impulsivity in preference for sports. *Personality and Individual Differences, 10*(1), 51–58.

Svebak, S., Storfjell, O., & Dalen, K. (1982). The effect of a threatening context upon motivation and task-induced physiological changes. *British Journal of Psychology, 73*, 505–512.

3

Into Sport: Aspects of Participation and Preference

The study of human personality in sport has been a popular and sometimes controversial subject since academic work in sport psychology began in earnest about 30 years ago. Probably the best recent review of personality theory and research in sport settings was provided by Vealey in 1992 (see also Morris, 1995). Although in her review Vealey neglected European work somewhat (e.g. Eysenck, Nias, & Cox, 1982; Furnham, 1990; Kirkcaldy, 1985), she described and discussed most of the important issues in sport and personality work, including definitional problems, different theoretical approaches, methods of assessment and research. Much of the review focused on the person–situation debate in the study of personality and sport, a general debate in psychology that is certainly not limited to sport psychology. This controversy concerned advocates of the trait, situational, and interactive (a combination of the other two) approaches to the study of personality, and which approach was most effective for understanding human behaviour (e.g. Bowers, 1973; Eysenck, 1970; Mischel, 1968, 1979). Similarly in sport psychology, a number of people aired their views on the topic in relation to sport (e.g. Martens, 1975; Morgan, 1980; Silva, 1984).

Looking briefly at the developments in personality theory, personality traits (e.g. extraversion, neuroticism) have traditionally been seen as relatively fixed and enduring aspects of human functioning. They are thought to be consistent across situations, and combinations of traits have a unique nature within each individual. Those psychologists convinced of the value of the trait approach (e.g. Cattell, 1957; Eysenck, 1970) have attempted to measure personality traits

27

and the links between different traits using reliable and valid psychometric methods. However, efforts to identify an assortment of traits able to represent human personality in all its diversity have proved only partially successful. One of the major problems with the trait approach is that, although people may appear to be, for example, generally extraverted, their behaviour does seem to vary across time and in different situations.

A rival approach to explaining personality developed in psychology, which emphasised the importance of situational or environmental factors on human behaviour. It is known as the social learning approach and can be linked back to the early work of the behaviourist approach to learning (Skinner, 1938). Social learning theorists (e.g. Mischel, 1968, 1979) contend that human behaviour is shaped by situational conditions and the kinds of learning experiences a child encounters in those situations while growing up. As Atkinson et al. (1990, p.519) point out:

> According to social-learning theorists, a person's actions in a given situation depend on the specific characteristics of the situation, the individual's appraisal of the situation, and past reinforcement for behavior in similar situations (or observations of others in similar situations). People behave consistently insofar as the situations they encounter and the roles they are expected to play remain relatively stable.

The interactionist approach (see e.g. Bowers, 1973) argued that human behaviour is determined by a combination of personal dispositions and situational factors.

Vealey (1992, see also 1989), pointed out that the popularity of the trait approach in sports personality research decreased substantially from 1974–1981. Furthermore, in the period 1974–1988, 55% of research literature was concerned with studies that had used an interactional approach to study aspects of personality in sport. Martens (1975), in particular, argued for the use of the interactional approach in sport research. Some studies incorporated his notions of trait and situational elements in the study of anxiety in sport and, for example, utilised sports-specific measures for use in competitive situations (e.g. Martens, Vealey, & Burton, 1990). The work of Martens and his colleagues on anxiety in sport will be examined in more detail in Chapter 6.

In the conclusion to her chapter, Vealey (1992, p.53) states:

> Overall a comprehensive view of personality is advocated in which sport psychology moves beyond the measurement of traits to a multitheory, multi-method approach to understanding the structure and process of personality as it relates to sport and exercise.

It is argued here that the multitheory and multimethod approach to the study of personality in sport, which Vealey recommended in 1992, already exists in the form of reversal theory. However, rather than being a multitheory approach, reversal theory is a single, but *multilevel* theoretical approach to personality. In addition, reversal theorists have already adopted a multimethod approach to understanding personality (e.g. Svebak & Murgatroyd, 1985) and sports-based research has been ongoing for almost 10 years (e.g. Braathen & Svebak, 1990, 1992; Kerr, 1987; Kerr & Cox, 1988; Svebak & Kerr, 1989; Summers & Stewart, 1993).

In terms of its multilevel approach, at the macro level is reversal theory's notion of stability, metamotivational dominance. This is overlaid, at the meso level, by metamotivational processes and states which, for example, dictate preferred levels of arousal. Finally, at the micro level are the 16 possible emotions that individuals experience in connection with various meta-motivational state combinations (see Chapter 2). As Apter (1984, p.265) pointed out, reversal theory:

> . . . provides a systematic way of looking at the essential changeability of human nature, the innate forces and structures which inevitably lead to inconsistency of one kind or another. In this it differs from most other theories of personality, since on the whole these tend to emphasize consistency and stability. This is not to deny that there may be important types of personality stability, and indeed, reversal theory itself is concerned with consistent biases and predispositions underlying inconsistencies of behavior and experience. Nor is it to deny that there may be certain kinds of situational consistency, and this is taken into account in the theory. But to concentrate on consistencies alone leads to a picture of human beings which is over-simple and unlife-like—and also unhelpful when it comes to explaining many of the seeming paradoxes of human life, and to helping people solve their personal problems.

For the study of personality, both in general and in the sports context, reversal theory may be the catalyst required for an eventual reconciliation between the *trait-* and *state*-based approaches (Fontana, 1983). However, as well as stimulating a possible melding of these two approaches, reversal theory goes one step further and argues that even in the same situation individuals will behave differently at different times, thus also taking the interactionist approach beyond its current limitations. At times a person's dominance may be over-ridden by state considerations and, in turn, situational influences may on some occasions be over-ridden by metamotivational and reversal processes.

Reversal theory sports-based research has attempted to discover the role of macro-, meso-, and micro-level influences on human behaviour in sport. In the remainder of this chapter the results of studies that have examined the importance of the macro-level concept, metamotivational dominance and, particularly but not exclusively, telic and paratelic dominance, will be reviewed. Research work focusing on the meso and micro levels will be discussed in detail later in this book.

METAMOTIVATIONAL DOMINANCE AND SPORT

There are some sports that seem tailor-made for a certain personality type, in terms of metamotivational dominance, and orienteering would appear to be one of them. Orienteering is a sport in which planning and the execution of those plans in a natural environment are crucial to success. Competitors make use of topographical maps to choose and plan routes to a number of control points usually located in wooded terrain. Competitors must check in at each control point and complete the course (perhaps encountering obstacles like valleys, dense forest, or rough stony ground) on foot as rapidly as possible. Each control acts as a separate goal for which the competitor must plan carefully. Route choice and planning must take into account the physical abilities of the individual competitor, who must also balance the advantage of a longer, easy running and/or technically simple route with a shorter but steep, hard running and/or technically demanding route. Choosing an optimal route prior to the event is considered one of the most important aspects of orienteering (Murakoshi, 1989; Seiler, 1989, 1990). Once the orienteer has set off, he or she must continue to make sense of the complex information presented in the map, selecting the most relevant information for anticipating the condition of the terrain ahead. Often, this has to be done on the move, while traversing rough ground and when the orienteer may be physically tired (Seiler, 1989). The point is that amongst the requirements for being successful in orienteering there is little place for impulsive, paratelic, or risk-taking behaviour. Sound prior planning, and the implementation of those plans during the event, suggest that a telic-oriented serious approach to the activity will be most appropriate. This is especially true if the orienteer encounters a rocky precipice or some other undetected obstruction, and plans have to be changed and a detour route taken. Should this occur, impulsive or badly planned decisions will probably only force the orienteer into further problems and difficulties at a later stage. Taking extra time to develop well-thought-out solutions is much more likely to be of benefit. Hence, telic-oriented behaviour would appear to be much more suited to this sport than paratelic-oriented behaviour and perhaps, therefore, more suited to the telic dominant than the paratelic dominant individual.

Conversely, consider sports that involve a high element of physical risk of injury such as mountaineering, parachuting, bungee jumping, or motorcycle racing. The characteristics of these sports appear to be particularly suited to paratelic behaviour and paratelic dominant individuals. Participants are usually intent on experiencing the thrills of risk-taking and seeking high or very high levels of arousal. Understanding why people risk injury and death by taking part in risk sports is so intriguing that a separate chapter (Chapter 4) is devoted to a discussion of the motivational factors involved. A range of sports (that does not, as yet, include orienteering) have been the subject of dominance research and some of the results are outlined next. A table summarising the reversal theory studies reviewed in this chapter can be found in Appendix A at the end of the book.

Sport-based Metamotivational Dominance Research

A number of different parameters of sport have been investigated in dominance research. These have included studies aimed at identifying differences in dominance: (a) between recreational, amateur, and professional performers (Kerr, 1987); (b) between Masters athletes and other performers (Kerr & van Lienden, 1987); (c) between athletes at different skill levels within one sport (Cox & Kerr, 1989; Kerr & Cox, 1988; Sell, 1991); (d) between top performers from different cultures playing the same sport (Kerr, 1988); (e) within different groups of subjects (high-level performers, human movement specialists, general student subjects, talented teenage athletes) who prefer and/or perform certain types of sports; (Braathen & Svebak, 1992; Chirivella & Martinez, 1994; Kerr, 1991, Kerr & Svebak, 1989; Summers & Stewart, 1993; Svebak & Kerr, 1989; Vlaswinkel & Kerr, 1990). The majority of these studies tested specific hypotheses or predictions from reversal theory. The results obtained, that generally were found to support reversal theory arguments and concepts, are reviewed next (with the exception of those investigations that examined risk or dangerous sports—these are reviewed in the following chapter).

Professional, Amateur and Masters Athletes

Using the Telic Dominance Scale (TDS; Murgatroyd, Rushton, Apter, & Ray, 1978), the telic dominance (i.e. the predisposition to have the telic state operative more frequently than the paratelic state) personality characteristics of 120 professional, serious amateur and recreational male sports performers were examined (Kerr, 1987). Cyclists and soccer players (N = 37) comprised the professional group; field hockey and table tennis players along with show jumpers (N = 38) made up the serious amateur group; the recreational group (N = 45) included participants from a range of different sports. In addition, a control group (N = 20) of non-sports participants were included in the study. The professionals were all dependent on sport for their income; serious amateurs were all involved in regular practice, training, and competition; and members of the recreational group did not practice or train regularly and participated in sports only infrequently as a form of recreation. The results of the statistical analysis using analysis of variance are summarised in Fig. 3.1.

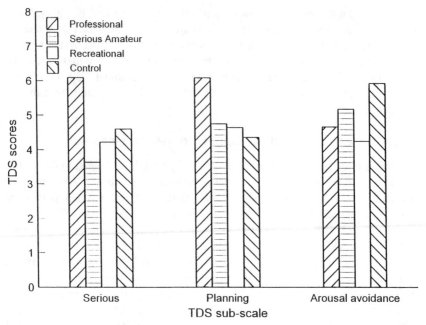

FIG. 3.1. TDS subscale characteristics of professional, serious amateur, and recreational sports performers and control subjects (from Kerr, 1987).

The professional group scored significantly higher than the serious amateur and recreational and control groups on two TDS subscales, planning orientation ($P = .05$) and seriousmindedness ($P < .05$), as well as total telic dominance score ($P < .05$). With the exception of the recreational group, the professional group had the lowest group mean score on the TDS arousal avoidance subscale, with group differences approaching significance ($P = .06$). The professional group were found to be more telic dominant than serious amateur and recreational sport groups and the control group.

The extreme goal-oriented telic nature of professional sport is supported by the comments of a Dutch professional cyclist in an interview (Kerr, 1991, p.49). He described:

The changes involved in becoming a professional:
It changed everything because cycling then is the most important thing in your life. Everything you do has to do with cycling.

The changes in training on becoming a professional:
I changed my training because I never trained more than 1½ hours and that was maybe 3 times a week. That wasn't very much. I tried to start training for 5 hours a day. I couldn't do it in the beginning; it was more like 3 hours in the morning and 2 hours in the afternoon, but not really that fast. . . . if you are a professional,

you have to do the races in the early season of 6–8 hours and I was only used to doing 2 hours.

Why cyclists become professionals:
> In the end, for professional racers, it's just the money. In the beginning, you want to race and you want to be good and afterwards they do it just for the money and publicity. . . There's one other thing that I want to say. There's a difference between amateur sports and professional sports; professionals have other standards and attitudes because it has to do with a lot of money.

A second study undertaken by Kerr and van Lienden (1987), examined telic dominance characteristics in 38 Masters swimmers (27 males, 11 females; mean age 39.4 years). The subjects included 8 former national, 12 former international, and 5 former Olympic level swimmers. Masters athletes are former elite-level athletes, who continue to train seriously and compete against other top athletes in their age groups. Regular competitive tournaments, sports events, and the Masters Games are organised for these performers. In this study, when Masters swimmers' TDS scores were compared with those of the serious amateur and recreational groups, described earlier in the Kerr (1987) study, significant differences were found on planning orientation, serious-mindedness and total telic dominance (see Fig. 3.2). When compared to the professional group, no significant differences were obtained between the Masters swimmers for total TDS and subscale scores.

It would appear, therefore, that even though they are not dependent on sport for extrinsic financial rewards, the telic dominant pattern in Masters swimmers' motivational dominance characteristics is rather similar to that of professional sports performers.

Sell (1991) undertook a study of professional and amateur triathletes. He studied independent groups of male (N = 13) and female (N = 19) professional, and an amateur male group (N = 15), of triathletes, using the TDS. He was interested in determining if there were differences in the groups' telic dominance characteristics and telic–paratelic state characteristics during a triathlon competition of international distance or greater. Both groups of professional triathletes had been competing longer, spent more time training, and participated in more competitions (almost double) than the amateur group. Statistical analysis of TDS scores revealed no important differences between groups with the exception of the arousal avoidance subscale scores. Serious minded and planning subscale and total TDS scores were in the telic direction, supporting the results of previously described studies and Svebak and Kerr's (1989) view (see later) that endurance sports like the triathlon are telic-oriented sports. The amateur male triathletes' mean score on arousal avoidance was significantly higher (i.e. more telic) than the scores of the male professional group. No clear reason for differences only on this subscale was apparent (Sell, 1991).

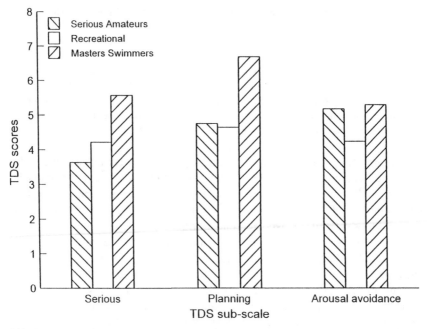

FIG. 3.2. TDS subscale characteristics of Masters swimmers, serious amateur, and recreational sports performers (from Kerr & van Lienden, 1987).

SPORTS, DOMINANCE, AND LIFESTYLE

Clearly, for the professional, Masters, and amateur athletes in some sports like triathlon, their sports activity occupies a central role in their lifestyle. One reversal theory research study (Svebak & Kerr, 1989) investigated the motivational differences associated with sport and the role that it can play within telic and paratelic lifestyles. Svebak and Kerr (1989) explored the possibility of a relationship between preference for and participation in certain types of sports and telic or paratelic dominant lifestyles. A pre-supposition of the study was that the motivational disposition of individuals with a predomi-nantly serious goal-directed lifestyle (i.e. telic dominant) would be to avoid impulsive behaviour in general and specifically sports involving impulsive or *explosive* action (e.g. baseball, basketball, cricket, soccer). Conversely, those individuals with a motivational disposition for a predominantly unplanned impulsive lifestyle would attempt to avoid *endurance* sports, that involve repetitive, monotonous activity (e.g. cycling, long-distance running, rowing). Responses on the TDS and the Barratt Impulsiveness Scale (BIS; Barratt, 1985) were examined in a series of three independent samples.

The first analysis compared a group of top tennis players from Sydney combined with members of the Australian Universities women's field hockey team (explosive sports) with high-level runners competing at the New South

Wales Cross-country Championships (endurance sport). The results of the analysis (shown in Fig. 3.3) indicated that the explosive sport performers were significantly less planning-oriented and arousal-avoiding than the endurance sport group. When the groups were balanced for age (previous work by Murgatroyd, 1985, had shown that a positive relationship existed between age and telic dominance) the differences between groups on these TDS subscales were more marked, underlining the higher impulsivity and high arousal seeking tendencies of the explosive sport group (field hockey, tennis) compared with the endurance group (long-distance running). However, these findings were confounded by gender differences, there being a majority of female subjects in the explosive group and a majority of male subjects in the endurance group. Problems associated with gender differences were eradicated in a second analysis.

In the second analysis 64 students, specialising in Human Movement Education at the University of Sydney, were asked to complete the TDS and BIS and list a maximum of three winter and three summer sports that they actually performed regularly during their leisure time. This approach allowed those sports performed by individuals with telic or paratelic dominant lifestyle patterns to be identified. Five sports, baseball, cricket, touch football, surfing and windsurfing, were found to be associated with extreme paratelic dominant

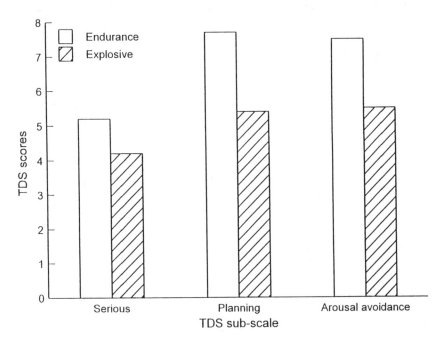

FIG. 3.3.   TDS subscale characteristics of endurance and explosive sports subjects (from Svebak & Kerr, 1989).

subjects, and long distance running and rowing with extreme telic dominant subjects. The paratelic dominant group were compared statistically with a non-paratelic group, balanced for age and gender, who did not perform any paratelic sports in their leisure time, but who were selected using a random recruitment procedure. Again significant results on TDS subscales were obtained that were supported by significant findings on the BIS non-planning subscale, indicating that a less planned lifestyle was characteristic of subjects who performed baseball, cricket, touch football, surfing and windsurfing (see Fig. 3.4).

The study's authors hypothesised that sport might play a more important role in the lives of specialist students of Human Movement Education than in the lives of students following other courses, and that the differences noted earlier might be less clearly associated with students from other courses who participated in paratelic sports. In addition, it was thought that there might be differences in the association between motivational styles and a *preference* to participate in certain sports, and *actual* participation amongst other student groups. For example, social norms, gender, interpersonal relations, economy, geography, and climate are real-life restraints that might lead to discrepancies between preferred sports and those sports that are actually performed. The third analysis explored possible relationships between motivational styles and sport preference and participation amongst female (N = 116) and male (N = 65) students following courses in arts, economics, education, science and engineer-

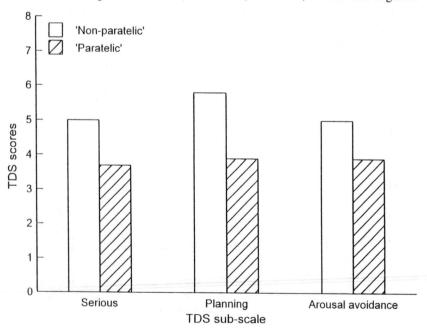

FIG. 3.4. TDS subscale characteristics of "paratelic" (human movement studies) and "non-paratelic" (leisure time) sports participants (from Svebak & Kerr, 1989).

ing, and others. These subjects completed the TDS and BIS and listed a maximum of three winter and three summer sports that they actually performed, as well as a maximum of three winter and three summer sports that, if given a free choice, they would have preferred to perform.

As expected, only some 20% of this student population reported actually performing the paratelic sports identified earlier, compared with 37.5% of Human Movement Education subjects. Also, participation in these sports was equally split between sexes in the Human Movement Education sample, but only about a third of females from the present sample participated in these paratelic sports. These subjects, 25 males and 11 females, were compared with a similar group recruited using a random procedure from the remainder of the student population, who indicated that they neither performed any of these sports, nor wished to do so, Initial *t*-test results indicated no TDS and BIS subscale differences between group mean scores, suggesting that the motivational lifestyles of these general university students were not related to the actual performance of paratelic sports. Further analysis, however, revealed the important role of gender in participation and preference for baseball, cricket, touch football, surfing, and windsurfing (paratelic sports). Those subjects who performed these sports were compared with 35 subjects who indicated that they would have liked to participate in one or more of them but, in reality, did not actually perform them. Statistical analysis indicated that females who preferred to perform these paratelic sports had TDS scores characteristic of a paratelic motivational lifestyle (playful, impulsive) and similar to those of male subjects who actually performed such sports. Svebak and Kerr (1989, p.57) came to the conclusion that as paratelic sports tend to be traditional male sports in Australia, "an extrinsic (social norms related to sex roles) rather than an intrinsic (motivational) 'barrier' explained why these females did not fulfil their wishes."

Also, those male students who did not perform, but reported a preference for paratelic sports appeared to have motivational lifestyles (telic, seriousminded, planning-oriented) least suited to performing these explosive, spontaneous, impulsive, sports. Svebak and Kerr (1989, p.57) went on to suggest that:

> In this sense their preference for these sports appeared to reflect an intrinsic desire to use these sports now and then in their otherwise dominantly goal-directed everyday lives to obtain excitement.

This quote is particularly important because it directs attention back to the complexity of the state–trait relationship in reversal theory's explanation of personality. Although it is correct that people may prefer and perform certain sports because they are telic or paratelic dominant, there is always the possibility that telic dominant individuals, for example, may reverse to the paratelic state in order to enjoy paratelic-oriented sports like baseball. In the same way, paratelic dominant individuals could reverse to the telic state when participating in long-distance running or rowing. Indeed, in the quote, Kerr and Svebak are suggesting that some telic dominant individuals may actually participate in paratelic-oriented sports deliberately, in order to experience pleasant high arousal in the form of excitement on an occasional basis. For similar reasons, there is also a certain danger in labelling sports as telic or paratelic, as the following example illustrates.

Muir (1991) carried out participant observation in a recreational tennis club setting. He found was that what was ostensibly a leisure sport, or in reversal theory terms a paratelic-oriented activity, was in fact conducted in a highly work-like manner. To Muir (1991) himself, tennis was enjoyable for its pleasant fellowship, challenging sport, and healthy exercise, and he was generally willing to play with anyone at the club. However, after a short period during the first days of his membership when he received many invitations to play, he found himself ignored by the better players who had previously defeated him easily. His invitations were declined with weak excuses. He later discovered that the best players insisted on only playing amongst themselves and had developed several ingenious and sophisticated means of temporal and spatial segregation that selectively excluded lesser players. Temporal segregation took place through, for example, careful scheduling to avoid busy or open periods as Muir (1991, p.72) describes:

> Spatial segregation was the next line of defense. To the casual eye all courts might appear equivalent, but a subtle ecology had become established—not just for playing but also for waiting to play. It would be reasonable to assume that everyone would prefer to sit in the main seating area, that provided comfortable chairs in the shade, ceiling fans, ice and water, as well as the best view of the courts. Top players, however, "rested" as a group away from this area whenever it contained lesser players waiting to play. When courts became open they rushed to the most remote one available, that they occupied, set after set, as a closed group. Lesser players thus consistently found themselves playing on courts with most access, not only to the comforts of the seating area but also to other lesser players intently waiting and hoping to be asked to rotate in. Juniors, some of whom could beat top club players (but, perhaps consequently, were excluded from club tournaments) were exiled to two isolated hard courts whenever the clay courts filled.

Muir (1991) went on to detail other examples of how play at the tennis club had become so fiercely competitive that it no longer had a recreational quality. The apparently paratelic activity had, in reality, taken on a highly telic nature. Consequently, there is a danger in labelling any particular activity as being exclusively, for example, telic or paratelic. Without access to the thinking of those individuals concerned, as in the tennis example, erroneous assessments about operative metamotivational states could be made.

Most of the discussion thus far has been concerned with telic and paratelic state dominance. There are, of course, four pairs of metamotivational states and eight possible types of state dominance. As well as people being telic or paratelic dominant they may also be negativism or conformity dominant, mastery or sympathy dominant, autic or alloic dominant. Most reversal theory research on dominance has concentrated on the telic and paratelic pair. Although some work has been carried out on negativism and conformity dominance amongst sports performers, mastery, sympathy, autic and alloic dominance have not as yet been addressed in reversal theory sports research.

The Negativism Dominance Scale (NDS; McDermott & Apter, 1988) has two subscales, one dealing with proactive negativism and one with reactive negativism. Proactive negativism is concerned with the frequency with which a person engages in negativistic behaviour in order to provoke situations that are exciting and fun. Reactive negativism is concerned with the frequency with which a person reacts to disappointments and frustrations with resentful feelings and sometimes vindictive or vengeful behaviour (see McDermott, 1988). In the following sections, the topic of negativistic and conformist behaviour and dominance research is taken up.

NEGATIVISM AND CONFORMITY IN SPORT

Much of the time top sports performers spend on their sports is concerned with conformity. Athletes must adhere strictly to training schedules and other aspects of the top performer's lifestyle like proper nutrition, having plenty of sleep, and often abstaining from alcohol, cigarettes, and late-night socialising. In addition, the coach's instructions must be followed and, when competing, the rules of the various events or laws of the different games, along with the directives of referees and officials, must be observed.

Generally speaking, negativistic behaviour amongst sports performers, when it occurs, is not tolerated for long. For example, the rebellious and negativistic attitude of North American baseball players who went on strike over a salary dispute during the 1994–95 season resulted in players being locked out by team owners and the cancellation of the season's fixture list. In Japan in the 1994–95 season international and Olympic female volleyball players, Tomoko Yoshihara and Motoko Obayashi, were sacked by their Hitachi company team coach after rebelliously sticking to their demands for professional status in the newly set up V-league.

Several other incidents and episodes where sports people have exhibited different types of negativism come to mind. For example, many people will remember the Black Power demonstration during the 1968 Olympic Games in Mexico. In an act of reactive negativism against US politicians and their policies, track athletes Tommie Smith and John Carlos raised black gloved fists while on the podium during the medal ceremony and the playing of the US national anthem. They were subsequently expelled from the Olympic village in a storm of controversy. The negativistic attitude of the England team towards the media during the Italia '90 European soccer tournament was also an example of reactive negativism. The media, especially the tabloid press, who had subjected the team and manager to heavy criticism in the period prior to the tournament and during the games in Italy, became largely ignored by the players, who reacted to their poor treatment by refusing to give interviews or provide information. Another Olympian, Australian swimming champion Dawn Fraser's rebelliousness led to a flag-stealing incident at the Tokyo Olympics in 1964 that virtually ended her Olympic career. Her attempt to steal one of the huge Olympic flags from outside the Emperor's' Palace, that led to a confrontation, chase, and apprehension by Japanese police, was an obvious act of proactive negativism (Gordon & Fraser, 1965).

It could be argued that most of the examples just described are on the periphery of sport and are not directly connected with performance. However, negativistic behaviour has also been associated with creativity (Apter, 1982, p.305) and there are some examples that relate to performance. Australian rugby player David Campese's unconventional tactics went against established playing procedures, but resulted in a brilliant World Cup try. In a game against New Zealand, he received the ball on one side of the pitch and ran across the face of the defence at an unusual angle. Each of the New Zealand threequarters covered their own defensive zones and did not chase him. Campese ended up scoring a brilliant try on the other side of the pitch outside defending New Zealand winger, John Kirwan. By not conforming, his creativity led to a piece of outstanding play (Dwyer, 1992). Then again, as legend has it, the game of rugby first began with an act of negativism when William Webb Ellis, playing soccer at Rugby School in England in 1823, picked up the ball and ran with it, an action that was totally against the laws of soccer.

The notorious case of the underarm bowling incident during the third World Series Cup game between Australia and New Zealand illustrates the reciprocal relationship between negativism and conformity. There was just one ball remaining and the New Zealanders needed six runs to win the match. Greg Chappell, captain of the Australian cricket team, instructed his brother, who was bowling at the time, to bowl underarm. It is virtually impossible to hit a six off an underarm ball and New Zealand batsman Brian McKechnie could only block the ball and throw his bat away in disgust (Brayshaw, 1981). Technically, underarm bowling is within the laws of cricket, but it caused an outcry because the act was seen as being against the spirit of the game. Cricket has long been held as a standard-setter in sportsmanship and fair play, both within and outside sport (see Marqusee, 1994) and this bowling tactic was considered by many cricket followers as definitely "not cricket". The controversy led to calls for the sacking of Chappell as captain. This is a useful example because it shows neatly how Chappell's conformist action, in terms of the laws of cricket, was seen by others as negativistic. It is important to remember that, according to reversal theory, it is the subjective interpretation of the individual concerned that determines whether an act is conformist or negativistic, not the way the action is interpreted by others.

A good example of conformity in a sports setting is provided by Nixon's (1986) research, that found that swimmers using a university pool structured and maintained their interaction in predictable and sociable patterns. Nixon (1986) claimed that this was necessary to allow participants to enjoy their swimming activity. Among those people using the pool for swimming, Nixon (1986) found four distinct groups: (a) serious and ex-competitive swimmers highly committed to skill improvement and personal performance; (b) casual swimmers interested in swimming as a leisure activity for exercise and enjoyment; both of these groups were subdivided into regular and irregular participants. The intensity of social control was strongest in the fast section of the pool used by serious swimmers and least in the casual section. On occasions, newcomers unaware of the rules, or uncooperative swimmers, generated aggression, rudeness, anger, and even confrontation. Regulars were sometimes observed to resort to aggressive retaliation in an attempt to make deviants conform to the code of conduct. Reversal theorists would probably classify the behaviour of the serious regular swimmers as characteristic of a telic–conformity state combination and recognise the paratelic orientation of the casual swimmers. In the latter case, behaviour in the paratelic state could be combined with the conformist state, operative in those who followed the code of conduct. However, if the norms were not broken through ignorance, the paratelic state could also have been combined with the negativistic state, perhaps leading to rule-breaking and disruptive behaviour as a negativistic response to the conformity of the serious regular swimmers.

Reversal Theory Research into Negativism and Conformity in Sport

The research that has been carried out has, in a similar way to telic dominance sport research, attempted to pinpoint differences in dominance: (a) between recreational and professional performers (Vlaswinkel & Kerr, 1990); (b) between athletes at different skill levels (Braathen & Svebak, 1992); (c) within different groups of subjects (high-level performers, general student subjects, talented teenage athletes) who perform certain types of sports (Braathen & Svebak, 1992; Vlaswinkel & Kerr, 1990). The results obtained are summarised next (again, those investigations that examined risk or dangerous sports are reviewed in the following chapter).

Vlaswinkel and Kerr (1990) examined negativism dominance in high-level performers of team and individual sports. Professional (N = 22) and recreational (N = 22) soccer players were found to exhibit no differences in NDS subscale and total scores. However, when the professional soccer players were compared with a group of long distance runners (N = 38), they were found to score significantly higher on the reactive negativism subscale.

Braathen and Svebak (1992) included the NDS in a batch of questionnaires administered to 228 male and 124 female talented teenage Norwegian athletes, aged 15 and 16 years. They were interested in trying to establish whether differences in performers' motivational characteristics would be related to gender, type of sport, and level of excellence. Amongst the analyses carried out by the authors, one differentiated between *endurance* (e.g. rowing, kayaking, race walking, distance running, cycling, swimming, cross-country skiing, and orienteering) *explosive* (e.g. sprinting, ski jumping, slalom skiing, 50m freestyle swimming, tae kwon do, boxing, gymnastics, and racquet sports), and *team* sports (e.g. basketball, soccer, volleyball, and European handball). Another differentiated between levels of excellence, national or international performers and moderately successful participants in local competitions.

Amongst various significant findings, Braathen and Svebak (1992) found that performers in endurance and explosive sports scored significantly higher on the reactive negativism scale than team sport performers. A significant interaction with gender was obtained, with male athletes in explosive sports scoring highest and female team sport athletes scoring lowest on reactive negativism. With regard to proactive negativism, again there were significant differences between sports, team sport performers scored lowest and explosive sport performers highest. This finding confirmed an earlier similar result from a general population that indicated higher levels of reactive negativism amongst males when compared to females (McDermott, 1988). Braathen and Svebak (1992) suggested that the trend for both male and female team sport performers to score low on reactive and proactive negativism (compared with, for example, male athletes in explosive sports), might indicate that negativistic lifestyles are in conflict with the social demands for the development of excellence in team sports. Finally, this study found that the most successful athletes (who performed at national or international level), scored significantly higher on proactive negativism than those who performed at local level only.

Although Vlaswinkel and Kerr's (1990) study did not provide much evidence that negativism dominance differences were related to type of sport for high-level Dutch participants, Braathen and Svebak's (1992) data confirmed this relationship among top-level teenage Norwegian athletes. The Norwegian data also showed that differences in negativism dominance are mediated by gender differences and appear to be important for those who reach a high level of excellence.

These results are early indications that negativism and conformity dominance may have important roles to play in sport. However, further research, not only with the NDS, but also with dominance scales belonging to the mastery–sympathy and autic–alloic pairs, is necessary before more comprehensive statements about metamotivational dominance and sport can be made.

CONCLUDING COMMENTS

Furnham (1990), provides a good summary of the criticisms that have been levelled at personality research in sport. He was not complimentary about the standard of previous studies, pointing out that a number of problems (definitional, epistemological, interpretational) were intrinsic to many of them. He claimed (1990, p.220) that a major problem arose from the state–trait dichotomy and the fact that those looking at the topic come from two opposing theoretical backgrounds:

> Personality theorists tend to see personality as the independent variable and sports' [sic] performance the dependent variable while the opposite is true of sports scientists. The implicit assumption of the former is that sports' [sic] preference and performance is a consequence of personality functioning, while the latter assume personality can be shaped by sporting competitions and exercise.

Whether Furnham's comments are justified is a matter for discussion elsewhere, but in highlighting the problem he states neatly the classic question in sport personality research, the answer to which has generally evaded researchers from both camps. This chapter has been largely concerned with the notion that personality, at least in terms of telic and paratelic dominance, determines preference for and participation in sports. Later in this book, via the intricacies of meso- and micro-level reversal theory concepts, the latter notion that motivation and personality, in terms of dominance, can be affected by people's experience in sports competition and exercise will also be expanded on. In doing so, it will be shown that reversal theory has the potential to go beyond conventional state–trait approaches and provide, as Fontana (1983) suggested, an eventual reconciliation between the two approaches.

However, before that process begins in earnest, some time will be spent in the following chapter examining the special circumstances that attract people to take part in risk or dangerous sports.

FURTHER READING

1. Svebak, S. (1990). Personality and sports participation. In G.P. Hermans (Ed.), *Sports, medicine and health* (pp.87–96). Amsterdam: Elsevier.
2. Apter, M.J. (1989). *Reversal theory: Motivation, emotion and personality.* London: Routledge. Chapter 4.
3. Apter, M.J. (1982). *The experience of motivation: The theory of psychological reversals.* London: Academic Press. Chapter 10.

4. Vealey, R.S. (1992). Personality and sport: A comprehensive view. In T.S. Horn (Ed.), *Advances in sport psychology* (pp.25–59). Champaign, IL: Human Kinetics.
5. Eysenck, H.J. Nias, D.K., & Cox, D.N. (1982). Sport and personality. *Advances in Behavioural Research and Therapy, 4*, 1–56.

REFERENCES

Apter, M.J. (1982). *The experience of motivation: The theory of psychological reversals.* London: Academic Press.

Apter, M.J. (1984). Reversal theory and personality: A review. *Journal of Research in Personality, 18*, 265–288.

Atkinson, R.I., Atkinson, R.C., Smith, E.E., Bem, D.J., & Hilgard, E.R. (1990). *Introduction to psychology.* New York: Harcourt Brace Jovanovich.

Barratt, E.S. (1985). Impulsiveness subtraits: Arousal and information processing. In J.T. Spence & C.E. Izard (Eds.), *Motivation, emotion and personality* (pp.137–146). New York: Elsevier.

Bowers, K.S. (1973). Situationism in psychology: An analysis and a critique. *Psychological Review, 80*, 307–336.

Braathen, E.T., & Svebak, S. (1990). Task-induced tonic and phasic EMG response patterns and psychological predictors in elite performers of endurance and explosive sports. *International Journal of Psychophysiology, 9*, 21–30.

Braathen, E.T., & Svebak, S. (1992). Motivational differences among talented teenage athletes: The significance of gender, type of sport and level of excellence. *Scandinavian Journal of Medicine and Science in Sports, 2*, 153–159.

Brayshaw, I. (1981). *The wit of cricket.* Sydney: Currawong Press.

Cattell, R.B. (1957). *Personality and motivation structure and measurement.* New York: Harcourt Brace Jovanovich.

Chirivella, E.C., & Martinez, L.M. (1994). The sensation of risk and motivational tendencies in sports: An empirical study. *Personality and Individual Differences, 16*, 777–786.

Cox, T., & Kerr, J.H. (1989). Arousal effects during tournament play in squash. *Perceptual and Motor Skills, 69*, 1275–1280.

Dwyer, B. (1992). *The winning way.* Auckland: Rugby Press.

Eysenck, H.J. (1970). *The structure of human personality.* London: Methuen.

Eysenck, H.J., Nias, D.K., & Cox, D.N. (1982). Sport and personality. *Advances in Behavioural Research and Therapy, 4*, 1–56.

Fontana, D. (1983). Individual differences in personality: Trait based versus state based theories. *Educational Psychology, 3*, 189–200.

Furnham, A. (1990). Personality and demographic determinants of leisure and sports performance. *International Journal of Sport Psychology, 21*, 218–236.

Gordon, H., & Fraser, D. (1965). *Gold medal girl: Confessions of an Olympic champion.* Melbourne: Circus.

Kerr, J.H. (1987). Differences in the motivational characteristics of "professional", "serious amateur" and "recreational" sports performers. *Perceptual and Motor Skills, 64*, 379–382.

Kerr, J.H. (1988). A study of motivation in rugby. *Journal of Social Psychology, 128(2)*, 269–270.

Kerr, J.H. (1991). Sport: Work or play? In J.H. Kerr & M.J. Apter (Eds.), *Adult play: A reversal theory approach* (pp.43–53). Lisse: Swets & Zeitlinger.

Kerr, J.H., & Cox, T. (1988). Effects of telic dominance and metamotivational state on squash task performance. *Perceptual and Motor Skills, 67*, 171–174.

Kerr, J.H., & Svebak, S. (1989). Motivational aspects of preference for and participation in risk sports. *Personality and Individual Differences, 10*, 797–800.

Kerr, J.H., & van Lienden, H.J. (1987). Telic dominance in masters swimmers. *Scandinavian Journal of Sports Sciences, 9*(3), 85–88.

Kirkcaldy, B.D. (1985). The value of traits in sport. In B.D. Kirkcaldy (Ed.), *Individual differences in movement* (pp.257–277). Lancaster: MTP Press.

Marqusee, M. (1994). *Anyone but England: Cricket and the national malaise.* London: Verso.

Martens, R. (1975). The paradigmatic crises in American sports personology. *Sportswissenschaft, 1,* 9–24.

Martens, R., Vealey, R.S., & Burton, D. (1990). *Competitive anxiety in sport.* Champaign, IL: Human Kinetics.

McDermott, M.R. (1988). Measuring rebelliousness: The development of the Negativism Dominance Scale. In M.J. Apter, J.H. Kerr, & M.P.Cowles (Eds.), *Progress in reversal theory* (pp.297–312). Amsterdam: North-Holland/Elsevier.

McDermott, M.R., & Apter, M.J. (1988). The Negativism Dominance Scale. In M.J. Apter, J.H. Kerr, & M.P. Cowles (Eds.), *Progress in reversal theory* (pp.373–376). [Advances in psychology series, 51]. Amsterdam: North-Holland/Elsevier.

Mischel, W. (1968). *Personality and assessment.* New York: Wiley.

Mischel, W. (1979). On the interface of cognition and personality: Beyond the person–situation debate. *American Psychologist, 34,* 740–754.

Morgan, W.P. (1980). Sport personology: The credulous–sceptical argument in perspective. In W. Straub (Ed.), *Sport psychology: An analysis of athlete behavior* (pp.330–339). Ithaca, NY: Mouvement Publications.

Morris, T. (1995). Psychological characteristics and sports behaviour. In T. Morris & J. Summers (Eds.), *Sport psychology: Theory, applications and issues* (pp.3–28). Brisbane: Wiley.

Muir, D.E. (1991). Club tennis: A case study in taking leisure very seriously. *Sociology of Sport Journal, 8,* 70–78.

Murakoshi, S. (1989). On psychological study of orienteering. *Scientific Journal of Orienteering, 2,* 67–73.

Murgatroyd, S. (1985). The nature of telic dominance. In M.J. Apter, D. Fontana, & S. Murgatroyd (Eds.), *Reversal theory: Applications and developments* (pp.20–41). Cardiff: University College Cardiff Press.

Murgatroyd, S., Rushton, C., Apter, M.J., & Ray, C. (1978). The development of the Telic Dominance Scale. *Journal of Personality Assessment, 42,* 519–528.

Nixon, H.L. (1986). Social order in a leisure setting: The case of recreational swimmers in a pool. *Sociology of Sport Journal, 3,* 320–332.

Seiler, R. (1989). Route planning and route choice. *Scientific Journal of Orienteering, 2,* 74–83.

Seiler, R. (1990). Decision making processes in orienteering. *International Journal of Sport Psychology, 21,* 36–45.

Sell, L. (1991). *Motivational characteristics of elite triathletes.* Master of Science Thesis, Department of Physical Education, West Chester University, USA.

Silva, J.M. (1984). Personality and sport performance: Controversy and challenge. In J.M. Silva & R.S. Weinberg (Eds.), *Psychological foundations of sport* (pp.59–69). Champaign, IL: Human Kinetics.

Skinner, B.F. (1938). *The behavior of organisms.* New York: Appelton.

Summers, J., & Stewart, E. (1993). The arousal performance relationship: Examining different conceptions. In S. Serpa, J. Alves, V. Ferriera, & A. Paula-Brito (Eds.), *Proceedings of the VIII World Congress of Sport Psychology* (pp.229–232). Lisbon, Portugal: International Society of Sport Psychology.

Svebak, S., & Kerr, J.H. (1989). The role of impulsivity in preference for sports. *Personality and Individual Differences, 10*(1), 51–58.

Svebak, S., & Murgatroyd, S. (1985). Metamotivational dominance: A multimethod validation of reversal theory constructs. *Journal of Personality and Social Psychology, 48*(1), 107–116.

Vealey, R.S. (1989). Sport personology: A paradigmatic and methodological analysis. *Journal of Sport and Exercise Psychology, 11,* 216–235.

Vealey, R.S. (1992). Personality and sport: A comprehensive view. In T.S. Horn (Ed.), *Advances in sport psychology* (pp.25–59). Champaign, IL: Human Kinetics.

Vlaswinkel, E.H., & Kerr, J.H. (1990). Negativism dominance in risk and team sports. *Perceptual and Motor Skills, 70,* 289–290.

4 Skating on Thin Ice: The Special Attraction of Dangerous Sports

It has been estimated that in 1993 in Australia alone, about 4500 people went skydiving for the first time and nearly 12,000 made their first tandem jump clipped to an experienced jumper (Scott, 1994). What is it that makes people put themselves at risk by taking part in dangerous sports like skydiving? After all, even at the top level, the most highly skilled can suffer awful injuries or death, as witnessed by the recent deaths of downhill skier Ulrike Maier, radical wave surfer Mark Foo, and Formula One motor racing driver Ayrton Senna.

Take Ayrton Senna, who had won the Formula One World Championship on three previous occasions. On the seventh lap of the 1994 Monaco Grand Prix, Senna died after he crashed into a wall at the Tamburello curve, while travelling at 310kph. The Brazilian media later revealed that a detailed video of the fatal crash showed that Senna's Williams–Renault car went out of control because of steering failure. There was some evidence that the left front wheel came loose and slipped out of control and the black box on Sennas's car indicated that the hydraulic pressure had failed when the car was doing 310kph. There were also indications of hard braking and a rapid slowing of the car as Senna fought to avoid the crash. Why the crash had been fatal was not immediately obvious, as the angle of impact, about 24 degrees, was one that experts thought could easily be absorbed in modern motor racing. Senna did, however, suffer a massive and fatal head injury.

Senna, Foo, and Maier are not the first participants in dangerous sports to lose their lives. There is a long list of well-known sports personalities, especially from motor sports, who have died as a result of their participation in

47

dangerous sports. Also, relatively frequently the newspapers report the deaths or serious injury of less well-known individuals who have come to grief in some way through risk sports. When Wayne Rainey (1994), former champion motorcycle racer was asked the question, "Was first place worth risking almost dying and losing the ability to walk?" he answered, "Yes it was." So, just what is the attraction of risk sports? This chapter will review the experience of individuals in a range of risk sports and reversal theory's original explanation for why they participate. The chapter begins by continuing the discussion on personality and metamotivational dominance from the last chapter and, using the pertinent concepts of parapathic emotions and protective frames, proceeds to examine the emotional experience of the risk sport participant.

RISK SPORTS AND PERSONALITY

A good example of studies on risk sport participants was provided by Ewert (1985). He undertook a study of the motives of some of those who engage in risk sports. The subjects in the study sample were 460 mountaineers who deliberately went climbing (sometimes in hostile weather conditions) in the beautiful, but often dangerous terrain of Mount Rainier National Park in America's Washington State. He found, using factor analysis, that the most important motives for mountaineers were the challenge/risk of the activity, the physical setting, and reasons of catharsis (total involvement and high concentration). These are characteristics that are closely related to arousal-seeking behaviour in the paratelic state.

Another example of research on the motivation behind risk sport participation was a study on surfers by Farmer (1992). Fifty surfers responded to questionnaires distributed at surf shops in twelve US cities. The questionnaire contained a modified version of Kenyon's (1968) Physical Activity Attitudinal Scale, including questions related to the six categories of motives from the scale (vertigo, catharsis, aesthetic, social, health and fitness, competition), which subjects were asked to rank in order of importance. The results from Kenyon's (1968) scale indicated that reasons for participation associated with the vertigo, aesthetic, and catharsis categories were highest. However, when the rankings were examined, surfers overwhelmingly (79%) ranked the most important reasons for surfing as those that fell under Kenyon's category labelled *the pursuit of vertigo*. Motives associated with the other categories were ranked in first place by only a minority: catharsis 9%, aesthetic 6%, social 0%, health and fitness 2%, competition 4%. Vertigo is a term that was used by Callois (1961) in his classification of games to represent those activities that involve the confusion of balance and perception and result in what Callois (1961) termed *voluptuous panic*. The characteristics of these activities include speed, acceleration, change of direction, overcoming the body's limitations, and the risk and thrill intrinsic to sports like surfing. Vertigo activities are usually sought after for their own sake, purely for pleasure as a form of excitement-seeking, paratelic activity (see Kerr, 1988). A quote from Edwards and Ottum (1967), included in Farmer's (1992, p.14) paper, illustrates how the surfer may experience vertigo:

> I'll tell you what neat is. The force of a monster wave can pin you right down to the bottom. You lie there on your back—spread-eagle and heavy and helpless—and if you look up you can see those spinning fingers of turbulence reaching down to get you. They scoop you up into a ball, and for a few seconds you are spinning crazily in a world that is neither land nor sea nor air.

If the results of these two studies are correct, then differences in the dominance characteristics of people who take part in risk sports and those who participate in other less risky sports might be expected. The next section outlines metamotivational dominance research that has focused on risky sport activities.

TELIC AND PARATELIC DOMINANCE

The first study of risk and safe sports participants' dominance characteristics was carried out using the Telic Dominance Scale (TDS; Murgatroyd, Rushton, Apter, & Ray, 1978; see Appendix D) by Kerr and Svebak (1989). In an extension to the Svebak and Kerr (1989) study on impulsivity in preference for sports, Kerr and Svebak (1989) also analysed the data to explore possible differences in those who took part in sports with a strong element of physical risk (e.g. caving, canoeing, downhill skiing, motor racing, surfing, waterskiing, and windsurfing) and relatively safer sports (e.g. archery, bowling, frisbee, golf, snooker, walking/hiking, and yoga). Subjects had been asked to list their first three preferences for summer and winter sports and also up to three summer and winter sports in which they actually participated (Svebak & Kerr, 1989).

In Kerr and Svebak's (1989) first analysis a strong significant difference was found on the TDS arousal avoidance subscale between those who opted for risk (N = 27) and those who opted for safe (N = 9) sports. Group mean differences on the TDS seriousmindedness and planning orientation subscale also approached significance. The authors interpreted this result as indicating that a preference for risk sports is strongly associated with a generally paratelic lifestyle.

Next, subjects who *did* participate in these sports in summer (risk N = 14, safe N = 8) and winter (risk N = 11, safe N = 10) were compared. In both cases, risk sport participants scored much lower on the TDS arousal avoidance subscale. No other important differences were identified, with the exception of winter sports activities where a similar significant difference was revealed for the TDS seriousmindedness subscale. Safe winter sport participants scored higher and were therefore more serious than risky winter sport performers.

Kerr and Svebak's (1989) study was carried out on student subjects, but how would the telic dominance characteristics of more experienced risk and safe sport performers compare? Kerr (1991) first compared Australian male surfers (N = 32) and sailboarders (N = 31), both considered risk sport participants, with weight trainers (N = 39), by comparison a relatively safe sport. Surfers and sailboarders were found to score significantly lower on all three subscales of the TDS, as well as on total telic dominance scores (see Fig. 4.1a).

Second, Dutch male parachutists (N = 21) and motorcycle racers (N = 18) were compared with marathon runners (N = 17). These were expert performers as opposed to recreational participants. Parachutists and motorcycle racers group mean scores on total telic dominance and arousal avoidance were significantly lower than those of marathon runners (see Fig. 4.1b). There were no differences between groups on the TDS seriousminded and planning subscales in this study. It may be that in sports like parachuting and motorcycle racing, which involve a very high degree of risk, careful planning and serious pre-event preparation are important aspects of the activity, which then allow the arousal-seeker to enjoy the subsequent high arousal experience.

This argument was supported by Kerr and Svebak (1989) who found no relationship between impulsiveness (as measured by the Barratt Impulsiveness

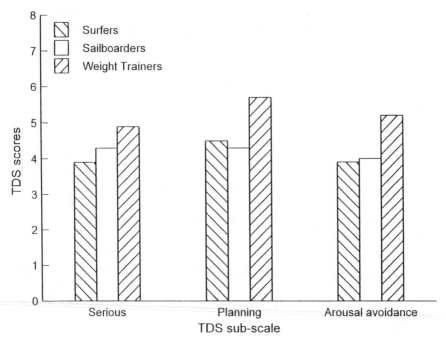

FIG. 4.1a.   TDS subscale characteristics of surfers, sailboarders, and weight trainers (from Kerr, 1991).

Scale, BIS; Barratt, 1985) and participation in risk sports. Impulsive people who do not plan their risk activities carefully might be subjecting themselves to greater levels of risk than those who are arousal seekers, but who plan well.

McGuane's (1990, p.37) observations of motorcross certainly seem to support the need for planning in risk sports:

> With the International to be run soon, it would have been a mistake not to notice the tension. Earlier, the riders had walked the course, looking for tracks that only they could see, looking for the fall lines on the steep drops and those particularly bad spots on the course where a special ability would let one pass another rider who was trying to maintain control. To a great extent the machinery is all fairly matched so it is hard to pick up advantages on the parts or "components", of the track where everyone can ride flat out. But, if for instance, there is a place where a sharp crown of hill makes most riders slow down to keep control going over the face, a certain number of hot shoes will pass there by hitting the crown full tilt, going by the other riders in midair, and maybe only touching with the rear wheel sixty or seventy feet down the face of the hill, and not till then easing the front wheel down for "stability". It seems unwarranted to use the word "stability" in any connection here, but the fine riders bring to the most elaborate forms of violence a kind of order.

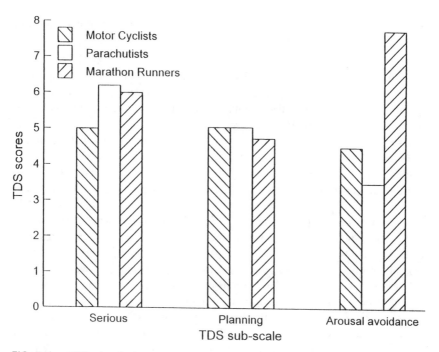

FIG. 4.1b.   TDS subscale characteristics of motorcycle racers, parachutists, and marathon runners (from Kerr, 1991).

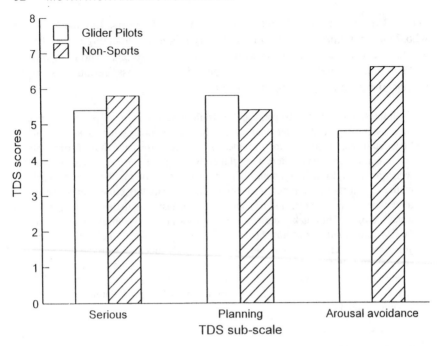

FIG. 4.1c. TDS subscale characteristics of glider pilots and non-sport participants (from Kerr, 1991).

Third, British glider pilots (N = 25) were compared with non-sporting individuals (N = 25). No significant differences were found on the serious-minded and planning subscales or total TDS score, but were again revealed by arousal–avoidance subscale scores (see Fig. 4.1c).

Also using the TDS, Summers and Stewart (1993) found that skydivers (N = 25) (high risk) scored significantly lower on TDS subscale arousal avoidance than groups of rowers (N = 25), semi-professional baseballers (N = 25), university baseballers (N = 25), and a non-sport group (N = 25) (low risk).

The finding of significantly lower scores on arousal–avoidance amongst risk sport participants was consistent across all analyses, thus supporting reversal theory arguments that risk sport participants are, in general, more likely to be paratelic dominant than safe sport performers. However, future work needs to explore the role of planning and seriousmindedness in risk sport participants. The empirical results obtained using the TDS suggest that there are no differences on these two subscales between participants in some very high-risk sports and those who participate in other types of sport. The planning and serious aspects of telic–paratelic dominance may be linked to the need for mastery and control that some people who engage in risky activities desire (see later).

Other, non-reversal theory studies have also found a similar link between excitement or sensation seeking and risk sport participation (see e.g. Goma, 1991; Rowland, Franken, & Harrison, 1986; Zuckerman, 1983). Evidence linking these findings to reversal theory was provided by Chirivella and Martinez (1994), who looked at motivational tendencies in a sample of Spanish sports performers. They gathered data using the TDS (Murgatroyd et al., 1978), the Negativism Dominance Scale (NDS; McDermott & Apter, 1988), and Zuckerman's Sensation Seeking Scale (SSS, Zuckerman, 1979) which has four separate factors (disinhibition, experience seeking, thrill and adventure seeking, and boredom susceptibility). The SSS subscales have previously been found to be related to TDS subscales (especially arousal avoidance, see e.g. Trimpop, Kirkcaldy, & Kerr, 1996; Murgatroyd, 1985) and similar relationships were found in this study.

Spanish subjects in the study were involved in three sports with three different levels of risk. These were tennis (low risk), karate (intermediate risk), and parasailing (high risk). The data collected included information about age, gender, educational background, the degree of risk in these sports (as perceived by participants), the length of time subjects had been participating in their sports, and other sports in which they took part.

Important differences were found between the three groups with respect to seeking high arousal. Consistent with previous findings, parasailors scored lowest on the TDS arousal avoidance subscale, followed by tennis players, and highest were the karate group. This result was supported by significant differences between the parasailors and the other two groups on sensation seeking in general and the SSS's disinhibition, experience seeking, and thrill and adventure seeking factors. However, parasailing was also associated with higher levels of seriousmindedness than karate and tennis.

The researchers also found that there was a link between type of sport and the second sport practised by subjects. Those who performed tennis also tended to perform a second low-risk sport (swimming, golf); those who took part in karate also tended to take part in a second intermediate-risk sport (e.g. horse riding, judo); those who took part in parasailing also tended to take part in a second high-risk sport (e.g. pot-holing, deep sea diving).

NEGATIVISM AND CONFORMITY DOMINANCE IN RISK SPORTS

To date, negativism dominance in risk sport participants has not been explored in as much detail as telic dominance. However, in the Chirivella and Martinez (1994) study which used the Negativism Dominance Scale (NDS; McDermott & Apter, 1988; see Appendix E), tennis players scored significantly higher on both total negativism dominance and the NDS *reactive negativism* subscale (which measures reaction to interpersonal frustration or affront) than the parasailing and karate groups, who were by comparison rather more conformist.

Different findings were obtained by Vlaswinkel and Kerr (1990) in their investigation of negativism dominance in high-level performers of risk and team sports. They thought that taking part in risk sports might be associated with higher scores on negativism dominance than non-risk sport participants (see e.g. Van Reusel & Renson, 1982) and that team sport performers might, by necessity, be less negativistic dominant than individual sport performers. A Dutch version of the NDS was used to compare sports groups. First, a small group (N = 10) of student participants in risk sports, identified from a larger student sample (N = 184), scored significantly higher on the reactive negativism subscale than student participants in safe sports (N = 27) from the same larger group. Second, at the elite level of performance, statistical analysis of NDS responses from groups of motorcycle racers (risky N = 28), Olympic sailors (less risky N = 25), and long-distance runners (safe N = 38) revealed no significant differences between groups on NDS subscale or total score. Goma (1991) had found that subjects who engaged in high physical risk sports generally conformed to social norms.

Braathen and Svebak (1992) found that talented teenage Norwegian male athletes in risk sports scored significantly higher on reactive negativism subscales as compared with female risk sport athletes. Furthermore, gender was found to interact with the risk–safe sport criterion, showing strong differences between male and female risk sport performers. A table summarising the results of reversal theory research into dominance in risk (and safe) sports can be found in Appendix B at the end of the book.

The most consistent finding from risk sport dominance research is the relationship that has been found to exist between arousal-seeking (as reflected in scores on the TDS arousal–avoidance scale) and participation in risk sport activities. This relationship appears to hold true across subject populations ranging from general student samples to highly specialised and skilled, elite-level performers and for a variety of samples from different countries. In addition, the findings obtained from the TDS have been generally supported by results from the SSS (Zuckerman, 1979) when the two scales have been used together in studies (see earlier, and Trimpop et al., 1996). Paratelic dominant people usually prefer high arousal, high intensity, and the pleasure of immediate sensation. It would appear that at least some paratelic dominant people use risk sports to this end, pushing the limits further and further and cashing in on the emotional rewards.

THE PERCEPTION OF RISK

One should not lose sight, however, of the fact that reversal theory is about more than personality dispositions. It is also about the individual's subjective experience, in this case, of risky and dangerous situations. In the following example, one sportsman describes his own personal perception of risk and illustrates how the reversal theory notion of *protective frames* may operate in practice. Emotions accompanied by high levels of felt arousal, such as fear, are experienced as unpleasant in the telic state. In particular situations, paratelic protective frames allow the person concerned to experience these same emotions as pleasant.

Carl Llewellyn is a British National Hunt jockey who regularly puts himself at risk riding horses at break-neck speed over jumps and hurdles. He knows, better than most, that the risks are real. A litany of injuries are testament to the fact that he has not always managed to remain in the saddle. As a result of falls, in 1986 he broke his jaw and right cheekbone; in 1988 he broke his left forearm; in March 1990 he received a compound fracture of the right leg, ankle, and foot; in August 1990 he suffered a hairline fracture of his left wrist and had surgery on a dislocated elbow; in 1993 he broke his left collar bone; in March 1994 he broke his left ankle; in November 1994 he broke his right ankle and foot; and in December 1994 he fractured two vertebrae at bottom of his back. Injuries forced him to stop racing for a total of more than 25 months for recovery and rehabilitation. In the six year period from 1988–94, he was out of action for over two years. Yet he said in a recent interview (Muscat, 1994):

> I know others think it strange but it's what I live for. I love winning; it gets your blood up. I love the speed, the jumping, the competition. Sure we're in it so deep that we can't see out, but to us it's just a normal job.

and, as his interviewer pointed out:

> There are, he says, a thousand dangerous things he would never dream of trying. The prospect of bungee-jumping, a common enough experience these days, would positively terrify him even though accidents are so few and far between as to constitute little or no risk. Llewellyn's idea of unbridled pleasure is to conquer the Grand National course, as he did with his victory aboard Party Politics in 1992.

This interview and these quotes are useful because they provide a good example of the importance of an individual's perception of risk. In spite of frequent injuries, Carl Llewellyn does not perceive the activity as dangerous or particularly risky ("it's just a normal job"), in fact, quite the opposite. He relishes the speed and jumping and the thrill of competing and winning ("it's what I live for"). However, while Llewellyn positively enjoys the danger involved in National Hunt racing, he is terrified of other risk activities, like bungee jumping, where the level of risk may be less. In other words, he perceives the risk involved in horse racing is much less than (or much different from) his perception of risk associated with other risky activities. How can this (apparent) paradox be explained?

In reversal theory terms, he has developed what is termed a *protective frame* (see Chapter 2) around steeplechasing which does not exist (for him) with respect to other risk sports or activities. It is not a frame in the physical sense, but according to Apter (1993, p.31) is rather a psychological, phenomenological frame that, under certain conditions, is associated with the paratelic state:

> ...a protective frame gives the individual a feeling of safety, even when the dangers and threats are part of the phenomenal field, and that this produces the paradox of danger-which-is-not-danger. The presence of the frame is concomitant with the arousal-seeking state, and the possibility of experiencing one or another type of excitement or pleasurable high arousal.

In order to understand further how protective frames work in everyday life, the notions of *detachment, safety, danger,* and *trauma zones* need to be included in the discussion. Think about the everyday expression "skating on thin ice", in both the literal and figurative sense. First the literal sense: suppose a wide river has frozen over during winter and ice has formed which is thick enough to skate on. The ice is thickest near the bank of the river; towards the middle the ice is a good deal thinner and skating on it could be dangerous. A thin strip of water right in the middle of the river is not frozen. Some people will not wish to venture onto the ice at all, preferring to stay on the river bank watching other people taking risks. These people, somewhat removed from events on the ice, are in what reversal theorists call the *detachment zone*.

Others, skaters, perhaps beginners or those whose level of proficiency is not too high, will go onto the ice, but tend to remain close to the bank of the river, as will those who feel anxious and do not like to take risks by venturing too far out. For these skaters, the *safety zone* exists in the area close to the river bank. There will undoubtedly be others who, attracted by the danger of the thin ice, skate out towards the middle of the river into the *danger zone*, perhaps hearing the thin ice crack from their weight, as they skate over it. For these people, the perception of danger is much less than for those who stay near or on the bank. In a sense, their psychological protective frame extends much farther out from the bank than the frames of those who remain closer in. Those skaters who come close to what Apter (1992) has called *the dangerous edge* of the thin ice, are seeking and enjoying the high levels of pleasant arousal that can be obtained by courting danger close to the *trauma zone*.

What is important here, is that protective frames are likely to be more or less extensive for different people, and their safety and danger zones extended or reduced to a greater or lesser extent accordingly. Equally, although the real place where trauma can occur is the point farthest from the bank, in the middle of the river where the ice is thinnest and some of the water remains unfrozen, individuals will perceive the extent of the trauma zone differently. For some, the thrill of flirting with the danger zone may only be a few metres from the bank, while for others, toying with the danger zone takes place a good deal farther out. In each case, the attraction and thrill for each individual is obtained from pushing up to *their own* dangerous edge, as it is in many other risk sports and dangerous activities.

Figuratively, the phrase "skating on thin ice" is used in a more general sense in everyday language to cover an almost limitless range of activities and situations, in which a person is usually taking risks in the same way as just described. For example, the stockbroker, car salesman, genetic scientist, teacher, and defending attorney may all at times, in their peculiar situations, be said to be skating on thin ice. Similarly, for each individual the safety, danger, and trauma zones will vary, but the thrills concerned will be obtained in the same way: by approaching the dangerous edge, albeit in a totally different context.

Apter (1991, p.22) has used the metaphor of the tiger in a cage to illustrate the notion of protective frames. He pointed out that a tiger without a cage produces anxiety in people (danger); a cage without a tiger produces boredom (safety) but only a combination of the two, a tiger in a cage produces excitement (danger-within-safety). In addition, he went on to say (p.26):

> Some people seem to be inveterate adventure-seekers and to find their natural habitat in the danger zone, while the rest of us prefer to pass our lives basking in those areas of experience which I have described as the safety and detachment zones, playing with danger in more circumspect or vicarious ways when the opportunity arises.

Those individuals who engage in risk sports are likely to belong to the group of adventure seekers that Apter describes. By means of a protective frame, the high levels of arousal intrinsic to most risk sport activities, which paratelic dominant people prefer, can be created and enjoyed. Those individuals who regularly experience the dangerous edge at close quarters do, on occasion, find that their protective frames have been broken and they experience anxiety as a result of reversal to the telic state. Moreover, now and then even the most skilled risk sport participants end up in the trauma zone and receive painful injuries (see Carl Llewellyn, quoted earlier, and Kerr, Frank-Regan, & Brown, 1993). Their attitude is typified in the words of Steve Podborski (former downhill ski racing champion) quoted in *The Sunday Times* newspaper (Podborski, 1981):

> ...the only thing I want to do when I go fast is to go faster. Just imagine yourself in the point where you are scared silly. You get tunnel vision, and the only things you can see are the absolute necessities to maintain life. I'm never afraid.... I think I can handle any pain that comes along, so there is not much to fear.

Podborski is like many risk sport participants, who report their experiences of risk as having a kind of duality. In Podborski's case it is characterised by both being *scared silly* and at the same time *never being afraid*. On the one hand, this may be a reflection of the emotions associated with reversals back and forth, between, for example, paratelic and telic states where high arousal is experienced as pleasant excitement or unpleasant anxiety respectively. On the other hand, if the anxious and fearful feelings associated with downhill skiing were so unpleasant, it seems likely that Podborski, and others, might have dropped out long before they reached elite status, even allowing for the possible emotional compensation offered (e.g. post-event) by pleasant high-arousal emotions. What is more likely is that the only way that dangerous sport performers can deal with the powerful cocktail of emotions their activities induce is to experience the usually unpleasant emotions like telic anxiety in a pleasant paratelic way, through reversal theory's *parapathic emotions*. In a similar manner, in other leisure contexts (e.g. science fiction horror films and murder mystery fiction) otherwise unpleasant emotions are experienced as pleasant parapathic emotions when the protective frame is in operation (see Apter, 1993, pp.66–70). It is important to emphasise again that the pleasant experience of risk and danger is coupled with the protective frame. Should the frame for any reason fail, the pleasant parapathic emotions will revert to the usual unpleasant telic-oriented type.

This chapter began at the macro level, examining metamotivational dominance in risk sports. It moved on to look at the meso level and the way that high and very high levels of arousal are experienced. Now, at the micro level, a concentrated examination of the sports of skydiving and parachuting will move the discussion on to the specific emotions and metamotivational state combinations allied with dangerous sports participation.

EMOTIONAL EXPERIENCE DURING PARACHUTING

A convenient place to begin this part of the chapter is with the results of two oft-quoted studies by Epstein and Fenz (Epstein & Fenz, 1965; Fenz & Epstein, 1967). In their first experiment they set out with two groups of parachuting subjects. One group was made up of 33 beginners (1–5 previous jumps) and a second group comprised 33 experienced jumpers (>100 jumps). Subjects were asked to rate their feelings of *approach* (looking forward to the jump, wanting to go ahead) and *avoidance* (wanting to turn back and call the jump off, fear). For the novice jumpers, the greatest fear built up through the week prior to the jump, reaching a peak slightly before the actual parachute jump when the *ready* signal was given. For experienced jumpers, maximum fear was experienced on the morning of the jump and decreased from then until they left the plane. Once they left the plane (the point of greatest danger), the experienced jumpers' level of fear increased with the opening of the parachute and continued to increase for quite a time after landing.

In a second experiment (Fenz & Epstein, 1967), as well as self-reported fear, the researchers monitored psychophysiological parameters of anxiety, including heartrate, respiration rate, and skin conductance. Ten experienced

(>100 jumps) and 10 inexperienced (1–10 jumps) parachutists were monitored from the time that they arrived at the airport to landing after the jump. Group differences in the results for the three physiological measures were found, but the overall pattern for each group was similar. Inexperienced jumpers were found to report increasing levels of fear, reaching a maximum when the plane had reached its final altitude and then decreasing again. Experienced jumpers also reported increases in fear until take-off, after which, Fenz and Epstein (1967) argued, they were able to control their responses to some degree through an anxiety inhibition process (Epstein, 1967).

In an attempted replication of the work of Epstein and Fenz, Schedlowski and Tewes (1992), again comparing novice and experienced parachutists, found a different pattern to that of the earlier experiments (Epstein & Fenz, 1965; Fenz & Epstein, 1967). They studied 18 novice (1–6 jumps) and 18 experienced (107–2500 jumps) male parachutists using both physiological measures of respiration and heartrate and subjective measures of arousal. Measurements were taken at 12 different points in time, beginning the evening before the jump, and at regular intervals throughout the jump, including just before exit and just before deployment of the parachute (the time of maximum danger, exit to landing). Schedlowski and Tewes (1992) considered that they had improved on the original Fenz and Epstein experimental design, by asking subjects to self-rate their level of bodily arousal rather than make subjective estimates of fear or anxiety. Thus, no emotional *labels* concerned with the interpretation of bodily arousal levels were used. This avoided possible problems of denial tendencies and allowed a direct comparison with measures of respiration and heartrate and an assessment of awareness of bodily state to be made. (A detailed theoretical discussion of the relationship between arousal, anxiety, and excitement will be the main subject matter in Chapter 6.)

Overall, novices reported higher levels of arousal than the experienced parachutists. Maximum levels of arousal for both groups were found during exit and just before deployment of the parachute. Although the heartrate measurements for novices were higher than for experienced jumpers, heartrate value curves paralleled each other, reaching maximum scores just after entering the plane and, as with self-rated arousal, just before exit. No significant differences were found in respiration rates. The results of this study not only failed to replicate the results of the earlier study, but also did not support inverted-U shaped curves for either novice or experienced groups identified earlier (Epstein & Fenz, 1965; Fenz & Epstein, 1967).

In a reversal theory study, Apter and Batler (1996) set out to probe subjects' parachuting experience in detail and identify whether reversals occurred during parachuting. The majority of their male (N = 51) and female (N = 10) parachuting subject sample (mean age 33.7 years) considered themselves to be experienced amateurs or higher in ability (mean parachuting time 4.7 years). The researchers' general hypothesis was that, in parachuting, anxiety would be felt before the moment of maximum danger and excitement afterwards. In addition to testing their general hypothesis, Apter and Batler (1996) were interested in identifying the different sources of satisfaction that emanate from parachuting and how those sources of satisfaction would relate to the four pairs of metamotivational states. In the description of the results that follows, subject numbers vary due to a small number of questionnaire responses which (for different reasons, see Apter & Batler, 1996) could not be included in the analysis.

For the 50 subjects whose responses were relevant to this part of the analysis, the moment of maximum danger was always reported by subjects as the period between leaving the plane and the opening of the parachute canopy, as in the Schedlowski and Tewes (1992) study. Subjects were also asked to pinpoint the times that maximum anxiety and excitement were experienced. Maximum anxiety was experienced by almost two-thirds (64%) of the subjects (eight subjects were excluded) 1–2 minutes before the point of maximum danger, by 10% of subjects at that moment, and by 7% of subjects 1 minute after the point of maximum danger. Of the remaining 19%, 2% experienced maximum anxiety 3 minutes before, 12% 8 minutes before and, 5% 10 minutes before the point of maximum danger (see Fig. 4.2).

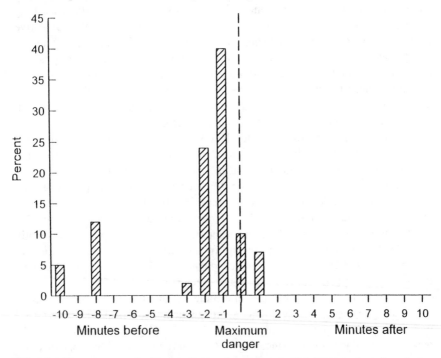

FIG. 4.2.   The percentage of subjects indicating the moment at which they experienced maximum anxiety, for each minute before or after the moment of maximum danger (from Svebak & Apter, 1996).

With respect to the experience of maximum excitement, 36% of subjects (three subjects were excluded) reported experiencing maximum excitement within 2 minutes after, 19% 3–6 minutes after, and 9% 10 minutes after the point of maximum danger; 13% of subjects reported maximum excitement at the moment of maximum danger, 15% 1 minute before, and the remainder, 2% 6 minutes and 2% 10 minutes before (see Fig. 4.3).

As can be seen from Figs. 4.2 and 4.3, subjects' responses about the moments of maximum anxiety and excitement are congregated just before and just after the point of maximum danger. This finding underlines the very rapid changes that occur between the two emotions in parachuting, and supports the arguments of reversal theory. In fact, 30 out of 50 subjects conformed to the general hypothesis; 8 subjects reported experiencing an anxiety to excitement reversal, but not at the moment of maximum danger; and a further 8 subjects reported no anxiety during the activity. Only 4 subjects reversed from excitement to anxiety, contrary to the hypothesis.

Consequently, although Schedlowski and Tewes (1992) found that maximum levels of arousal were experienced during exit and just before deployment of the parachute, Apter and Batler (1996) have demonstrated that these high

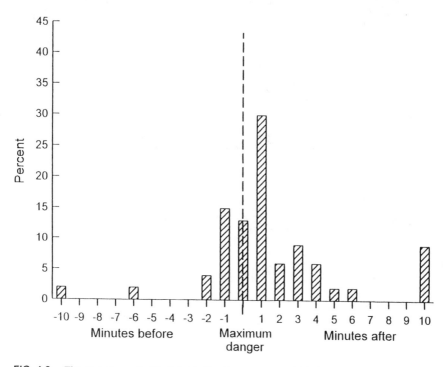

FIG. 4.3. The percentage of subjects indicating the moment at which they experienced maximum excitement, for each minute before or after the moment of maximum danger (from Svebak & Apter, 1996).

arousal levels could be experienced as either anxiety or excitement and that, for the majority of subjects, reversals took place from anxiety to excitement close to the moment of maximum danger. Unlike Fenz and Epstein (Epstein & Fenz, 1965; Fenz & Epstein 1967), who restricted their study to unpleasant emotions (i.e. fear and anxiety), Apter and Batler (1996) used both pleasant and unpleasant high arousal emotions (i.e. excitement and anxiety) and allowed subjects to report exactly when they were experiencing these two specific emotions.

Apter and Batler (1996) also attempted to identify the particular motives allied with participation in dangerous sports. Subjects (N = 61) were presented with a list of possible sources of pleasure and asked to indicate which of these corresponded with their reasons for participating in parachuting. Subjects were permitted to choose more than one item. As reflected by frequency of citation, the most important reasons given were (in descending order of importance) excitement/thrill, immediate fun, serious achievement, control and mastery, being part of a community or group, helping others master the situation, defying convention, relief afterwards, being concerned for others, and finally being the centre of concerned attention.

Subjects were also asked to list the reason for participation that provided them with the greatest pleasure. The responses were then grouped according to

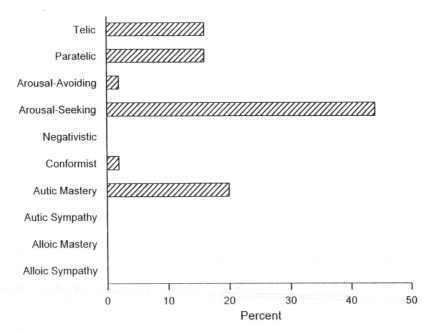

FIG. 4.4. The percentage of subjects endorsing, as their primary reason for parachuting, statements representing different basic motives (from Svebak & Apter, 1996).

reversal theory's metamotivational state terminology. The most frequently cited reasons were concerned with arousal seeking, paratelic, telic, and autic-mastery motives (see Fig. 4.4). However, negativistic or sympathy-based motives also played a part in some subjects' metamotivational patterns. Therefore, with such a range of answers, pinpointing particular metamotivational combinations associated with risk sport participation becomes hazardous. In searching for a predominant metamotivational pattern, individual idiosyncrasies may become hidden. Of course, as reversal theory argues, metamotivational patterns are not fixed and, when parachuting, different combinations are undoubtedly operative at different times. The results of this study have helped to emphasise the value of reversal theory for analysing individual motivation in sport.

CONCLUDING COMMENTS

Apter and Batler's (1996) study is, to date, one of the few reversal theory studies (see also Males & Kerr, 1996) which have studied the emotional experiences of risk sport participants in situ. It not only provided the details of subjects' experience of high arousal (anxiety/excitement) and reversals, but also identified a sizeable proportion of subjects who indicated mastery-based reasons for taking part in parachuting. This is an important finding which links in with the findings of other research and helps to pinpoint how individuals construct their protective frames while carrying out dangerous sports and activities. As Trimpop (1994, p.141) pointed out:

> The importance of perceived control, familiarity, security and predictability to induce the paratelic state has also been stressed by Apter (1982). This in turn means, that in the case of paratelic arousal, we deal with a kind of planned arousal in a subjectively controlled situation. This assumption is strongly supported by Piët (1987), who reported that stuntmen experienced their profession as generally risky but individually and situationally controlled, and that they spent a lot of their time with making the situation controllable, while maintaining the pleasantness of arousal.

The results of the Piët (1987) study mentioned by Trimpop are of interest in this context. Being a stuntman is a risky occupation, but her results showed that the risks involved are perceived as an opportunity to improve mastery and control elements in their lives, rather than being the origin of fear. She also found that, while they perceive themselves as having high personal control in their occupation, they are less certain about everyday activities like, for example, driving in traffic. Piët (1987, p.210) also argued that the objectively risky actions in their profession are perceived by stuntmen as a challenge: "The reward of danger seeking is thus to be found in the sense of mastery and competence."

In many forms of risk sport, people compete against nature and the elements, without necessarily having other human competitors present. In other forms of sport and games, people compete against each other, either individually or in teams. For many of these individuals, pleasure and satisfaction come from being successful and winning. The next chapter explores this experience, examining the motivation and emotions associated with being successful, and contrasting this experience with the experience of those who are less successful.

FURTHER READING

1. Apter, M.J. (1992). *The dangerous edge*. New York: Free Press.
2. Apter, M.J. (1991). A structural-phenomenology of play. In J.H. Kerr & M.J. Apter (Eds.), *Adult play* (pp.13–29). Amsterdam: Swets & Zeitlinger.
3. Trimpop, R.M. (1994). *The psychology of risk taking behaviour*. Amsterdam: North Holland.

REFERENCES

Apter, M. J. (1982). *The experience of motivation: The theory of psychological reversals*. London/ New York: Academic Press.

Apter, M.J. (1991). A structural phenomenology of play. In J.H. Kerr & M.J. Apter (Eds.), *Adult play* (pp.13–29). Amsterdam: Swets & Zeitlinger.

Apter, M.J. (1992). *The dangerous edge*. New York: Free Press.

Apter, M.J. (1993). Phenomenological frames and the paradoxes of experience. In J.H. Kerr, S. Murgatroyd, & M.J. Apter (Eds.), *Advances in reversal theory* (pp.27–39). Amsterdam: Swets & Zeitlinger.

Apter, M.J., & Batler, R. (1996). Gratuitous risk: A study of parachuting. In S. Svebak, & M.J. Apter (Eds.), *Stress and health: A reversal theory perspective*. Washington, DC: Taylor & Francis.

Barratt, E.S. (1985). Impulsiveness subtraits: Arousal and information processing. In J.T. Spence, & C.E. Izard, C.E. (Eds.), *Motivation, emotion and personality* (pp.137–146). New York: Elsevier.

Braathen, E.T., & Svebak, S. (1992). Motivational differences among talented teenage athletes: The significance of gender, type of sport and level of excellence. *Scandinavian Journal of Medicine and Science in Sports, 2*, 153–159.

Callois, R. (1961). *Man, play and games*. New York: The Free Press.

Chirivella, E.C., & Martinez, L.M. (1994). The sensation of risk and motivational tendencies in sports: An empirical study. *Personality and Individual Differences, 16*, 777–786.

Edwards, P., & Ottum, B. (1967). *You should have been here an hour ago*. New York: Harper & Row.

Epstein, S. (1967). Toward a unified theory of anxiety. In B.A. Maher (Ed.), *Progress in experimental personality research* (pp.1–89). New York: Academic Press.

Epstein, S., & Fenz, W.D. (1965). Steepness of approach and avoidance in humans as a function of experience. *Journal of Experimental Psychology, 70*, 1–12.

Ewert, A. (1985). Why people climb: The relationship of participant motives and experience level to mountaineering. *Journal of Leisure Research, 17*(3), 241–250.

Farmer, R.J. (1992). Surfing: Motivations, values and culture. *Journal of Sport Behaviour, 15* (3), 241–257.

Fenz, W.D., & Epstein, S. (1967). Gradients of psychological arousal in parachutists as a function of the approaching jump. *Journal of Psychosomatic Medicine, 29*, 33–51.

Goma, M. (1991). Personality profile of subjects engaged in high physical risk sports. *Personality and Individual Differences, 12*, 1087–1093.

Kenyon, G.S. (1968). Six scales for assessing attitudes toward physical activity. *Research Quarterly, 39*, 96–105.

Kerr, J.H. (1988). Play, sport and the paratelic state. In M.J. Apter, J.H. Kerr, & M.P. Cowles (Eds.), *Progress in reversal theory* (pp.77–88). [Advances in psychology series, 51]. Amsterdam: North Holland/Elsevier.

Kerr, J.H. (1991). Arousal-seeking in risk sport participants. *Personality and Individual Differences, 12*(6) 613–616.

Kerr, J.H., Frank-Regan, E., & Brown, R.I.F. (1993). Taking risks with health. *Patient Guidance and Counselling, 22*, 73–80.

Kerr, J.H., & Svebak, S. (1989). Motivational aspects of preference for and participation in risk sports. *Personality and Individual Differences, 10*, 797–800.

Males, J.R., & Kerr, J.H. (1996). Stress, emotion and performance in elite slalom canoeists. *The Sport Psychologist, 10*, 17–36.

McDermott, M.R., & Apter, M.J. (1988). Negativism Dominance Scale. In M.J. Apter, J.H. Kerr, & M.P.Cowles (Eds.), *Progress in reversal theory.* [Advances in psychology series, 51]. Amsterdam: North-Holland/Elsevier.

McGuane, T. (1990). *An outside chance.* Boston: Houghton Mifflin/Seymour Lawrence.

Murgatroyd, S. (1985). The nature of telic dominance. In M.J. Apter, S. Murgatroyd, & D. Fontana (Eds.), *Reversal theory: Applications and developments* (pp.20–41). Cardiff: University College Cardiff Press.

Murgatroyd, S., Rushton, C., Apter, M.J., & Ray, C. (1978). The development of the Telic Dominance Scale. *Journal of Personality Assessment, 42*, 519–528.

Muscat, J. (1994, 17 December). Bones of contention curb Llewellyn. *The Times.*

Piët, S. (1987). What motivates stunt men? *Motivation and Emotion, 11*, 195–213.

Podborski, S., (1981, 8 February). *The Sunday Times.*

Rainey, W. (1994, May). *Inside Sport, 29*, 13.

Rowland, G.L., Franken, R.E., & Harrison, K. (1986). Sensation seeking and participation in sporting activities. *Journal of Sport Psychology, 8*, 212–220.

Schedlowski, M., & Tewes, U. (1992). Physiological arousal and perception of bodily state during parachute jumping. *Psychophysiology, 29*, 95–103.

Scott, D. (1994, May). Stepping out in style. *The Australian Way*, 70–74.

Summers, J., & Stewart, E. (1993). The arousal performance relationship: Examining different conceptions. In S. Serpa, J. Alves, V. Ferriera, & A. Paula–Brito (Eds.), *Proceedings of the VIII World Congress of Sport Psychology* (pp.229–232). Lisbon, Portugal: International Society of Sport Psychology.

Svebak, S., & Apter, M.J. (Eds.) (1996). *Stress and health: A reversal theory perspective.* Washington, DC: Taylor & Francis.

Svebak, S., & Kerr, J.H. (1989). The role of impulsivity in preference for sports. *Personality and Individual Differences, 10*(1), 51–58.

Svebak, S., & Murgatroyd, S. (1985). Metamotivational dominance: A multimethod validation of reversal theory constructs. *Journal of Personality and Social Psychology, 48*(1), 107–116.

Trimpop, R.M. (1994). *The psychology of risk taking behaviour.* Amsterdam: North Holland.

Trimpop, R.M., Kirkcaldy, B., & Kerr, J.H. (1996). *Comparing personality constructs of risk-taking behavior.* Manuscript submitted for publication.

Van Reusel, B., & Renson, R. (1982). The social stigma of high-risk sport subcultures. In A.O. Dunleavy, A.W. Miracle, & R.C. Rees (Eds.), *Studies in the sociology of sport. Proceedings of the Annual Conference of the North American Society for the Sociology of Sport* (pp.183–202). Fort Worth, Texas (12–15 November , 1981). Fort Worth Texas Christian University Press.

Vlaswinkel, E.H., & Kerr, J.H. (1990). Negativism dominance in risk and team sports. *Perceptual and Motor Skills, 70,* 289–290.

Zuckerman, M. (1979). *Sensation seeking: Beyond the optimal level of arousal.* Hillsdale, NJ: Lawrence Erlbaum Associates Inc.

Zuckerman, M. (1983). Sensation seeking and sports. *Personality and Individual Differences, 4,* 285–293.

5

We are the Champions!: Winning and Losing in Sport

For some top performers, taking part in and having pleasure from sport is a major source of satisfaction. For example, Evonne Goolagong, the former Australian tennis player and Wimbledon winner enthused about the joy of playing (Goolagong, Collins, & Edwards, 1975, p.33):

> Some players feel that winning is everything, and losing a disaster. Not me. I want the spectators to take home a good memory. If I'd lost my 1972 Wimbledon semi-final to Chris Evert in three sets instead of winning in three, I'd have been disappointed. But not displeased or angry. Because of the occasion, the tension, the fight we both displayed, and our shot-making, it will rank as one of the memorable matches. I was told that it was an emotionally draining experience for the viewers. Above all: An experience. Playing a part in a gripping sporting drama is all I ask.

More recently, Davies (1991, p.258) reports an interview with England and Liverpool player John Barnes, a top performer in the fiercely competitive sport of professional soccer:

> Throughout, talking about football, he talked about pleasure much more than he talked about winning. Sure, winning was great, and a good run gave you confidence—but it didn't come over as a motivating force for him personally, in the way that the pure pleasure of playing did.

The sentiments of Barnes and Goolagong are in sharp contrast to those of some other sports performers for whom, as Goolagong says, "winning is everything, and losing a disaster". Novak (1976, pp.86–87) astutely described the fine line between success and failure and the reality of winning and losing in sport:

> It is true that for coaches "winning is the only thing." No matter how much they enjoy the game, coaches are fired if they do not produce winners. But players go on playing, win or lose; and on the average, all lose as often as they win . . .
>
> Often, in victory, a player will know that his own performance was beneath his ideals; in defeat, that he never played better. Victory tastes sweet; defeat is like death. But the seasons march on, next week is another game. Winning is a priceless and lovely thing, but for players it cannot be the only thing, for losing is very much a part of every career.

Sport psychologists have shown a keen interest in psychological aspects of successful performance for some time. In addition to trying to understand the motor processes involved, their interest has had two primary focuses. First, they have tried to pinpoint the psychological responses that accompany the experience of winning and losing and, second, the mental states that are associated with successful (or unsuccessful) performance. To some extent, reversal theory research on successful performance has followed similar lines. In some cases, reversal theory studies have looked exclusively at the psychological parameters of success, in others, a combined approach examining the parameters of success and ongoing changes in mood response during performance have been undertaken. These research studies have examined a number of different sports and exercise activities (rugby, gymnastics, squash, and canoeing) and sports performers, both male and female at a wide range of ability levels (international, national, county, club, and recreational). Furthermore, a number of different research methodologies have been adopted in order to reveal the experience of performers in the sports context. These investigations, reviewed next, have included field experiments and field studies, comprising ecologically valid "real-life" competitive simulations and actual competitive events.

SUCCESS IN RUGBY

Kerr and Van Schaik (1995) monitored possible changes in the mood of top-level Dutch rugby players as a result of game outcome (win or loss). At each of four rugby games during the 1992–93 rugby season, Dutch versions of the Telic State Measure (TSM; Svebak & Murgatroyd, 1985; see Appendix F) and the Stress–Arousal Checklist measures (SACL; Mackay, Cox, Burrows, & Lazzerini, 1978) were administered to players five minutes before and just after playing. (The conceptual basis for the SACL is provided by a two-dimensional model of mood. The checklist comprises two independent measures of self-reported mood: arousal and stress. Subjects are asked to respond on a four-point rating scale to 18 positive and negative stress adjectives and 12 positive and negative arousal adjectives.) Two games were won and two lost. Analysis of the results indicated that players' psychological experience after winning games was considerably more pleasant than after losing games (see also Abadie, 1989). Specifically, after winning players' scores were significantly less serious (TSM) and more spontaneous (TSM) than after losing. Also, arousal (SACL) scores were significantly higher and stress (SACL) scores significantly lower after winning games than after losing games.

The sample of rugby players who took part in this study were mature male subjects. By way of contrast, in the study that follows, young female gymnasts, heavily involved in training for and competition in gymnastics, comprised the subject sample.

SUCCESS IN GYMNASTICS

An exploratory field study in competitive gymnastics was carried out by Kerr and Pos (1994). They were interested in comparing the psychological experience of two groups of female gymnasts of different ability, at training and in competition. One more successful group of gymnasts (A-level group; N=7) competed at the highest level in the Netherlands and trained for, on average, 20 hours per week. A second group of less successful gymnasts (B-level group; N=7) competed at the level just below the top A-level group and trained for 12–15 hours per week. Differences in age were not significant between the two groups. In training and competition there were four individual gymnastic disciplines (beam, floor, horse, and asymmetric bars). Gymnasts were asked to complete Dutch versions of the TSM and SACL immediately before and just after performing each discipline during two training sessions and two competitions.

Amongst the results obtained were important group differences in the patterns of mood experience between A- and B-level groups and between training and competition. The A-level group gymnasts' scores were consistent between training and competition on felt arousal (TSM), preferred arousal (TSM), arousal discrepancy (TSM), and effort (TSM). In contrast, the arousal pattern for B-level gymnasts was inconsistent between training and competition. B-level gymnasts, for example, reported mean scores on both felt arousal (TSM), and arousal discrepancy (TSM) that were significantly higher before competition than before training (see also, Krane & Williams, 1987; Mahoney & Avener, 1977; Mahoney, Avener, & Avener, 1983).

In addition, there were no important differences in the amount of effort (TSM) invested in competition and training by the A-level group, but group B's effort (TSM) scores were found to be significantly higher during competition than during training. B-level gymnasts were experiencing a greater mismatch between preferred and felt arousal levels and these higher effort (TSM) scores reflected greater efforts by the B-level group to cope with the demands of competition. These findings were supported by self-reported stress (SACL) scores (see also Chapter 9).

In this study, two different patterns of mood experience were identified. In particular, less successful performers were found to exhibit less stability in mood response than their more successful peers. In psychological terms, being successful in female gymnastics appears to require the ability to achieve and maintain appropriate levels of felt arousal both at training and in competition. Also, A-level gymnasts showed significantly lower seriousmindedness (TSM) scores before and after training, and significantly lower planning orientation scores after training, than B-level gymnasts. Thus, A-level athletes were generally more paratelic-oriented before and after training than their less successful gymnastic peers.

The results outlined here, however, should be interpreted with some caution due to the study's exploratory nature and the relatively small number of subjects involved. Gymnastics is primarily an individual sport. A series of studies on squash, another individual sport, are reported in the following section.

SUCCESS IN SQUASH

Sports performers are sometimes reluctant to take part in research studies, finding the completion of psychological instruments intrusive during competition. Performers typically want to keep their minds focused on the task at hand without distractions. This is especially true for those competing at a high level, where rankings and financial rewards may be at stake. One option for researchers is to re-create the natural conditions of real-life sports situations under controlled conditions in field experiments. This was the research strategy carried out in the first two squash studies (Cox & Kerr, 1989a, b; Kerr & Cox, 1988, 1990, 1991).

Squash Study 1

The first squash study (Kerr & Cox, 1988, 1990) was carried out in a squash court, which conveniently allowed experimental conditions during skill performance to be controlled. Forty volunteer males, divided into groups of skilled, average, and novice squash players, equipped with their own racquets, completed a squash practice task (frequently performed in games) with two levels of difficulty. Extra lines were placed on the squash court to mark out targets on the front wall and the rear corners of the court (see Kerr & Cox, 1990; and Figs. 5.1a & b). Using a mixed blocks research design, squash subjects were required to hit 30 continuous forehand shots from the back of the court (a) at the front wall target only (easy), and (b) at the front wall and the rear corner targets (difficult). The player's score for each squash task was the total number of hits on the front wall target.

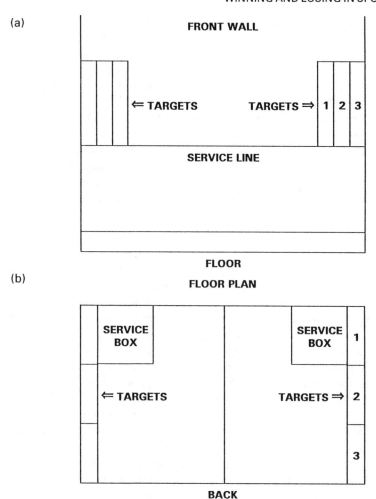

FIG. 5.1a/b. Front wall and floor plan with targets used in the squash tasks (easy and difficult) (from Kerr & Cox, 1990).

Prior to and just after finishing the squash tasks, players completed the TSM and SACL measures. The Telic Dominance Scale (TDS; Murgatroyd, Rushton, Apter, & Ray, 1978) was also administered on an earlier occasion, but no significant differences between ability groups were revealed. Amongst other results, performance scores in the experiment confirmed the ability classification. Also, significant increases (in the telic direction) in planning–spontaneous (TSM) scores and increases approaching significance in serious–playful (TSM) scores were obtained pre- to post-task for all groups. This result indicated that carrying out the squash task appeared to make all three groups more telic-oriented and may have induced paratelic to telic reversals in a considerable number of players.

With respect to arousal and stress measures, high levels of arousal (SACL and TSM) were reported by all three ability groups and remained high throughout the field experiment. However, the skilled players reported significantly lower levels of arousal discrepancy (TSM) scores pre- and post-task, than the average and novice groups. Stress (SACL) supported arousal discrepancy (TSM) scores. All of this pointed to a difference in experience while performing the squash tasks. For the skilled group, the squash task experience (one of high arousal and low arousal discrepancy and stress) was pleasant and accompanied by high levels of hedonic tone. Conversely, for the average and novice groups, (high arousal levels were accompanied by high levels of arousal discrepancy and stress) the experience was considerably less pleasant and accompanied by low levels of hedonic tone (see also Dowd & Innes, 1981).

Squash Study 2

Cox and Kerr (1989a, b) monitored squash players' psychological reactions to competitive play, in a series of three specially arranged tournaments in which independent squash experts selected and approached players about participating, organised and controlled the separate tournaments, and awarded cash prizes to the winner and runner-up. The three tournaments involved English club, county, or international level players. In each tournament, ten players of similar ability were organised in two leagues of five players who played off against each other. Squash players played four games, the winner of each game being the first to reach 15 points. One player from each league, who had scored most points overall, progressed to the tournament final.

Before the beginning of the tournament, players completed a batch of questionnaires which included the TDS. No significant differences in telic dominance were found between groups. Prior to and after the four preliminary games, players completed the TSM and SACL measures and data from these were collapsed across tournament groups to form different groups of the most successful (winners) and least successful (losers) players.

Aspects of the players' arousal scores were found to be important with respect to success and failure. Winners' arousal (SACL) scores were significantly higher than those of losers. Perhaps more important, the pattern of winners' arousal scores remained relatively stable across the four tournament games, as did their moderate stress (SACL) scores. Losers' arousal scores (SACL) did change significantly across games. Significant differences between winners' and losers' group means on arousal (SACL) were especially marked at games 3 and 4 (see Fig. 5.2a). Winners' stress (SACL) scores also decreased significantly across games, but losers' did not (see Fig. 5.2b). Losers' stress (SACL) scores were high initially, but decreased after game 2. Losers' arousal discrepancy (TSM) results supported their stress (SACL) results (see Fig. 5.2c).

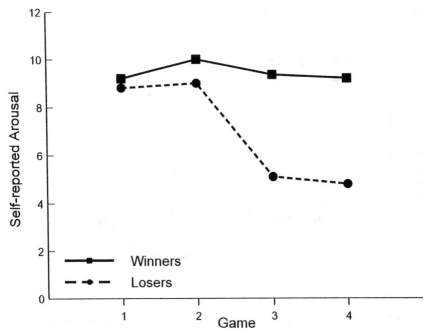

FIG. 5.2a. Mean arousal (SACL) scores for winners and losers at the four games of the squash tournament (from Cox & Kerr, 1989a).

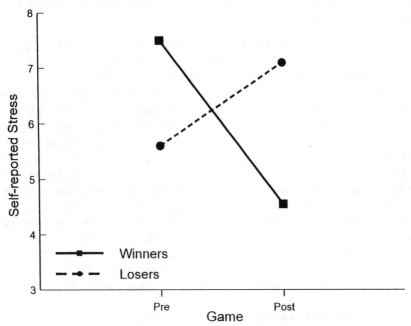

FIG. 5.2b. Mean pre- and post-game stress (SACL) scores for winners and losers (averaged over all games) (from Cox & Kerr, 1989a).

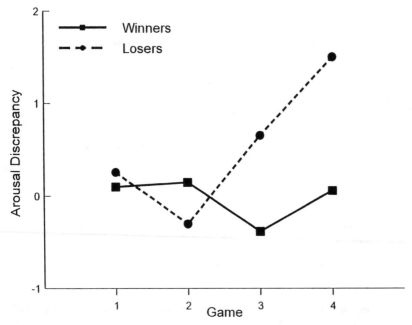

FIG. 5.2c. Mean arousal discrepancy scores (TSM) for winners and losers at the four games of the squash tournament (from Cox & Kerr, 1989a).

Cox and Kerr (1989a, b) argued that the stability of mood found in winners' scores was due either to winners being less affected by, or being better able to minimises any negative effects that might have arisen from the demands of playing. The high levels of arousal that were achieved and maintained during winners' squash performance were non-stressful and, as in the previous study, may be an important element in successful squash performance. In contrast, the mood pattern of losers appeared much less stable with, for example, significant differences revealed in arousal (SACL) scores at games 3 and 4 and significant differences on arousal discrepancy (TSM) scores across games. In general, TSM scores also revealed that more winners were in the telic state than the paratelic state, both pre- and post-game, throughout the tournament.

The study was concerned with an examination of metamotivational characteristics and arousal and stress effects amongst winners and losers in squash. Jonah Barrington, former world class squash player, was a frequent winner. As illustrated by the following quote (Barrington, 1982, p.43), he left no doubt about where he stood with respect to winning and losing:

I've always wanted to win. I'm convinced that all champion athletes hate defeat. A young person setting out in sport like squash, hungry to get out of his environment, hungry to be somebody, has to have this deep almost maniacal, hatred of being beaten. Ideally he must learn to control it, but he has to feel it inside.

It's pride, it's shame, it's a dread of being inferior. It's a throwback to more primitive times, when you had to be competitive in order to survive . . . This is not to say that there is no such thing as 'social' sport—sport for fun, and sport to make friends. But there's an enormous difference between social sport and high-level, professional, international sport. For people playing sport for fun, there is no life-and-death struggle—not at that level. For them, the crucial area for survival is not sport but some other sphere. Whereas sport at the highest level is absolutely brutal. The fun element is negligible. For the people involved, sport is the survival area.

As well as the tremendous drive and determination that is apparent here, Barrington's (1982) quote also draws attention to feelings like pride, shame, and the desire to master (not be inferior to) opponents, which are involved in winning at the top level in squash. Wilson and Phillips (1995) carried out an extension of the earlier research work in competitive squash (Cox & Kerr, 1989a, b; Kerr & Cox, 1988, 1990, 1991) which attempted to explore reversal theory's somatic and transactional emotions, groupings that include some of those emotions mentioned by Barrington (1982).

Squash Study 3

Wilson and Phillips' (1995) study enlisted Tasmanian male squash players (N = 60) involved in four different grades of a *real* squash competition as subjects. Subjects completed a number of reversal theory instruments which included the TDS and the Negativism Dominance Scale (NDS; McDermott & Apter, 1988), and a mood checklist (MC) comprising the eight somatic and eight transactional mood adjectives (see Chapter 2; Apter, 1989). Players were asked to choose the adjective that best fitted their feelings at the time of testing for both somatic and transactional sets of states. Players also provided match performance information comprising straightforward 10-point rating scales with descriptive adjectives at each end. This included a strength-of-opponent rating scale and post-game scales relating to how pleasant–unpleasant players felt, how satisfied–dissatisfied players were with their performance, and how close–not close they felt their match to have been regardless of score. The MC and the strength of opponent scale were completed 2–3 minutes pre-game, after the second set, and post-game. Games consisted of the best of five sets.

The findings of the study showed that winners experienced significantly more:

- pleasant than unpleasant somatic emotions;
- conformist than negativistic emotions;
- high than low felt transactional outcome emotions (associated with feelings of net gain);
- pleasant than unpleasant transactional emotions;
- mastery than sympathy emotions.

Conversely, losers were found to experience significantly more:

- negativistic than conformist emotions;
- telic than paratelic emotions;
- unpleasant than pleasant transactional emotions;
- mastery than sympathy emotions.

Furthermore, when games were not close-fought, there was little difference between winners and losers, but when games were close, losers were more telic than winners. In terms of satisfaction, there was no difference between winners and losers when games were close-fought, but losers were significantly more dissatisfied when games were not close (see Fig. 5.3a). Analysis of strength-of-opponent scores showed that, in general, players felt significantly more dissatisfied after playing a stronger player than either a player who was about the same strength or a weaker opponent. While winners revealed little variability in unpleasantness, losers revealed greater unpleasantness when, for example, they lost easily to a player of similar strength (see Figs. 5.3b & 5.3c).

Also of interest with regard to losers' results, was a low correlation obtained between NDS scores and unpleasantness. In other words, the more negativistic

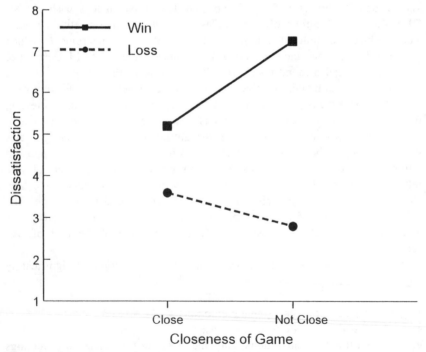

FIG. 5.3a. The effects of game closeness and game outcome on players' feelings of dissatisfaction post-game (from Wilson & Phillips, 1995).

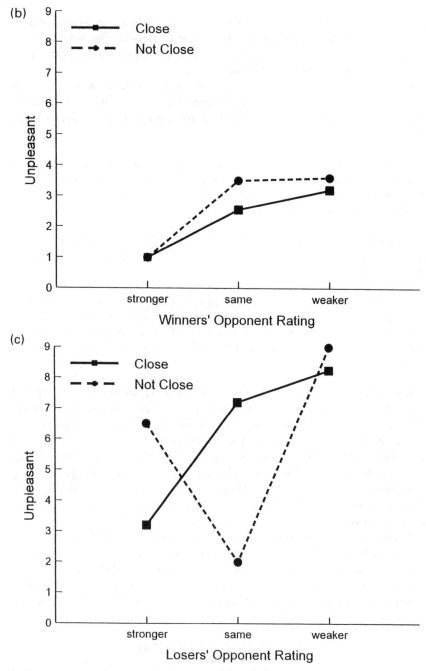

FIG. 5.3b/c. The effects of opponent strength and game closeness on post-game ratings of unpleasantness for winners (b) and losers (c) (from Wilson & Phillips, 1995).

dominant a player was, the greater the unpleasantness felt after losing. Wilson and Phillips (1995) pointed out that this result is important because it means that game outcome is a strong mediator of metamotivational state which, in turn is also related to aspects of dominance.

Anecdotal evidence concerning the emotional experience associated with winning and losing which supports the findings of this squash study can be found. For example, Cleary (1993, p.44) quotes top female tennis player Steffi Graf on the feeling associated with winning:

> For herself, her motivation lies not in a cheque book nor even in the scroll of honour which adorns Wimbledon. She is driven solely by a few moments of intangible joy. 'In those brief moments after a match is finished,' said Graf, 'you experience a high which you can't get anywhere else.'

In contrast, Daley Thompson, the highly successful decathlete describes the hell of losing after coming second in the 1978 European Championships (Rozin, 1983, p.17):

> ... I felt so bad. I couldn't shake that feeling of failure. I walked around the house for days, not answering the phone, not wanting to talk to anyone. It was like I'd died but nobody's buried me. It was the worst thing that had ever happened to me. I know it shouldn't be that bad, but it was. Nothing is worse. Nothing.

It is important to note that the results from the Wilson and Phillips' (1995) study go beyond telic and paratelic considerations and underline the important role that, for example, mastery can play in the individual's motivational experience in sport. This links back to the previous chapter on risk sports and Apter and Batler's (1996) study in which mastery motives were identified as important for participation in parachuting. As a professional cyclist being interviewed by the author stated when asked to describe the winning feeling, "It's very hard to describe. I think it's just the feeling that you're the best and that you can beat them all."

Another individual sport is the subject of the final section in this review. It is one in which the skills required, and the challenges met by participants, could hardly be more different than those encountered in squash. The individual sport at focus is white-water slalom canoeing and the researchers involved used a somewhat different investigative approach to uncovering the emotional experiences of the canoeists.

SUCCESS IN CANOEING

The research strategy selected for the study of canoeing comprised a joint approach using questionnaire and interview techniques (Males & Kerr, 1996;

Males, Kerr, & Gerkovich, 1997). Questionnaire data obtained was treated as a collection of individual case studies and analysed according to time-series analysis, which allowed subjects' best and worst performances to be compared (see e.g. Males & Kerr, 1996; Mueser, Yarnold, & Foy, 1991). In addition, the canoeists also took part in post-race semi-structured interviews (Males et al., 1997).

Nine elite male slalom canoeists from the top ten in their country were volunteer subjects and at the World Canoe Slalom Championships (one of the events at which data was gathered), three members of the group won individual and team medals. Their average length of involvement in canoeing was 10.1 years and they trained on average 13.1 hours per week.

Questionnaire Results

The canoeists completed a modified version of the Tension and Effort Stress Inventory (TESI; Svebak, 1993; Svebak, et al. 1991; see Appendix G) with added items from the TSM (3–felt arousal and 4–preferred arousal), within 30 minutes of the start of each slalom event over a seven-month slalom season. These events included non-ranking, national team selection, and the World Championships.

The TESI has four groups of items concerning pleasant somatic emotions (relaxation, excitement, placidity, provocativeness); unpleasant somatic emotions (anxiety, anger, boredom, sullenness); pleasant transactional emotions (pride, gratitude, modesty, virtue); unpleasant transactional emotions (humiliation, resentment, shame, guilt); as well as four items that relate to external and internal stress and coping (see also Chapter 9). Official race results were used as a measure of performance and these were compared to the canoeists' average performance scores for the season through the calculation of ipsative Z scores (see Males & Kerr, 1996).

Levels of pleasant emotions (TESI) were found to be consistently higher than levels of unpleasant emotions (see also Kerr & Svebak, 1994), but there were no important changes across performances. The same pattern was also apparent for the majority of canoeists on stress (TESI), effort (TESI), and felt arousal (TSM) scores (see also Chapter 9). All the best performances were preceded by null or low levels of arousal discrepancy (TSM).

The profiles of two canoeists, both experienced national team members and successful Olympic competitors, provide an interesting contrast. Subject F performed best in a local canoeing event and worst at the World Championships, and subject G performed best at the World Championships and worst in a local canoeing event. For canoeist F the majority of emotions (11 out of 16) were reported at similar levels, with no significant differences between scores for any emotion before best and worst performances. The emotion scores of canoeist G showed greater variation, but only scores on *anger* revealed a significant difference between best and worst performance. Both canoeists reported experiencing pleasant emotions such as *excitement, pride, relaxation* and *virtue,* and unpleasant emotions such as *anxiety.* However, as mentioned earlier, unpleasant emotions were experienced at lower levels than pleasant emotions.

It is interesting that arousal discrepancy (TSM) scores were zero before both subjects' best performances and both experienced a mismatch between preferred and felt arousal (TSM) levels before their worst performances (see Fig. 5.4). Although, at both events, canoeist G would have preferred an arousal level similar to his season's average, his arousal level before his worst performance (at a local event) was significantly lower than that reported at his best performance in the World Championships. Canoeist F experienced both felt and preferred levels of arousal higher than his season's average before his worst performance at the World Championship, (see Fig. 5.4).

To summarise, sports psychologists and coaches generally assume that pre-competitive mood affects performance. Yet the main finding from Males and Kerr's (1996) study of elite canoeists indicated a stable pattern for pre-competitive mood in elite-level canoeists.

Interview Results

The same nine male slalom canoeists who completed the questionnaires at each event during a competitive slalom season (Males & Kerr, 1996) also volunteered to take part in semi-structured interviews after each event. Using a modified version of the Metamotivational State Coding Schedule (Potocky, Cook, & O'Connell, 1993), interview transcripts were analysed and operative metamotivational states and state combinations identified and categorised in accordance with reversal theory criteria.

When the additional interview material from the same group of canoeists (Males et al., 1997) was considered, in general, consistent patterns in operative metamotivational states, specifically conformist–autic–mastery combinations, were obtained. Identification of telic and paratelic states was less clear and a discussion of this matter, along with full details of the methodology and results of this interview study, can be found in Males et al. (1997).

Even though these top performers were consistently found to be in particular metamotivational state combinations before competition, occasionally some individual canoeists found themselves in a state combination that was not typical and which turned out to be detrimental to their own high-level performance. Part of the interview transcript provided by one subject (subject C from the questionnaire study; Males & Kerr, 1996) is included here to illustrate how this occurred and how the athlete dealt with the problem.

The canoeing event concerned was the Grandtully International Competition held in Scotland at a venue that would be used a month later for selection of the British slalom team. The event comprised two races over one weekend, each race consisting of two runs down the slalom course.

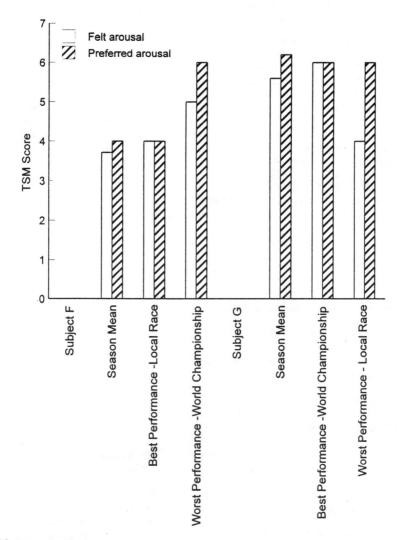

FIG. 5.4. Felt and preferred arousal scores (TSM) for canoeists F and G (from Males & Kerr, 1996).

This interview material is interesting for a number of reasons. The comments from subject C neatly illustrate the mechanism of the reversal process in operation at a top-level sports event. His comments also show that he is aware of the reversals that normally take place during his pre-race mental preparation, at least in terms of the switch between nervousness and excitement. He was also able to recognise (after his first run) that his pre-race mental build-up had not been appropriate and was capable of taking the necessary action to correct this prior to his second run. Although he could not

Interview Transcript	*Reversal Theory* *Interpretation*

Did you have a goal for this race?
I DIDN'T REALLY NO, I DIDN'T KNOW I WAS
RACING UNTIL THIS MORNING, BIT OF
CONFUSION IN THE ENTRIES AND WHAT WAS
GOING ON SO IT WAS A BIT OF A RUSHED JOB
THIS MORNING, I DIDN'T PREPARE REAL WELL.

Canoist C did not organise his entry to this event until the day of the race, a sign of a lack of planning and strategic goals and a generally paratelic approach to this race.

Now let's talk about what happened just before your first run. Can you give me three words to describe how you were feeling just before your first run?
PRETTY RELAXED, PRETTY HAPPY, UH,
ANOTHER WORD, UH, SORT OF WE WERE
JOKING AROUND A LOT—I DON'T KNOW IF
YOU'LL PUT THAT DOWN OR NOT (LAUGHS).

I'll just write down what you say (laughs). Is that the way you wanted to feel?
NO, I THINK I SHOULD HAVE BEEN A BIT MORE
FOCUSED IN.

And the way you were feeling, was it pleasant or unpleasant?
NO IT (WAS) PRETTY PLEASANT, IT WAS COOL.

What was the most important thing on your mind?
UM, WHAT YOU MEAN, IN THE ACTUAL . . .

Just before the race
I DUNNO I DON'T HAVE A LOT ON MY MIND, UH
NO I DON'T REMEMBER.

Was it like the race was a job you had to do, or was it something you really enjoyed because it was fun?
NO IT WAS JUST FUN.

His comments here about 'fun' and 'taking it as it came along' point to C being in the paratelic state prior to the first run which, although enjoyable, lacked the concentration and focus (related to control and mastery in terms of his skills and the demands of the slalom course) he wanted.

Were you planning ahead or just taking things as they came along?
UH, ON MY FIRST RUN I WAS JUST TAKING IT AS
IT CAME ALONG, I DIDN'T REALLY PREPARE
MUCH.

Now, what about the time between your runs. You said before that you came back here?
YEAH, THE BASIC THING WAS I WASN'T
FOCUSING ON THE RACE SO I THOUGHT I'D
BETTER COME BACK TO THE VAN, TOOK A
SLEEP, GOT MYSELF AWAY FROM MESSING
AROUND.

After the first run, one of C's poorest of the season, he decided that a change was necessary before the second run. This involved moving away from the crowded cafe where most of the paddlers were sitting,

Interview Transcript	Reversal Theory Interpretation

What was the most important thing on your mind? How would you describe it?
WELL NOT QUITE SURE REALLY, JUST TRYING TO GET INTO STATE OF MIND WHERE, LIKE THAT I'M USUALLY LIKE, WHICH I DIDN'T NORMALLY HAVE TO MAKE AN EFFORT TO DO, JUST COMING AWAY FROM (the crowd) FOCUSING ON WHAT I HAVE TO DO.

When you say you get focused does that mean getting more serious about what you do or doesn't that describe it?
NOT SERIOUS, I THINK ITS LIKE EXCITED IN THE RIGHT WAY, LIKE KNOW WHAT I MEAN? LIKE MESSING AROUND (in the cafe) IS A GOOD LAUGH, SO 'EXCITED' BUT FOCUSING THAT EXCITEMENT ON THE RIGHT THINGS, LIKE I WASN'T . . . (doing that before).

Yeah I know it's hard to get words for it, so rather than just stuffing around it was like taking that energy and taking it towards the course?
YEAH, YEP.

Where do you focus it on, or to?
I THINK YOU COME DOWN, I GET MYSELF TO A FAMILIAR RELAXED STATE WHICH I'M SORT OF FAMILIAR WITH WHEN I RACE, THEN I THINK I GO INTO A RACE, I GET A BIT NERVOUS BUT I CAN CONVERT THAT EXCITEMENT QUITE EASILY, THAT SORT OF HAPPENS NATURALLY, KNOW WHAT I MEAN?

Yeah
I DON'T REALLY HAVE TO MAKE AN EFFORT TO DO THAT, BUT TODAY I HAD TO MAKE AN EFFORT TO GET MYSELF AWAY FROM, SO I COULD GET LIKE A STATE I WAS FAMILIAR WITH SO I COULD BUILD ON IT FOR MY SECOND RUN.

And you turn the nervousness into excitement?
YEAH, I FIND THAT HAPPENS UH NOT LONG BEFORE MY RUN, LIKE TWENTY MINUTES.

Did something different happen before your first run?
I DIDN'T THINK. I DIDN'T HAVE THE NERVOUSNESS.

chatting, joking, eating, and drinking coffee. This paratelic–alloic–sympathy oriented environment was warm, comfortable and removed from the detail of the competition. Paddlers tended not to talk seriously about the race while inside the cafe, although by walking outside they could easily watch the race, check scores and so on. C, an experienced performer, realising that he had performed badly and was not in his usual pre-race state of mind, chose to spend some time alone and try and change his mental state.

When alone in the quiet self-contained environment of his van he concentrated on mental preparation. He induced the telic state by first taking a sleep and relaxing (a telic act in itself) before deliberately increasing the significance and importance of the event and his participation in it (by this stage the autic and mastery states would have also been operative). This led to increased arousal and nervousness which he could then 'turn into excitement' by reversing back to the paratelic state.

These additional comments from C confirm that usually before performing a telic to paratelic reversal occurs which characterises his normal pre-competitive mental state, i.e. pleasant paratelic high arousal ('excitement'). On this particular occasion (prior to the first run) the customary reversal did not occur. As a result he was forced to take action and use his experience and skill to induce the necessary reversal and the state of mind that he prefers prior to white-water slalom performance.

Interview Transcript	*Reversal Theory Interpretation*
So because you didn't have the nervousness you didn't have the excitement? THAT'S RIGHT, LIKE I WAS HAPPY AND THAT BUT IT WASN'T LIKE THE EXCITEMENT OF A RACE. *So what about your second run then?* YEAH I GOT MORE EXCITED ABOUT IT, LIKE THE WAY I WANTED TO. *So did you end up feeling the way you wanted to feel?* YEAH I FELT PRETTY FOCUSED IN. *Was it a job you had to do, or was it something you really enjoyed because it was fun?* NO I NEVER FIND IT A JOB I HAVE TO DO I ALWAYS FIND IT PRETTY FUN, I LIKE BEING IN THE COMPETITION SITUATION. *What about during the second run, did anything change once you had started?* NO THAT WENT QUITE WELL, I WAS QUITE HAPPY WITH MY SECOND RUN. *During the run, or at the end or both?* DURING, AGAIN I WAS A BIT DISAPPOINTED AT THE END CAUSE I GOT A COUPLE OF TOUCHES, BUT DURING THE RUN LIKE, I ONLY CONSIDERED THEM AFTERWARDS.	C's focus was on the present moment and trying to master the gates on the slalom course rather than on the consequences of the race and there was no comparison with others. He confirms his answers to earlier questions by describing his mental state as enjoyable and that competition is fun and a challenge. This is representative of a metamotivational combination of paratelic–autic–mastery. (Presumably C had to follow the competition rules while performing, therefore it might be assumed that the conformist state was the fourth part of his operative metamotivational combination.) Canoeist C ignored his gate penalties until the race was over, then experienced disappointment suggesting a paratelic to telic reversal when the consequences of his performance were realised. His basic time for the second run was much better than for the first run and very competitive in comparison with other paddlers' times. Unfortunately his basic time was marred by the addition of time penalties incurred at two gates.

voluntarily induce a reversal, he was able to create a set of environmental conditions that would precipitate the desired reversal to his usual pre-race state of mind. On his own initiative, he adopted an intervention strategy which utilised both arousal modulation and psychological reversals. Readers are referred to Kerr (1993) for more specific details of reversal theory-based psychological intervention in sport and some further discussion can be found in Chapter 10.

A NOTE FOR COACHES AND ATHLETES

There are a number of implications arising from the results of the research studies reviewed in this chapter (summarised in a table in Appendix C at the end of the book) which may be of importance to coaches and athletes:

1. In these sports, relatively high levels of felt arousal, experienced by the athletes as positive, pleasant, and non-stressful, were a feature of successful performance.
2. Successful athletes were consistently better than less successful athletes at achieving and maintaining the levels of felt arousal they desired when competing.
3. The experience of winning was more pleasant than losing in terms of somatic and transactional emotions.
4. Successful athletes exhibited more stable emotional patterns when competing than less successful athletes.
5. Patterns of pre-competitive affect tended to be consistent in successful athletes, although occasionally some athletes may have experienced a non-typical pattern. Athletes may know through experience, or should be taught, how to deal with these situations when they do arise.

CONCLUDING COMMENTS

In Chapter 3, features of participation and performance in sport associated with metamotivational dominance were explored. In this chapter, the emphasis has been on "state" characteristics (including, for example, felt arousal and to some extent felt transactional outcome) of performance as they are related to success and failure, winning and losing. When the psychological characteristics of successful performers were examined, the pattern was one of stability and little change. The pattern for unsuccessful performers was less consistent, more variable, and the act of losing for these performers was accompanied by unpleasant psychological responses. From the Wilson and Phillips (1995) study it was possible to compare players' predominant metamotivational combinations pre-, during and post-game. In addition, this squash study was one that found significant differences between successful and unsuccessful performers on a dominance measure. These researchers were able to link negativism dominance to squash players' state responses after losing. It is in this sense that Fontana's (1983) argument (mentioned in Chapter 3), that reversal theory can go beyond conventional state–trait approaches (e.g. Martens, Vealey, & Burton, 1990; Spielberger, 1966, 1972) in explaining motivational and emotional processes, gains credibility. However, it was the individually focused design used in the canoeing studies (Males & Kerr, 1996; Males et al., 1997) that revealed results which illustrated the inconsistency of human behaviour and the real advantage of reversal theory over state–trait approaches. As Apter (1982, p.8) stated:

> According to reversal theory, some important aspects of the way in which an individual interprets his world, and what he is doing in it, fluctuate in various ways which may involve radically different interpretations being made by him at various times.

In spite of the overall similar constellation of emotions pre-performance, personally specific motivational differences were revealed between canoeists at the same local and World Championship events. At these events, in opposite fashion, the two canoeists managed their best and worst performances, but the psychological responses of two elite canoeists performing highly tuned skills under pressure differed markedly, as did their performances (Males & Kerr, 1996; Males et al., 1997).

What comes through, from all of the reversal theory studies reviewed here, as with those summarised in Chapters 3 and 4, is the crucial importance of felt arousal in both participation and performance. Successful performers appear to be more able than less successful performers to achieve and maintain their desired levels of arousal and to experience them in a positive, pleasant, and non-stressful way. The concept of arousal has been a feature of theoretical discussion and research in sport psychology for some years. Over the last ten years, however, theoretical explanations and research activity related to the arousal–performance relationship in sport have gained special prominence in the literature. In Chapter 6, the main theoretical approaches will be examined and attempts made to show their inadequacy in the light of the broad and flexible approach of reversal theory.

FURTHER READING

1. Kerr, J.H., & Cox, T. (1991). Arousal and individual differences in sport. *Personality and Individual Differences, 12*(10), 1075–1085.
2. Thayer, R.E. (1989). *The biopsychology of mood and arousal.* Oxford: Oxford University Press.
3. Kerr, J.H. (1993). An eclectic approach to psychological interventions in sport: Reversal theory. *The Sport Psychologist, 7,* 400–418.

REFERENCES

Abadie, B.R. (1989). Effect of competitive outcome on state anxiety. *Perceptual and Motor Skills,* 69, 1057–1058.

Apter, M.J. (1982). *The experience of motivation: The theory of psychological reversals.* London: Academic Press.

Apter, M.J. (1989). *Reversal theory: Motivation, emotion and personality.* London: Routledge.

Apter, M.J., & Batler, R. (1996). Gratuitous risk: A study of parachuting. In S. Svebak & M.J. Apter (Eds.), *Stress and health: A reversal theory perspective.* Washington, DC: Taylor & Francis.

Barrington, J. (1982, 28 March). Murder in the squash court. *The Observer.*

Cleary, M. (1993, 4 June). The fat lady sings for Graf. *The Observer,* p.44.

Cox, T., & Kerr, J.H. (1989a). Self-reported mood in competitive squash. *Personality and Individual Differences, 11*(2), 199–203.

Cox, T., & Kerr, J.H. (1989b). Arousal effects during tournament play in squash. *Perceptual and Motor Skills, 69,* 1275–1280.

Davies, P. (1991). *All played out. The full story of Italia '90.* London: Mandarin Paperbacks.

Dowd, R., & Innes, J.M. (1981). Sport and personality: Effects of type of sport and level of competition. *Perceptual and Motor Skills, 53,* 79–89.

Fontana, D. (1983). Individual differences in personality: Trait based versus state based theories. *Educational Psychology, 3,* 189–200.

Goolagong, E., Collins, B., & Edwards, V. (1975). *Evonne.* London: Hart-Davis, McGibbon.

Kerr, J.H. (1993). An eclectic approach to psychological interventions in sport: Reversal theory. *The Sport Psychologist, 7,* 400–418.

Kerr, J.H., & Cox, T. (1988). Effects of metamotivational dominance and metamotivational state on squash task performance. *Perceptual and Motor Skills, 67,* 171–174.

Kerr, J.H., & Cox, T. (1990). Cognition and mood in relation to the performance of a squash task. *Acta Psychologica, 73*(1), 103–114.

Kerr, J.H., & Cox, T. (1991). Arousal and individual differences in sport. *Personality and Individual Differences, 12*(10), 1075–1085.

Kerr, J.H., & Pos, E. (1994). Psychological mood in competitive gymnastics: An exploratory field study. *Journal of Human Movement Studies, 26*(4), 175–185.

Kerr, J.H., & Svebak, S. (1994). The acute effects of participation in sports on mood. *Personality and Individual Differences, 16*(1), 159–166.

Kerr, J.H., & van Schaik, P. (1995). Effects of game venue and outcome on psychological mood states in rugby. *Personality and Individual Differences, 19*(3), 407–409.

Krane, V., & Williams, J. (1987). Performance and somatic anxiety, cognitive anxiety, and confidence changes prior to competition. *Journal of Sport Behavior, 10*(1), 47–56.

Mackay, C.J., Cox, T., Burrows, G.C., & Lazzerini, A.J. (1978). An inventory for the measurement of self-reported stress and arousal. *British Journal of Social and Clinical Psychology, 17,* 283–284.

Mahoney, M.J., & Avener, M. (1977). Psychology of the elite athlete: An exploratory study. *Cognitive Therapy and Research, 1*(2), 135–141.

Mahoney, M.J., Avener, J., & Avener, M. (1983). Psychological aspects of competitive athletic performance. In L.E. Unestahl (Ed.), *The mental aspects of gymnastics.* Oreboro, Sweden: Veje Forlag.

Males, J.R., & Kerr, J.H. (1996). Stress, emotion and performance in elite slalom canoeists. *The Sport Psychologist, 10,* 17–36.

Males, J.R., Kerr, J.H., & Gerkovich, M. (1997). Metamotivational states during canoe slalom competition: A qualitative analysis using reversal theory. Manuscript submitted for publication.

Martens, R., Vealey, R.S., & Burton, D. (1990). *Competitive anxiety in sport.* Champaign, IL: Human Kinetics.

McDermott, M.R., & Apter, M.J. (1988). The Negativism Dominance Scale (NDS). In M.J. Apter, J.H. Kerr, & M.P. Cowles (Eds.), *Progress in reversal theory.* Advances in Psychology series, 51. Amsterdam: North-Holland/Elsevier.

Mueser, K.T., Yarnold, P.R., & Foy, D.W. (1991). Statistical analysis for single case designs: Evaluating outcome of imaginal exposure treatment of chronic PTSD. *Behaviour Modification, 15,* 134–155.

Murgatroyd, S., Rushton, C., Apter, M.J., & Ray, C. (1978). The development of the Telic Dominance Scale. *Journal of Personality Assessment, 42,* 519–528.

Novak, M. (1976). *The joy of sports.* New York: Basic Books.

Potocky, M., Cook, M.R., & O'Connell, K.A. (1993). The use of an interview and structured coding system to assess metamotivational state. In J.H. Kerr, S. Murgatroyd, & M.J. Apter (Eds.), *Advances in reversal theory* (pp.135–150). Amsterdam: Swets & Zeitlinger.

Rozin, S. (1983, 17 May). The will to win and the hell of losing. *The Daily Express,* p.17. [Article based on Rozin, S. (1983). *Daley Thompson: The subject is winning.* London: Stanley Paul.].

Spielberger, C.D. (1966). Theory and research on anxiety. In C.D. Spielberger (Ed.), *Anxiety and behavior* (pp.3–22). New York: Academic Press.

Spielberger, C.D. (1972). Anxiety as an emotional state. In C.D. Spielberger (Ed.), *Anxiety: Vol.1. Current trends in theory and research* (pp.24–54). New York: Academic Press.

Svebak, S. (1993). The development of the Tension and Effort Stress Inventory (TESI). In J.H. Kerr, S. Murgatroyd, & M.J. Apter (Eds.), *Advances in reversal theory* (pp.189–204). Amsterdam: Swets & Zeitlinger.

Svebak, S., & Murgatroyd, S. (1985). Metamotivational dominance: A multimethod validation of reversal theory constructs. *Journal of Personality and Social Psychology, 48*(1), 107–116.

Svebak, S., Ursin, H., Endresen, I., Hjelmen, A.M., & Apter, M.J. (1991). Back pain and the experience of stress, efforts and moods. *Psychology and Health, 5,* 307–314.

Wilson, G.V., & Phillips, M. (1995, July). *A reversal theory explanation of emotions in competitive sport.* Paper presented at the Seventh International Conference on Reversal Theory, Melbourne, Australia.

6

Up for the Match? Experiencing Arousal and Emotion in Sport

In his younger days, the Dutchman Tom de Booij was an elite athlete—his sport was mountaineering. In the early 1950s he set out, with fellow countryman Egeler and Frenchman Terray, to climb the Nevado Huanstán, over 20,000 feet high and the highest unclimbed mountain in the Cordillera Blanca range in the Peruvian Andes. Their attempt to climb the Huanstán was successful, but not before de Booij had a perilous 300-foot fall down a steep wall of ice. Luckily, when he fell he was not injured, but he was left hanging upside down on the end of a rope over the abyss. His own account of his psychological reactions, as Terray tried to rescue him, is worth recounting here (Egeler & de Booij, 1955, pp.106–107).

> All I heard was an agonized French oath, then a panting voice urging me to have patience for another five minutes. It was then, at that precise moment, that I fully realized that as soon as my feet and the rope parted company, I would irrevocably plunge into the void. It was a strange sensation, to become conscious that I was going to die. Oddly enough, I felt calm and untroubled by pangs of fear. Death seemed so inevitable that I simply accepted my lot. Thus it was that, suspended head downwards, I was able to remark to Egeler: 'This is it Kees! It's all over with us!'
>
> If there had been the slightest chance of surviving, I should no doubt have been terribly scared. But I felt no apprehension; only a feeling of relief, coupled with curiosity as to what death would be like.

Although he has long since retired from climbing mountains, de Booij is now, at around 60 years of age, still very much active in the world of professional golf. None of this background was known to the author the first time he encountered de Booij during a period of time set aside for questions and discussion following a reversal theory presentation by the author at the annual Dutch Sport Psychology Conference. De Booij explained, after giving a few very brief details about his mountaineering exploits, that: "When I was hanging on the end of the rope after the fall down the mountain, I felt absolutely no fear, even though I was close to death, yet every time I have to take a putt in golf which is about one metre long I get so anxious that my hands start shaking." Contrary to what one might have expected, it was not during the life-threatening situation on the mountain, but in the safe context of carrying out a straightforward task on a golf course that de Booij experienced extreme anxiety. Tom de Booij's account is one piece of anecdotal evidence that underlines the different ways (sometimes contrary to expectations) that arousal can be interpreted by individuals in sport and other situations. This notion forms one of the fundamental building blocks of reversal theory.

Yet other anecdotal evidence links the importance of high levels of arousal to performance, and some of the many quotations from top sports performers have been reviewed by Kerr (1985a). A more recent example is provided by Stephen Hendry, the youngest ever winner of the World Snooker Championship. In 1992 (McIlvanney, 1992, p.42) he said:

> It's good when a major championship comes down to two tables but it is when there is only one that I get the real high, that I can feel the best coming out of my game.

However, before a detailed examination of relationship between arousal and performance (including the reversal theory and rival approaches) is undertaken, further clarification of reversal theory's individual approach to the experience of motivation is necessary.

REVERSAL THEORY AND AROUSAL

Probably the best place to start this discussion is to refer back to Chapter 2 and reversal theory's definition of arousal. Within reversal theory, arousal is defined phenomenologically as "the degree to which an individual feels him or herself to be worked up or emotionally intense about what one is doing" (Apter, 1989, p.9). In the theory, therefore, it is termed *felt arousal*. Although this definition is phenomenologically based, Apter has argued that felt arousal has close links with physiological arousal (Apter, 1982, p.81). Consequently, the concept of felt arousal in reversal theory includes both psychological (phenomenological) and physiological aspects of arousal (see e.g. Svebak, 1983, 1984, 1986; Svebak & Murgatroyd, 1985).

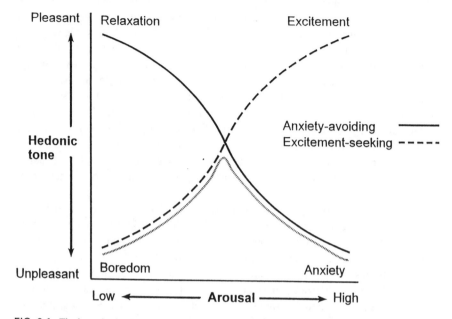

FIG. 6.1. The hypothesised relationship between arousal and hedonic tone for the telic (continuous line) and paratelic (dashed line) states respectively. The inverted-U curve from optimal arousal theory is included for comparison (from Apter, 1982).

An important relationship exists between operative metamotivational state and a person's experience of arousal. People with the telic state operative are thought to prefer low arousal and, with the paratelic state operative, high arousal. As a result, people with the telic (or arousal-avoiding) state operative experience low arousal as pleasant relaxation (i.e. high hedonic tone) and high arousal as unpleasant anxiety (i.e. low hedonic tone). Conversely, people with the paratelic (or arousal-seeking) state operative, experience low arousal as unpleasant boredom and high arousal as pleasant excitement (see Fig. 6.1).

There is also empirical research evidence that fits in with de Booij's experience and supports reversal theory's explanation about people's experience of arousal. Apter (1976) carried out an experiment in which 67 male and female undergraduates were asked to rate a list of 50 varied situations in terms of the degree of felt arousal and the affective tone associated with that level of arousal on two 7-point rating scales. For eleven out of the 50 items there was a consensus amongst subjects that these situations were highly pleasurable in terms of felt arousal. From these eleven situations, four (*arriving on holiday in a foreign country, playing an important game when the scores are level, building up to an orgasm, reading a particularly tense chapter in a thriller*) were considered highly arousing and highly pleasurable. Three situations (*going for a walk, just after having an orgasm, dancing at a discotheque*) were judged to be moderately arousing and highly pleasurable. (This is not inconsistent with reversal theory. Moderate levels of arousal can be pleasant and are represented in Fig. 6.1 by the cross-over area of the two curves. This area also corresponds with the peak section of the optimal arousal curve, included within the lower part of the X-shaped curve.) The final four situations (*just before going to sleep, having a bath, relaxing after a hard day's work, just after eating a good meal*) were also reported as being highly pleasurable, but low in arousal. In the present context, perhaps the most important result from this experiment is that it shows that there are a number of highly arousing situations which individuals experience as pleasant (see also Schachter & Singer, 1962).

The results of Apter's (1976) early experiment have been supported by the results of other reversal theory studies, such as the Kerr and Vlaswinkel (1993) running study described in Chapter 8 and Walters, Apter, and Svebak's (1982) study of arousal preferences in office workers over time.

The studies reviewed in Chapter 5 were concerned with performance in sport. Using subjects from a number of different cultures, ages, and skill levels, these studies investigated a range of different sports. What became apparent from the results of these studies was that successful performance was characterised by high levels of felt arousal which was experienced by the performers as positive, pleasant, and non-stressful. In addition, those who performed successfully were consistently more able than less successful performers to achieve and maintain their preferred levels of felt arousal when performing. These results directly challenge other theoretical explanations of arousal and performance common in contemporary sport psychology. For example, the findings are in conflict with the single intermediate optimal level of arousal advocated by optimal arousal theorists (e.g. Fiske & Maddi, 1961; Hebb, 1955; Hebb & Thompson, 1954) or the single zone of optimal functioning as proposed in Hanin's (1986, 1989) zones of optimal functioning model (ZOF). These findings are also at odds with the arguments of those advocating multidimensional anxiety theory (Martens et al., 1990a; Martens, Vealey, & Burton, 1990b) and catastrophe theory (Fazey & Hardy, 1988; Kirkcaldy, 1983), due to their exclusive focus on a single negative emotion, anxiety. Morgan's (1979, 1980) so-called mental health model, based on findings obtained from the Profile of Mood States (POMS; McNair, Lorr, & Droppleman, 1971), is also biased towards negative moods and negative affect. Reversal theory has a more balanced approach which incorporates both positive and negative emotions in relation to performance (e.g. Kerr & Svebak, 1994; Males & Kerr, 1996).

This is an opportune place to compare some of the main aspects of the rival approaches just mentioned with reversal theory. As optimal arousal theory (e.g.

Fiske & Maddi, 1961; Hebb, 1955; Hebb & Thompson, 1954) and its forerunner, the inverted-U hypothesis (Yerkes & Dodson, 1908), have played a major role in sport psychology over the past 25 years (e.g. Klavora, 1977; Martens & Landers, 1970; Sonstroem & Bernardo, 1982), it seems appropriate to begin the comparison with them.

COMPARING OPTIMAL AROUSAL THEORY AND REVERSAL THEORY

The main concepts of reversal theory have been set out in Chapter 2 and elaborated on in each of the chapters that follow. However, a brief description of optimal arousal theory (Fiske & Maddi, 1961; Hebb, 1955; Hebb & Thompson, 1954) is necessary before the two theories can be contrasted. Yerkes and Dodson's (1908) experimental work with rats was concerned with motivation and task complexity. They found that a graph representing the relationship between motivation and performance followed an inverted-U shape and that the peak of the inverted-U curve shifted as a function of task difficulty. Later, this relationship was incorporated into optimal arousal theory (Hebb, 1955), in which the importance of the optimal level of arousal was brought to the fore. Optimal arousal theory argued that increases in arousal were beneficial to performance up to a certain point, beyond which any further increases in arousal would lead to a decrease in the level of performance. This hypothesised relationship between arousal and performance, represented by the well known inverted-U-shaped graph, has often featured in explanations of sports performance.

Some researchers have carried out sport-based empirical studies in motor steadiness (Martens & Landers, 1970), high-school basketball (Klavora, 1977) and university basketball (Sonstroem & Bernardo, 1982) in which they purported to find an inverted-U relationship between arousal and performance. Sonstroem and Bernardo (1982), for example, studied the state anxiety scores of 30 female university basketball starters from six teams in relation to their performance scores. (State anxiety is subjective, consciously perceived feelings of apprehension and tension, accompanied by or associated with activation or arousal; Spielberger, 1966.) Composite performance scores were used, which took into account aspects of game performance such as success in shooting, rebounds, assists, turnovers, and fouls. Sonstroem and Bernardo (1982) argued that their results, which showed that high state anxiety scores were associated with the poorest performances, supported the inverted-U hypothesis.

Kerr (1985b) began to question the usefulness of the inverted-U hypothesis and optimal arousal theory for explaining the relationship between arousal and performance in sport. For a number of different reasons, others had similarly expressed criticism (e.g. Baddeley, 1972; Cooke, 1981; Martens, 1974;

Naatanen, 1973, Welford, 1976) but few of these (if any) had offered any alternative approach. In a series of publications, Kerr (1985a, 1987, 1989) argued that, contrary to the position of optimal arousal theory, not only was high arousal actively sought and enjoyed by many athletes, but it was also a crucial ingredient in many types of sports performance. He pointed to empirical evidence (e.g. Kerr, 1987; Sarason, 1980) and anecdotal reports and quotes from top sports performers (Kerr, 1985a). Kerr concluded that an alternative to optimal arousal theory was necessary and proposed the orthogonal model of stress and arousal (Mackay, Cox, Burrows, & Lazzerini, 1978) and reversal theory (Apter, 1982) as being more appropriate (Kerr, 1985a, b, 1987, 1989). At that time, these were relatively new theoretical approaches and exhibited more versatility than optimal arousal theory in providing a theoretical explanation of why high levels of arousal could be experienced as pleasant and might actually benefit the experience and performance of athletes in some sports. As noted in Chapter 5, since the mid to late 1980s, numerous reversal theory sport-based empirical studies have underlined the crucial role that relatively high levels of arousal play in performance (e.g. Cox & Kerr, 1989, 1990; Kerr & Cox, 1988, 1989, 1990; Kerr & Vlaswinkel, 1993; Males & Kerr, 1996).

Kerr was not the only sport psychologist disenchanted with applying optimal arousal theory in the sport context. Others were also searching for alternatives and several other theoretical approaches were put forward. These included, as already mentioned, the zones of optimal functioning model (ZOF; Hanin, 1986, 1989), multidimensional anxiety theory (Martens et al., 1990a; Martens et al., 1990b) catastrophe theory (Fazey & Hardy, 1988; Kirkcaldy, 1983), and the mental health model (Morgan, 1979, 1980). As far as sport psychology is concerned, these approaches might be seen as contemporary rivals to reversal theory in attempting to provide theoretical explanations of performers' emotional experiences in sport. In the next section, each of these approaches will be briefly described and some of the advantages and disadvantages of these approaches will be explored in relation to reversal theory.

OTHER APPROACHES TO EMOTION AND PERFORMANCE IN SPORT PSYCHOLOGY

Zones of Optimal Functioning Model

The zones of optimal functioning model (ZOF) proposed by Russian sports psychologist Hanin (1986, 1989) might be considered as an extension of the notion of an optimal level of arousal for maximum performance that forms the basis of the inverted-U hypothesis/optimal arousal theory approach. Instead of a single optimal point at which performance was theoretically maximised, Hanin (1986, 1989), using Spielberger's (1966) concept and measure (Spielberger, Gorsuch, & Lushene, 1970) of state anxiety, developed the concept of a band or zone. He argued that, for each athlete, performance would be optimal when anxiety levels remained within this specific zone. This *zone of anxiety* could be at any point low or high on the anxiety continuum, depending on the individual athlete.

Krane (1993) drew attention to some of the advantages of the ZOF model. The approach takes an idiographic rather than a nomothetic approach, concentrating on the intensive study of individual cases rather than the group-based designs used in other approaches and studies of anxiety. In addition, Krane (1993) also claimed that the approach might provide an explanation for the wide variability in state anxiety scores often found in field studies with different sports groups (e.g. Gould & Krane, 1992). She also considered the model to be an improvement on the non-specific approach of the inverted-U hypothesis/optimal arousal theory approach because, by using systematic monitoring of performers' levels of pre-competitive state anxiety and performance, ZOFs can be determined for each individual. A number of research studies have tested the utility of the ZOF model (e.g. Krane, 1993; Prapavessis & Grove, 1991; Raglin & Turner, 1993). Raglin and Turner (1993) claimed that their results supported the ZOF approach, but Krane's (1993) and Prapavessis and Grove's (1991) results only offered partial support.

Although there are some advantages associated with the ZOF approach, it would appear to suffer from some of the same weaknesses as the inverted-U hypothesis/optimal arousal theory approach outlined earlier. Furthermore, how can it deal with other, positive emotions like excitement or relaxation, at the high and low ends of the arousal range, which may also be important with respect to performance? The simple answer is that, in its original form, it cannot. This may be why, in more recent publications (Hanin, 1993; Hanin & Syrjá, 1995), the *individual zone of functioning model* (IZOF, as it was later renamed) was extended beyond anxiety to include positive and negative affect.

In the new IZOF model it is hypothesised that athletes will have individual optimal and non-optimal patterns of positive and negative affect which are related to their successful and unsuccessful performances. These patterns relate to both the particular emotions experienced and the "zones" of intensity of those emotions. It is considered possible that particular emotions may be optimal for some athletes but not for others, and that some emotions (both positive and negative) may be facilitating or debilitating or both (Hanin, 1993; Hanin & Syrjá, 1995).

In Hanin and Syrjá's (1995) study, and in a similar way to the original ZOF model, athletes were asked to recall their successful and unsuccessful performances and the positive and negative emotions (rather than just anxiety) that produced both performance-facilitating and performance-debilitating effects. The positive and negative affect scales from Watson and Tellegen's (1985) work were included in an item list which was used to help performers decide on the individual mood items for their idiosyncratic scales. Each performer selected 4–5 positive and 4–5 negative mood items. Watson and Tellegen (1985) re-analysed a number of studies of self-reported mood and, using a factor analysis statistical treatment, identified positive and negative affect as the first two and therefore most important factors in the structure of mood. These individual scales were then used to examine intra- and inter-individual differences amongst ice hockey players. Subsequent analysis of affect data (collected from the subjects over a series of games) led Hanin and Syrjá (1995) to conclude that their prediction that athletes would have individual optimal and non-optimal positive–negative affect patterns related to their individual successful and unsuccessful performances was confirmed.

The *new* IZOF is potentially a more powerful model than the previous ZOF model. Not only does it continue with a within-individual subject approach and include the notion of performance-facilitating and debilitating emotions, but it has also linked IZOF affect to the well known work of Watson and Tellegen (1985) on the structure of mood. However, although the new style IZOF model appears to be an improvement on the older version, does this mean that the original anxiety-based ZOF model is now obsolete? More importantly, to this author's knowledge Hanin has not really clarified why the change from anxiety to positive and negative affect was undertaken. Although the IZOF model is probably the closest, of the approaches reviewed in this chapter, to reversal theory's framework of emotions, unlike reversal theory, it does not appear to be based on a sound theoretical foundation. Hanin may have to invest more time and effort in specifying more clearly how the ideas in the IZOF model combine together theoretically, before it becomes truly acceptable to those advocating a broader approach to the study of emotions and performance in sport (see later).

The Multidimensional Anxiety Approach

The origins of the multidimensional approach to the study of anxiety in sport can be found in the work of Martens and his colleagues at the University of Illinois in the US during the 1980s. The multidimensional approach to anxiety is comprehensively described in the book *Competitive anxiety in sport* (Martens et al., 1990b). This approach has been popular with some sport psychologists, and work using the scales developed has been carried out in several other countries, including the work of Jones and his colleagues at Loughborough University in the UK (e.g. Jones & Cale, 1989; Jones & Swain, 1992).

Martens extended Spielberger's state–trait approach to the understanding and measurement of anxiety (Spielberger, 1966) by developing the Sport Competition Anxiety Test (SCAT; Martens, 1977), and the Competitive State Anxiety Inventory (CSAI; Martens, Burton, Rivkin, & Simon, 1980). These instruments were intended to measure trait and state anxiety in competitive sports situations. The CSAI instrument was further refined into the CSAI-2 (Martens et al., 1990a) to encompass the division of anxiety into separate *cognitive* and *somatic* components (see e.g. Davidson & Schwartz, 1976; Morris, Davis, & Hutchings, 1981). According to Martens et al. (1990b, p.6), cognitive anxiety is "the mental component of anxiety and is caused by negative expectations about success or by negative self-evaluation" and somatic anxiety is "the physiological and affective elements of the anxiety experience that develop directly from autonomic arousal."   Martens et al. (1990a) predicted that cognitive state anxiety would have a negative linear relationship with performance, and somatic anxiety a somewhat less powerful curvilinear (inverted-U) relationship with performance.

During the validation process of the CSAI-2, a third dimension, labelled *self-confidence* was added to the two original dimensions of cognitive and somatic anxiety. Research work using this scale has formed the backbone of what is now referred to as the *multidimensional approach to competitive state anxiety* and the scale has been used in a number of research studies in sport (e.g. Gould, Petlichkoff, Simons, & Vivera, 1987; Hammerstein & Burton, 1995); Jones & Cale, 1989; Krane & Williams, 1987). The study undertaken by Hammerstein and Burton (1995) provides a very recent example of research based on the multidimensional approach to anxiety. The subject sample for their study comprised 293 endurance athletes, including triathletes, distance runners, and cyclists, competing in their respective sports. The CSAI-2 was one of the measures the researchers used to collect pre-competitive state anxiety data from the endurance athletes.

Triathletes were found to be significantly more cognitively and somatically anxious than either runners or cyclists. Also, younger endurance athletes were found to experience significantly more cognitive anxiety than older endurance athletes. However, the results revealed non-significant relationships between pre-competitive anxiety levels and performance. Although Burton's (1988) study on swimmers was an exception, several other researchers in addition to Hammerstein and Burton (1995) have had only partial success in confirming Martens et al.'s (1990a) anxiety–performance predictions (e.g. Gould et al., 1987; Krane, 1990).

Jones and his colleagues (Jones, Hanton, & Swain, 1994; Jones & Swain, 1992; Swain & Jones, 1993) have argued that, in addition to measuring the intensity of anxiety (e.g. using CSAI-2), sports-based anxiety research studies need to take into account what has been termed the *direction of anxiety*. This label has been used to describe the *directional perceptions* of anxiety symptoms and the interpretation of those symptoms as being positive (facilitative) or negative (debilitative) with respect to forthcoming performance (e.g. Jones & Swain, 1995). Jones and Swain (1992), for example, found no significant differences in the intensity of cognitive and somatic anxiety, or in direction of somatic anxiety between high and low competitive sports groups (as measured by Gill & Deeter's (1988) Sport Orientation Questionnaire), but anxiety was reported by some athletes (those who were more competitive) in a positive way, as more facilitative than debilitative to good performance. However, arguments about the usefulness of considering the direction of anxiety appear to be an attempt to explain empirical results that have generally not supported Martens et al.'s (1990a) predictions about the effects of anxiety on performance. Although the idea of mental states having a facilitative or debilitative effect on performance is reasonable, tying this in with the multidimensional approach to anxiety may ultimately prove to be counter-productive.

The division of anxiety into cognitive and somatic components is an artificial division which is unhelpful to the study of anxiety and other emotions in sport. This is a position apparently shared by Krane (1992, p.77):

> The ostensibly equivocal results of multidimensional anxiety theory studies may lie in the fact that cognitive and somatic anxiety were examined independently. Possibly cognitive and somatic anxiety are not completely independent of one another.

For those researchers who have adopted and used the multidimensional approach, the majority of studies have provided, by their own admission, equivocal results (see e.g. Jones, 1995) which have done little to support the theoretical assumptions behind splitting anxiety into separate cognitive and somatic components (Jones & Swain, 1992; Jones et al., 1994; Hammerstein & Burton, 1995; Man, Stuchlíková, & Kindlmann, 1995; Swain & Jones, 1993). Furthermore, results from catastrophe model studies (see later) have raised doubts about the postulated theoretical relationship between cognitive anxiety, somatic anxiety, and successful performance (see Hardy & Parfitt, 1991; Hardy, Parfitt, & Pates, 1994).

After a comprehensive series of studies which examined the multi-dimensional approach to anxiety in sport, Jones (1995, p.464), was led to state:

> It is likely, of course, that a state in which cognitive and physiological symptoms, however intense, are perceived as being facilitative to performance does not represent 'anxiety' at all. Instead, it will probably be labelled by the performer as 'anticipatory excitement' or being 'psyched up'. This clearly has serious repercussions for the employment of conventional questionnaire measures of competitive anxiety.

Prior to a competitive sports event, competitors may well feel heightened arousal. In reversal theory terms, however, whether this is interpreted by the competitor as anxiety, or as being *psyched up* or excited, will depend on the prevailing metamotivational state combination of the competitor. This is the essence of what Jones (1995) is saying. In fact, the results from Jones and his colleagues' research lend more support to reversal theory than they do to the multidimensional anxiety approach.

Both the equivocal research results and the attempts to explain them reveal the basic flaw(s) in anxiety research. For example, even though validation work was carried out on this scale (Martens et al., 1990b), careful examination of the nine items from the CSAI-2 subscale labelled *somatic anxiety* raises questions about content validity. The first item (*I feel nervous*) is an anxiety item, but it would be more appropriately placed in the cognitive anxiety subscale. It can be seen that most of the somatic anxiety items (eight out of nine; e.g. *my body feels tense; my hands are clammy;* and *my heart is racing*) are describing symptoms of increased physiological arousal rather than anxiety per se. Subjects may well indicate that they experience these arousal symptoms prior to competition, but the CSAI-2, as an anxiety measure, can only categorise them as anxiety symptoms. Excitement is excluded as a possibility. Within reversal theory measures (e.g. the Tension and Effort Stress Inventory, TESI, Svebak, 1993) allowance is made for the different ways that individuals may interpret arousal. The nature of the CSAI-2 measuring instrument, particularly the contents of the somatic anxiety subscale, may be one reason why the multidimensional anxiety research has produced conflicting results.

Further support for reversal theory can be found in more recent work by Jones and Swain (1995), using an altered version of CSAI-2 into a trait or general measure. They carried out a study with elite and non-elite competitive cricketers which monitored how the performers usually felt before competition. No important differences were found between groups on the intensity of cognitive trait and somatic trait anxiety or self-confidence. However, the elite group reported cognitive trait and somatic trait anxiety as more facilitative than debilitative to their cricket batting performance. In other words, the elite group had a more positive interpretation of their "anxiety" in terms of facilitating their performance, to the extent that it was likely to be labelled as *excitement, psyched up*, or *motivated* (Jones & Swain, 1995). Elite performers were therefore concluded to be different from their non-elite peers in their predisposition to interpret cognitive trait and somatic trait anxiety. What is clear to reversal theorists from the results of this study is that what Jones and Swain (1995) have encountered are differences between the two groups in their predispositions to interpret and experience heightened *arousal* (not anxiety) in a positive way. Such a concept has been a basic notion in reversal theory from its inception and is termed telic and paratelic dominance.

It may be somewhat ironic that, while the results obtained from multi-dimensional anxiety studies sometimes appear difficult to explain under the terms of that approach, looked at from a different perspective, they provide some of the strongest support available in the sport psychology literature for reversal theory. This applies not only to notions like telic and paratelic states and dominance, but also to more fundamental concepts like the individual's subjective interpretation of arousal and hedonic tone.

Catastrophe Theory

Catastrophe model explanations of arousal and performance have attracted a certain amount of interest amongst sport psychologists because they appear useful in accounting for sudden decrements in performance, generally known in the sports world as "choking" under pressure (although they can also be applied to explain sudden increments in performance) (see also Baumeister & Showers, 1986). For example, Jana Novotna, the top tennis player, has become infamous, at least in the media, for her reputation as a player who often throws away an apparently insurmountable lead. It happened in the Wimbledon final in 1993 against Steffi Graf and again at the French Open in 1995 where she lost to Chandra Rubin. Although such examples seem to occur often enough for the notion to have become established amongst athletes, coaches, and media commentators, they are not typical of most performance situations in sport.

Catastrophe theory was originally developed by Thom (1975) and further revised by Zeeman (1976) for possible use in the social and behavioural sciences. The first reference made to catastrophe theory in the sports context was probably a paper by Kirkcaldy (1983) in the German journal *Sportswissenschaft*. In this paper, Kirkcaldy presented catastrophe theory as a possible way of explaining what he termed the *peak–flop phenomena* in sports performance. He suggested that the explosive effects, often concomitant with relatively small changes in arousal, that result in record-breaking maximal performance or sudden, unexpected collapses in performances (choking), could be explained by the mathematical models of catastrophe theory.

Somewhat later, Hardy and his colleagues at the University of Wales turned their attention to catastrophe theory (Fazey & Hardy, 1988; Hardy & Parfitt, 1991). They directed some criticism at Kirkcaldy's (1983) earlier attempts to apply catastrophe theory to sports performance because of what were claimed to be serious theoretical flaws and a failure to generate any subsequent empirical research (Hardy & Parfitt, 1991, p.167). They also carried out several empirical studies based on catastrophe theory (e.g. Hardy et al., 1994) and it is examples from this work that will be discussed here.

As space here does not allow for a full description of the application of catastrophe theory to performance in sport, readers should look to other sources for more complete explanations of the mathematical models concerned (e.g. Hardy, 1990; Kirkcaldy, 1983). Briefly, the simplest model, the cusp catastrophe used by Hardy and his co-workers, takes the general form of a three-dimensional cross-sectional view of a breaking wave (see Fig. 6.2).

The three dimensions underlying Fazey and Hardy's (1988) cusp catastrophe model were physiological arousal, cognitive anxiety, and performance, which represented what Zeeman (1976) termed the *normal factor*, the *splitting factor*, and the *dependent variable* respectively (see X, Y & Z in Fig. 6.2). In this case, like the ascending section of the inverted-U curve, increases in physiological arousal were thought to produce increases in performance, but this would be affected by the intensity of the splitting factor, cognitive anxiety. Fazey and Hardy (1988) postulated that, at high levels of cognitive anxiety, gradual increases in physiological arousal would lead to gradual increases in performance up to a certain point, beyond which (like a breaking wave) performance would suddenly fall to a much lower level at higher levels of cognitive anxiety (catastrophic effect; see Fig. 6.2). Gradual decreases in physiological arousal were thought to produce a similar effect, but in this case the point of discontinuity would occur at a different point on the x-axis. That performance follows different paths under physiological arousal increasing and physiological arousal decreasing conditions has been termed *hysteresis*. Hysteresis does not take place when cognitive anxiety is low, and the relationship between physiological arousal and performance is the same whether physiological arousal is increasing or decreasing.

Using the results of anxiety–performance research, Hardy and Parfitt (1991) argued that a negative correlation between cognitive anxiety and performance (see the right-hand face of Fig. 6.2) would exist if physiological arousal was high on the day before an important event. Cognitive anxiety would be associated with enhanced performance (see the left-hand face of Fig. 6.2) if, in

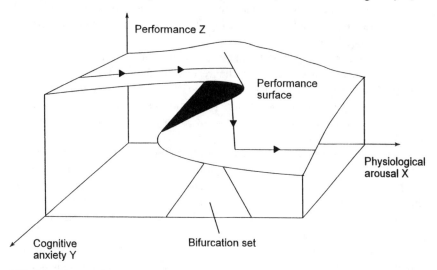

FIG. 6.2.   Fazey and Hardy's (1988) cusp catastrophe model of anxiety and performance.

the days prior to an important event, physiological arousal was low. However, depending how high cognitive anxiety and physiological arousal actually became, physiological arousal might either enhance or decrease performance, if cognitive anxiety was increasing in a time-to-event paradigm (see the cross-sectional view facing the reader in Fig. 6.2).

Hardy and Parfitt (1991), carried out an empirical study using the CSAI-2 to test the prediction that (a) physiological arousal (and the associated somatic anxiety; see Parfitt & Hardy, 1987) would not necessarily be detrimental to performance, but would be associated with catastrophic effects when cognitive anxiety was high, and (b) when cognitive anxiety was high, performance would follow a different path when physiological arousal was increasing than when it was decreasing (so-called hysteresis).

The researchers utilised female university basketball players and a time-to-event paradigm to manipulate cognitive anxiety (as measured by the CSAI-2) independent of physiological arousal. In previous work in basketball, high (day 1) and low (day 2) cognitive anxiety had been found, along with low physiological arousal and low somatic anxiety, on each of these days (Parfitt & Hardy, 1987). In this study, the authors claimed that the cognitive anxiety manipulation was achieved by testing players one day before (day 1) and one day after (day 2) an important match. (As a result of using the CSAI-2 measure of somatic anxiety was also obtained.) Physiological arousal (as measured by heart rate) was manipulated by having subjects perform shuttle runs to increase and rest to decrease heart rate to the desired bandwidth. Under conditions of both high and low cognitive anxiety, one group performed the experimental task with heart rate increasing and then decreasing and the other group with heart rate decreasing and then increasing. The basketball set shot was used as the experimental task.

The researchers purported to show, by using curve-fitting and non-parametric statistical procedures, that the results of the study were consistent with the hysteresis prediction (b). In addition, they also showed that maximum performances were higher, minimum performances lower, and decreases in performance greater under conditions of high rather than low cognitive anxiety.

There was, however, a problem with their results. Both cognitive and somatic anxiety were found to be significantly higher on the days before competition than on the day after. As mentioned earlier, previous work had shown that the patterns of cognitive and somatic anxiety were different before a competitive event (Parfitt & Hardy, 1987) The cognitive anxiety result was as predicted, but the somatic anxiety result was unexpected. As Hardy and Parfitt (1991) pointed out, the somatic anxiety result implies that cognitive anxiety had not been successfully isolated and hence control over the independent variables from the catastrophe model of performance had been lost. Hardy and Parfitt (1991) went to considerable lengths to explain why this might have occurred in order to justify proceeding with the analysis of the performance data.

Of interest to reversal theorists is one of Hardy and Parfitt's conclusions (1991, p.174):

> The performance results do offer support for the hysteresis hypothesis which was being tested. They also indicate some of the potential gains and catastrophic drops in performance that can occur under conditions of high cognitive anxiety. At the opposite end of the cognitive anxiety spectrum, the results demonstrate the great stability of skilled performers, even when performing complex motor tasks under conditions of low cognitive anxiety and extremely high physiological arousal.

Could it have been that what the performers were experiencing, at the low end of the cognitive anxiety spectrum under conditions of extremely high arousal, was not anxiety at all, but excitement?

A second experiment (Hardy et al., 1994), attempted to replicate the findings from Hardy and Parfitt's (1991) study with a different sport (crown green bowling) and a different cognitive anxiety manipulation (neutral and ego-threatening instruction sets). This second study provided results the authors claimed also supported the catastrophe model of anxiety and performance (Fazey & Hardy, 1988) and the notion of hysteresis. A three-way interaction was obtained which showed that performance followed a different path for heart rate increasing than for heart rate decreasing under conditions of high cognitive anxiety, but not under conditions of low cognitive anxiety, indicating that hysteresis had occurred. Also, under high cognitive anxiety conditions, subjects' best performances were significantly better and their worst performances significantly worse than under low cognitive anxiety conditions (see also Krane, Joyce, & Rafeld, 1994). However, the authors also reported that: "Even though hysteresis did occur in the high cognitive anxiety condition, there was no really clear evidence of a considerable reduction in heart rate being necessary before subjects 'flipped' back onto the upper performance surface," (Hardy et al., 1994, p.332) as predicted by Fazey and Hardy's (1988) model.

A study by Krane (1990) attempted to test the full catastrophe model, rather than use the specific hypothesis testing approach adopted in the two foregoing studies (Hardy et al., 1994). She decided to examine whether anxiety and performance data would fit Thom's (1975) original catastrophe model. Her analysis showed that significant portions of the performance data could not be explained by Thom's (1975) three-dimensional model.

The catastrophe theory model (Fazey & Hardy, 1988) and the multi-dimensional anxiety approach (Martens et al., 1990b) conceptualise anxiety in separate cognitive and somatic dimensions and share a common measuring instrument, the CSAI-2. This means that many of the criticisms directed at the multidimensional anxiety approach (Martens et al., 1990b), mentioned earlier in this chapter, can also be directed at the catastrophe theory model approach (Fazey & Hardy, 1988). A number of other criticisms of the catastrophe model approach have been outlined in the literature. Krane (1992, p.80) indicated that some problems exist with the applicability and efficiency of some of the methods of statistical analysis recommended for treating catastrophe theory data. In addition, she pointed out that catastrophes in experiments and real-life situations are impossible to predict, leading to practical difficulties in testing (Krane, 1992, p.82). Also, Gill (1994, p.24) argued that the catastrophe theory approach is too limited in comparison with other models (e.g. Lazarus, 1966) which she considered have broader implications for performance.

Incidentally, it may seem to some readers that there are similarities between reversals, as conceptualised within reversal theory, and the simplest forms of catastrophe. However, as Apter (1982 pp.45–46), in talking about meta-motivational systems has stated:

> Metamotivational systems are viewed here as being different systems, like alternative computer subroutines, so that a change from one to the other must necessarily be a discrete switch. It is therefore not the case that on some occasions the switch is discontinuous and on other occasions it is continuous to some degree or another. So, although a reversal is a form of catastrophe, it does not seem that it is in itself one to which 'catastrophe theory' (Thom, 1975) could usefully be applied, since the interest of catastrophe theory is mainly in explaining why sudden jumps sometimes occur in the value of a variable, in relation to one or more smoothly changing control factors, and not at other times.

In addition, the emphasis of reversal theory, with its phenomenological base, is on the psychological rather than the mathematical. For many psychologists, accepting that the complex mathematical computations that go along with catastrophe theory can really explain the great variations which occur in human behaviour might prove difficult. The two approaches do not appear to be compatible.

In summary, the major problem with the approaches reviewed here (the ZOF model [until very recently], the multidimensional anxiety approach, and the catastrophe theory model) is that they are all concerned with anxiety and performance. For reversal theorists, this is probably the biggest single problem associated with these approaches. Why are researchers in sport psychology so preoccupied with this one particular unpleasant emotion? This may have been due to the importance of the inverted-U hypothesis (Yerkes & Dodson, 1908) in motor skills research, historically a forerunner of applied sport psychology. A further reason was provided by Kerr and Svebak (1994), who suggested that a bias existed in the availability and expedience of anxiety-based measuring instruments. Whatever the reason, there would appear to be little real justification for restricting investigations of performance to anxiety when clearly there are other emotions, both pleasant and unpleasant, that may play an important role in performance.

These anxiety-based approaches comprise one major thrust in the performance research. A second major thrust has involved the monitoring of performance-related moods through the use of the POMS instrument (McNair et al., 1971).

The Mental Health Model

Instead of being restricted to one emotion, anxiety, the Profile of Mood States (POMS) measures tension, depression, anger, vigour, fatigue, and confusion. Use of the POMS was pioneered in sport psychology by Morgan (e.g. 1979, 1980). In a succession of studies, Morgan and his colleagues (e.g. Morgan & Johnson, 1978; Morgan & Pollock, 1979) found a relatively consistent pattern amongst sports groups of high scores on the (positive) vigour subscale and low scores on the other (negative) scales. Due the placement of vigour in the middle of the other moods, a graphical representation of scores assumed what became known as the *iceberg* profile. According to Morgan (1980), this iceberg profile reflected mental health in successful performers. As a result, some commentators (e.g. Prapavessis, & Grove, 1991) have termed this *Morgan's mental health model*.

Although in some respects the use of the POMS in mood performance research has moved beyond the preoccupation with anxiety, Morgan's (1980) mental health model has recently been subjected to heavy criticism (e.g. Renger, 1993; Rowley, Landers, Blaine Kyllo, & Etnier, 1995; Terry, 1995). Rowley et al. (1995) have argued that the scale is susceptible to social desirability and other response sets. They also point out that, in some studies using the scale, successful performance was assumed from team membership rather than measured directly. This problem was further exacerbated by the use of between-subjects research designs (see also Krane, 1992). Furthermore, there was inconsistency and variability in the time between the measurement of mental health and performance. Terry (1995) drew attention to a tendency in Morgan's early studies (e.g. Morgan & Johnson, 1978; Morgan & Pollock, 1979) to consider profiles of mood states as stable dispositions without setting them in a situational context. Also, in these same studies, Prapavessis and Grove (1991) pointed to an erroneous interpretation of correlational findings as indicating a causal relationship between POMS mood scores and performance. Findings that qualifiers for national squads had different mood profiles before competition than non-qualifiers were interpreted to mean that higher performance was a result of the profile. This interpretation was confounded by the pre-performance status of the athletes. Highly ranked athletes assured of selection were less likely to be stressed during qualification and therefore might have exhibited relatively positive moods prior to performance. Finally, methodological problems associated with lack of control groups and the comparison of athletes' mood profiles with extremely limited normative data, in Morgan's (1980) mental health model studies, have been identified by Rowley et al. (1995).

One study that did incorporate the POMS into a direct study of performance in cross-country running was carried out by Cockerill, Nevill, and Lyons (1991). They used the POMS, completed one hour prior to running in two cross-country races involving experienced competitive distance runners (N=81). The results from race one were used to develop a mood model and those from race 2 to test the validity of the model for predicting performance (race times). From race 1 data, no significant differences were found between the mood scores of successful runners (those 15 runners who finished in the top 50 places) and less successful runners (those 19 runners who finished in the last 50 places). Also, no clear relationships were found when each of the POMS six mood factors were plotted against the times from race 1. However, when all six were analysed using a multiple-regression statistical technique a *best subset* of mood factors was identified, which involved tension, depression, and anger.

Prior to race 2, POMS data was collected from 14 competing runners and used to predict their times. Analysis of actual and predicted times yielded a significant correlation coefficient. Cockerill et al. (1991) argued that, as the race was over a different course, it was the relative finishing position of the runners rather than absolute times that was of interest for testing the model. When the predicted finishing order was ranked against their actual rank order, a stronger correlation coefficient was revealed. Thus, some but not all POMS mood factors were successfully used as performance predictors in cross-country running. Nevertheless, in considering their overall results, Cockerill et al., (1991, p.210) warn that, "... while it might eventually be possible to describe a 'winner's profile' for a given sport, it is likely to be different from the iceberg referred to by Morgan."

Also, Rowley et al. (1995) carried out a meta-analysis of some 33 sport-based POMS studies. Their results indicated that pre-competitive mood states accounted for less than 1% of the variance in determining performance. Thus, the difference between successful and unsuccessful sports performers in terms of their mental health mood profiles is extremely small and casts doubt on the usefulness of the POMS in predicting successful performance.

In terms of a balance between mood items and scales, the POMS favours unpleasant or negative moods to the extent that some researchers have attempted to redress the balance by adding extra positive mood items (invigorated, refreshed, uplifted; Steptoe & Cox, 1988). By concentrating on mood profiles, derived from instruments like the POMS, that are biased towards negative moods and negative affect, sport psychology researchers and practitioners are missing a major part of the mood and performance jigsaw. Examining changes that may be taking place in other states or emotions (e.g. excitement, relaxation), within an approach balanced for positive and negative emotions, may prove more beneficial. What Kerr and his co-workers (e.g. Kerr & Svebak, 1994; Males & Kerr, 1996) have argued for, is a broader approach to the study of psychological mood states in the sports context through reversal theory. Such a balanced approach is possible based on the eight positive and eight negative emotions, which are thought to occur as a result of metamotivational state combinations (see Chapter 2 and Apter, 1988). A measuring instrument that includes these 16 positive and negative emotions (the Tension and Effort Stress Inventory, TESI; Svebak, 1993) has been developed and used successfully in both medical (e.g. Svebak et al., 1991) and sports research (Kerr & Svebak, 1994; Males & Kerr, 1996). What is more, the 16 emotions identified within reversal theory have the advantage of being built on a comprehensive theoretical framework which lends itself to hypothesis testing.

CONCLUDING COMMENTS

The main purpose of this chapter has been to examine the relationship between arousal and performance in sport as it has been explained by traditional and more contemporary theoretical explanations. The gist of each approach was presented, some details of how the approach had been used in sports research were included, and some of the criticisms of each that have been recorded in the literature were listed. In addition, an attempt was made to show the advantages pertaining to the use of reversal theory in sport psychology theory and research on arousal and performance.

The impression may have been given from the discussion here that pre-competitive emotions and levels of arousal are relatively unstable and that top-level performers are not very skilful at modulating them. In fact, the results of the reversal theory studies reviewed in Chapter 5 suggest that this is not the case and that skilled performers are consistently good at achieving and maintaining their desired mental state.

Leaving aside research evidence for a moment, a commonsense view of top sports performers might consider that, as these athletes have reached the top, they must (in addition to a number of other aspects of performance like technique and fitness) have become reasonably proficient in getting themselves into the right frame of mind for competition. It seems likely that, as they have progressed from young performers, through age-group competitions and the representative ranks, to become senior national and international competitors, they have undergone (whether consciously or otherwise) a process that has toughened them mentally. This process may work in a manner similar to systematic desensitisation or stress inoculation training (Meichenbaum, 1985). All other things being equal, if they have not developed a good degree of mental toughness, they are likely to have dropped out well before reaching the top. A similar process may also be at work in the development of pre-competition mental skills. Although there may be exceptions, it seems probable that young sports performers as they progress would, perhaps through trial and error, learn to recognise which pre-competition moods or emotions (including excitement) are most appropriate for their forthcoming performance. Again, failure to do so might well result in performers dropping out.

There is considerable evidence from the non-sport psychological literature that people are more than capable of manipulating arousal levels and moods or emotions in everyday life through, for example, smoking, drinking, eating, and exercise (see e.g. Thayer, 1989). Morris and Reilly (1987) have called this *the self-regulation of mood* and Thayer (1989, p.174) *personal planning to optimise mood*. Kerr (1993) argued that athletes use pre-competition performance routines (see Boutcher, 1990) in a similar way to the other methods of mood modulation used in everyday life, to regulate pre-competitive metamotivational states and emotions. There may well be times when some sports performers will need the assistance of a sport psychologist to help them regulate pre-competitive emotions, but sport psychology, in general, may have underplayed the ability of performers to develop mental skills by themselves through experience (see e.g. Keating & Hogg, 1995).

The following chapter concentrates on aggression and violence in sport and, yet again, felt arousal comes into the picture. In the discussion, it will be shown that felt arousal has a very important underlying part to play in the pleasure participants obtain from physical contact sports, where being aggressive is an intrinsic element, and also when behaviour in some sports goes outside the rules and participants become violent towards each other.

FURTHER READING

1. Kerr, J.H. (1985b). The experience of arousal: A new basis for studying arousal effects in sports. *Journal of Sports Sciences, 3,* 169–179.
2. Apter, M.J. (1989). *Reversal theory: Motivation, emotion and personality.* London: Routledge. Chapter 2.
3. Apter, M.J. (1988). Reversal theory as a theory of the emotions. In M.J. Apter, J.H., Kerr, & M.P. Cowles, (Eds.), *Progress in reversal theory.* (pp.43–62). [Advances in Psychology series, 51]. Amsterdam: North-Holland/Elsevier.

REFERENCES

Apter, M.J. (1976). Some data inconsistent with the optimal arousal theory of motivation. *Perceptual and Motor Skills, 43,* 1209–1210.

Apter, M.J. (1982). *The experience of motivation: The theory of psychological reversals.* London: Academic Press.

Apter, M.J. (1988). Reversal theory as a theory of the emotions. In M.J. Apter, J.H., Kerr, & M.P.

Cowles (Eds.), *Progress in reversal theory* (pp.43–62). [Advances in psychology series, 51]. Amsterdam: North-Holland/Elsevier.

Apter, M.J. (1989). *Reversal theory: Motivation, emotion and personality.* London: Routledge.

Baddeley, A.D. (1972). Selective attention and performance in dangerous environments. *British Journal of Psychology, 63*, 537–546.

Baumeister, R.F., & Showers, C.J. (1986). A review of paradoxical effects: Choking under pressure in sports and mental tests. *European Journal of Social Psychology, 16*, 361–383.

Boutcher, S.H. (1990). The role of performance routines in sport. In G.L. Jones & L. Hardy (Eds.), *Stress and performance in sport* (pp.231–245). London: Wiley.

Burton, D. (1988). Do anxious swimmers swim slower? Re-examining the elusive anxiety-performance relationship. *Journal of Exercise and Sports Psychology, 10*, 45–61.

Cooke, L.E. (1981). A critical appraisal of the Yerkes-Dodson law. Unpublished doctoral dissertation, University of Leeds, UK.

Cockerill, I.A., Nevill, A.M., & Lyons, N. (1991). Modelling mood states in athletic performance. *Journal of Sports Sciences, 9*, 205–212.

Cox, T., & Kerr, J.H. (1989). Arousal effects during tournament play in squash. *Perceptual and Motor Skills, 69*, 1275–1280.

Cox, T., & Kerr, J.H. (1990). Self-reported mood in competitive squash. *Personality and Individual Differences, 11*(2), 199–203.

Davidson, R.J., & Schwartz, G.E. (1976). The psychobiology of relaxation and related states: A multiprocess theory. In D.I. Mostofsky (Ed.), *Behavioral control and modification of physiological activity* (pp.399–442). Englewood Cliffs, NJ: Prentice-Hall.

Egeler, C.G., & de Booij, T. (1955). *Challenge of the Andes: The conquest of Mount Huanstán.* New York: David Mackay Company.

Fazey, J.A., & Hardy, L. (1988). *The inverted-U hypothesis: A catastrophe for sport psychology.* British Association of Sports Sciences Monograph No.1. Leeds: National Coaching Foundation.

Fiske, D.W., & Maddi, S.R. (1961). A conceptual framework. In D.W. Fiske & S.R. Maddi (Eds.), *Functions of varied experience* (pp.11–56). Homewood, IL: Dorsey Press.

Gill, D.L. (1994). A sport and exercise psychology perspective on stress. *Quest, 46*, 20–27.

Gill, D.L., & Deeter, T.E. (1988). Development of the Sport Orientation Questionnaire. *Research Quarterly for Exercise and Sport, 59*, 191–202.

Gould, D., & Krane, V. (1992). The arousal–athletic performance relationship: Current status and future direction. In T. Horn (Ed.), *Advances in sport psychology.* Champaign, IL: Human Kinetics.

Gould, D., Petlichkoff, L., Simons, J., & Vivera, M. (1987). Relationship between Competitive State Anxiety Inventory–2 subscale scores and pistol shooting performance. *Journal of Sport Psychology, 9*, 33–42.

Hammerstein, J., & Burton, D. (1995). Anxiety and the Ironman: Investigating the antecedents and consequences of endurance athletes' state anxiety. *The Sport Psychologist, 9*, 29–40.

Hanin, Y. (1986). The state–trait anxiety research on sports in the USSR. In C.D. Spielberger & R. Diaz-Guerrero (Eds.), *Cross-cultural anxiety* (pp.45–64). Washington: Hemisphere.

Hanin, Y. (1989). Interpersonal and group anxiety in sports. In D. Hackfort & C.D. Spielberger (Eds.), *Anxiety in sports: An international perspective* (pp.137–151). Series in Health Psychology and Behavioral Medicine. New York: Hemisphere Publishing.

Hanin, Y. (1993). Optimal performance emotions in top athletes. In S. Serpa, J. Alves, V. Ferriera, & A. Paula-Brito (Eds.), *Proceedings of the VIII World Congress of Sport Psychology* (pp.229–232). Lisbon, Portugal: International Society of Sport Psychology.

Hanin, Y., & Syrjá, P. (1995). Performance affect in junior ice hockey players: An application of the individual zones of optimal functioning model. *The Sport Psychologist, 9*, 169–187.

Hardy, L. (1990). A catastrophe model of performance in sport. In G. Jones & L. Hardy (Eds.), *Stress and performance in sport* (pp.81–106). Chichester, UK: John Wiley.

Hardy, L., & Parfitt, G. (1991). A catastrophe model of anxiety and performance. *British Journal of Psychology, 82,* 163–178.

Hardy, L., Parfitt, G., & Pates, J. (1994). Performance catastrophes in sport: A test of the hysteresis hypothesis. *Journal of Sports Sciences, 12,* 327–334.

Hebb, D.O. (1955). Drives and the C.N.S. (Conceptual Nervous System). *Psychological Review, 62,* 243–254.

Hebb, D.O., & Thompson, W.R. (1954). The social significance of animal studies. In G. Lindzey (Ed.), *Handbook of social psychology* (pp.532–561). Cambridge, MA: Addison-Wesley.

Jones, G. (1995). More than just a game: Research developments and issues in competitive anxiety in sport. *British Journal of Psychology, 86,* 449–478.

Jones, G., & Cale, A. (1989). Relationships between multidimensional and competitive state anxiety and cognitive and motor components of performance. *Journal of Sports Sciences, 7,* 229–240.

Jones, G., Hanton, S., & Swain, A.B.J. (1994). Intensity and interpretation of anxiety symptoms in elite and non-elite sports performers. *Personality and Individual Differences, 17,* 657–663.

Jones, G., & Swain, A.B.J. (1992). Intensity and direction dimensions of competitive state anxiety and relationships with competitiveness. *Perceptual and Motor Skills, 74,* 467–472.

Jones, G., & Swain, A.B.J. (1995). Predispositions to experience debilitative and facilitative anxiety in elite and non-elite performers. *The Sport Psychologist, 9*(2), 201–211.

Keating, J., & Hogg, J. (1995). Precompetitive preparations in professional hockey. *Journal of Sport Behavior, 18,* 270–285.

Kerr, J.H. (1985a). A new perspective for sports psychology. In M.J. Apter, D. Fontana, & S. Murgatroyd (Eds.), *Reversal theory: Applications and developments.* Cardiff: University College Cardiff Press/New York: Lawrence Erlbaum Associates Inc.

Kerr, J.H. (1985b). The experience of arousal: A new basis for studying arousal effects in sports. *Journal of Sports Sciences, 3,* 169–179.

Kerr, J.H. (1987). Structural phenomenology, arousal and performance. *Journal of Human Movement Studies, 13*(5), 211–229.

Kerr, J.H. (1989). Anxiety, arousal and sport performance: An application of reversal theory. In D. Hackfort & C.D. Spielberger (Eds.), *Anxiety in sports: An international perspective* (pp.137–151). [Series in Health Psychology and Behavioral Medicine.] New York: Hemisphere Publishing.

Kerr, J.H. (1993). An eclectic approach to psychological interventions in sport: Reversal theory. *The Sport Psychologist, 7,* 400–418.

Kerr, J.H., & Cox, T. (1988). Psychological preparation for competitive squash. *Journal of Human Movement Studies, 14,* 205–218.

Kerr, J.H., & Cox, T. (1989). Effects of metamotivational dominance and metamotivational state on squash task performance. *Perceptual and Motor Skills, 67,* 171–174.

Kerr, J.H., & Cox, T. (1990). Cognition and mood in relation to the performance of a squash task. *Acta Psychologica, 73*(1), 103–114.

Kerr, J.H., & Svebak, S. (1994). The acute effects of participation in sport on mood. *Personality and Individual Differences, 16*(1), 159–166.

Kerr, J.H., & Vlaswinkel, E.H. (1993). Self-reported mood and running. *Work & Stress, 7*(3), 161–177.

Kirkcaldy, B.D. (1983). Catastrophic performances. *Sportswissenschaft, 1,* 46–53.

Klavora, P. (1977). An attempt to derive inverted-U curves based on the relationship between anxiety and athletic performance. In D.M. Landers & R.W. Christina (Eds.), *Psychology of motor behavior and sport* (pp.369–377). Champaign, IL: Human Kinetics.

Krane, V. (1990). *Anxiety and athletic performance: A test of multidimensional anxiety and catastrophe theories.* Unpublished doctoral dissertation. University of North Carolina at Greensboro.

Krane, V. (1992). Conceptual and methodological considerations in sport anxiety research: From the inverted-U hypothesis to catastrophe theory. *Quest, 44,* 72–87.

Krane, V. (1993). A practical application of the anxiety–athletic performance relationship: The zone of optimal functioning hypothesis. *The Sport Psychologist, 7,* 113–126.

Krane, V., Joyce, D., & Rafeld, J. (1994). Competitive anxiety, situation criticality and softball performance. *The Sport Psychologist, 8,* 58–72.

Krane, V., & Williams, J.M. (1987). Performance and somatic anxiety, cognitive anxiety and confidence changes prior to competition. *Journal of Sport Behavior, 10,* 47–56.

Lazarus, R.S. (1966). *Psychological stress and the coping process.* New York: McGraw-Hill.

Mackay, C.J., Cox, T., Burrows, G.C., & Lazzerini, A.J. (1978). An inventory for the measurement of self-reported stress and arousal. *British Journal of Social and Clinical Psychology, 17,* 283–284.

Males, J.R., & Kerr, J.H. (1996). Stress, emotion and performance in elite slalom canoeists. *The Sport Psychologist, 10,* 17–36.

Man, F., Stuchlíková, I., & Kindlmann, P. (1995). Trait–state anxiety, worry, emotionality and self-confidence in top-level soccer players. *The Sport Psychologist, 9*(2) 212–224.

Martens, R. (1974). Arousal and motor performance. In J.A. Wilmore (Ed.), *Exercise and sports science reviews.* New York: Academic Press.

Martens, R. (1977). *Sport competition anxiety test.* Champaign, IL: Human Kinetics.

Martens, R., Burton, D., Rivkin, F., & Simon, J. (1980). Reliability and validity of the Competitive State Anxiety Inventory (CSAI). In C.H. Nadeau, W.C. Halliwell, K.M. Newell, & G.C. Roberts (Eds.), *Psychology of motor behavior and sport* (pp.91–99). Champaign, IL: Human Kinetics.

Martens, R., Burton, D., Vealey, R.S., Bump, L.A., & Smith, D.E. (1990a). Development and validation of the Competitive State Anxiety Inventory–2 (CSAI-2). In R. Martens, R.S. Vealey, & D. Burton (Eds.), *Competitive anxiety in sport.* Champaign, IL: Human Kinetics.

Martens, R., & Landers, D.M. (1970). Motor performance under stress: A test of the inverted-U hypothesis. *Journal of Personality and Social Psychology, 16,* 29–37.

Martens, R., Vealey, R.S., & Burton, D. (Eds.) (1990b). *Competitive anxiety in sport.* Champaign, IL: Human Kinetics.

McIlvanney, H. (1992, 12 April). Coolest nerve at the Crucible. *The Observer.* (p.42).

McNair, D.M., Lorr, M., & Droppleman, L.F. (1971). *Manual for the Profile of Mood States.* San Diego, CA: Educational and Industrial Testing Service.

Meichenbaum, D. (1985). *Stress inoculation training.* New York: Pergamon.

Morgan, W.P. (1979). Prediction of performance in athletics. In P. Klavora & J.V. Daniels (Eds.), *Coach, athlete and the sport psychologist* (pp.173–186). Champaign, IL: Human Kinetics.

Morgan, W.P. (1980). The trait psychology controversy. *Research Quarterly for Exercise and Sport, 51,* 50–76.

Morgan, W.P., & Johnson, R.W. (1978). Personality correlates of successful and unsuccessful oarsmen. *International Journal of Sport Psychology, 11,* 38–49.

Morgan, W.P., & Pollock, M.L. (1979). Psychologic characterization of the elite distance runner. *Annals of the New York Academy of Sciences, 301,* 382–403.

Morris, L.W., Davis, M.A., & Hutchings, C.H. (1981). Cognitive and emotional components of anxiety: Literature review and a revised Worry–Emotionality Scale. *Journal of Educational Psychology, 73,* 541–555.

Morris, W.N., & Reilly, N.P. (1987). Toward the self-regulation of mood: Theory and research. *Motivation and Emotion, 11,* 215–249.

Naatanen, R. (1973). The inverted-U relationship between activation and performance: A critical review. In S. Kornblum (Ed.), *Attention and performance* (pp.155–174). London: Academic Press.

Parfitt, C.G., & Hardy, L. (1987). Further evidence for the differential effects of competitive anxiety upon a number of cognitive and motor subcomponents. *Journal of Sports Science, 5*, 62–63.

Prapavessis, H., & Grove, J.R. (1991). Precompetitive emotions and shooting performance: The mental health and zone of optimal function models. *The Sport Psychologist, 5*, 223–234.

Raglin, J.S., & Turner, P.E. (1993). Anxiety and performance in track and field athletes: A comparison of the inverted-U hypothesis with zone of optimal function theory. *Personality and Individual Differences, 14*, 163–171.

Renger, R. (1993). A review of the Profile of Mood States (POMS) in the prediction of athletic success. *Journal of Applied Sport Psychology, 5*, 78–84.

Rowley, A.J., Landers, D.M., Blaine Kyllo, L., & Etnier, J.L. (1995). Does the iceberg profile discriminate between successful and less successful athletes? A meta-analysis. *Journal of Sport and Exercise Psychology, 17*, 185–189.

Sarason, I.G. (1980). *Test anxiety: Theory, research and applications*. Hillsdale, NJ: Lawrence Erlbaum Associates Inc.

Schachter, S., & Singer, J. (1962). Cognitive, social and physiological determinants of emotional state. *Psychological Review, 69*, 283–290.

Sonstroem, R.J., & Bernardo, P. (1982). Intraindividual pre-game state anxiety and basketball performance: A re-examination of the inverted-U curve. *Journal of Sport Psychology, 4*, 235–245.

Spielberger, C.D. (1966). Theory and research on anxiety. In C.D. Spielberger (Ed.), *Anxiety and behavior* (pp.3–20). New York: Academic Press.

Spielberger, C.D., Gorsuch, R.L., & Lushene, R.E. (1970). *Manual for the State–Trait Anxiety Inventory*. Palo Alto, CA: Consulting Psychologists Press.

Steptoe, A., & Cox, S. (1988). Acute effects of aerobic exercise on mood. *Health Psychology, 7*, 329–340.

Svebak, S. (1983). The effect of information load, emotional load and motivational state upon tonic physiological activation. In H. Ursin & R. Murison (Eds.), *Biological and psychological basis of psychosomatic disease: Advances in the biosciences* (pp.61–73). Oxford: Pergamon Press.

Svebak, S. (1984). Active and passive forearm flexor tension patterns in the continuous perceptual–motor task paradigm: The significance of motivation. *International Journal of Psychophysiology, 2*, 167–176.

Svebak, S. (1986). Cardiac and somatic activation in the continuous perceptual–motor task: The significance of threat and serious-mindedness. *International Journal of Psychophysiology, 10*, 155–162.

Svebak, S. (1993). The development of the Tension and Effort Stress Inventory (TESI). In J.H. Kerr, S. Murgatroyd, & M.J. Apter, (Eds.), *Advances in reversal theory* (pp.189–204). Amsterdam: Swets & Zeitlinger.

Svebak, S., & Murgatroyd, S. (1985). Metamotivational dominance: A multimethod validation of reversal theory constructs. *Journal of Personality and Social Psychology, 48*(1), 107–116.

Svebak, S., Ursin, H., Endresen, I., Hjelmen, A.M., & Apter, M.J. (1991). Psychological factors in the aetiology of back pain. *Psychology and Health, 5*, 307–314.

Swain, A.B.J., & Jones, G. (1993). Intensity and frequency dimensions of competitive state anxiety. *Journal of Sports Sciences, 11*, 533–542.

Terry, P. (1995). The efficacy of mood state profiling with elite performers: A review and synthesis. *The Sport Psychologist, 9*, 309–324.

Thayer, R.E. (1989). *The biopsychology of mood and arousal*. Oxford: Oxford University Press.

Thom, R. (1975). *Structural stability and morphogenesis* [D.H. Fowler, Trans.] New York: Benjamin-Addison Wesley.

Walters, J., Apter, M.J., & Svebak, S. (1982). Color preference, arousal and the theory of psychological reversals. *Motivation and Emotion, 6*, 193–215.

Watson, D., & Tellegen, A. (1985). Towards a consensual structure of mood. *Psychological Bulletin, 98*, 219–235.

Welford, A.T. (1976). *Skilled performance*. Brighton, UK: Scott, Foresman & Co.

Yerkes, R.M., & Dodson, J.D. (1908). The relation of strength of stimulus to rapidity of habit formation. *Journal of Comparative Neurology and Psychology, 18*, 459–482.

Zeeman, E.C. (1976). Catastrophe theory. *Scientific American, 234*, 65–82.

7

Get Your Retaliation in First: Aggression and Violence in Team Contact Sports

Team contact sports, like rugby union and rugby league, American football, Australian rules football, ice hockey, and perhaps Gaelic football and soccer are all characterised by a high degree of aggression and physical, often violent, contact. In this sense, they are different from other team games such as basketball, netball, field hockey, and volleyball (in theory non-contact games). In studying the motivation behind, and the emotion involved in, participation in team contact sports, there is a need to address the fact that much of the pleasure and satisfaction to be gained from these sports is associated with the element of physical contact. No one who has ever sacked a quarterback in American football, brought off a punishing crash tackle in rugby or a powerful body check in ice hockey, or fought for a 50-50 ball in soccer could deny the tremendous feelings of pleasure and satisfaction that arise from carrying out these skills successfully. These physical and violent plays are an intrinsic part of each of these sports and are a major reason why many people enjoy them.

Before proceeding any further, it might be useful to clarify what exactly is understood in this chapter by the terms *aggression* and *violent plays* in team contact sports. Academic writers on aggression have had difficulty in agreeing on a definition of aggression (see e.g. Geen, 1990, p.2–4) and the task becomes even more difficult when aggression and violence in sport are considered. According to reversal theory, the permissible aggression and violent plays that are intrinsic to team contact sports are of a special nature, in that they take place within a protective frame. Therefore, these actions are not the same as the aggressive and violent acts that occur outside the sports context. In general, aggression can be seen as unprovoked hostility or attacks on another person which are not sanctioned by society. However, in the sports context, the aggression is provoked in the sense that two opposing teams have willingly agreed to compete against each other. Aggression in team contact sports is intrinsic and sanctioned, provided the plays remain permissible within the boundaries of certain rules, which act as a kind of contract in the pursuit of aggression (and violence) between consenting adults. Violence generally can be considered as violent conduct of an unlawful kind, yet crash tackles, quarterback sacks, and ice hockey body checks are violent, sometimes very violent plays. All of these actions require strong physical force to be exerted against another person. What is special about sport is that these actions, which might be illegal elsewhere, are legal in sport. This is not to say that illegal actions cannot or do not take place in team contact sports; they do, but these acts are of a fundamentally different nature. The motivation and emotion involved in both sanctioned violent plays and unsanctioned violent acts in sport are central topics in the discussion that follows.

A few sport psychology writers have tried to explain aggression and violence in the team contact sports context (e.g. Russell, 1993; Smith, 1983). They have based their discussions on explanations of aggression from other areas of psychology, such as those of Zillman (1979) on excitation transfer and Bandura's (1973) social learning theory. However, many of the other texts on psychology and sport have tended to avoid or skirt around the topic of aggression and violence in sport, getting bogged down in ethical debates or getting side-tracked into discussions of spectator violence. Kerr (1994) has provided, in detail, the reversal theory view of violent and aggressive behaviour in the most enduring form of spectator violence, soccer hooliganism. Although some mention of the theoretical models used to explain hooliganism will be made, the intention in this chapter is to concentrate on the players themselves and what motivates them to take part in dangerous team contact sports. Ethical aspects of aggression and violence in sport will not be discussed.

Brink's (1995, p.29) perceptive description of rugby draws attention to three essential points which need to be considered in any discussion about motivation and team contact sports:

Much of the attraction of rugby lies in its extreme physicality. But its full fascination is determined by the way in which brute force and athletic speed are married to quick thinking, the ingenuity and anticipation of a chess player, the absorption of the individual within a large, fluid motion, the creation of moving patterns and changing rhythms.

At its best rugby acquires a poetry of its own, characterised by rapid changes of tempo, and unexpected switches of direction, played at many levels simultaneously, and involving the totality of the human person: body, mind and imagination; memory and foresight—all of it pushed to the extreme. Which is why it is balanced on such a precarious knife-edge: if a good game accords physical and emotional delight, a bad one can be awful beyond description.

If rugby has the potential to demonstrate the best of which a sportsperson is capable, it can also encapsulate the worst. The way a game turns out may be determined by the players, the coach, the referee, the spectators, the overall cultural context with which it is played. And this is where foul play becomes a marker of larger meanings.

Because the game is so relentless by its very nature, the borders between the permissible and the inadmissible are not always very clear-cut. Both are inherently violent. But surely the distinction between hard play and foul play lies in the resort of the latter to violence of an underhand, malicious, treacherous kind. It is a condition of foul play that it is not supposed to come to light, to be exposed, because it is not directed to the unfolding of the game but to the private goals of rage or revenge, to "get at" a specific opponent, to "prove" oneself. It foregrounds the individual, not the team.

The essential points that require discussion here are concerned with the facts that: (a) although the sport is dangerous, the nature of the game, including hard physical play, makes it attractive; (b) brute force and sanctioned violence are important features of the game; and (c) unsanctioned, malicious violence in the form of foul or dirty play can also occur. It may be useful to point out at this stage that theme (a) relates mainly to the paratelic state, theme (b) to the mastery state, and theme (c) to the negativistic state. Each of these themes will be dealt with in more detail in the following sections.

THE DANGEROUS BUT ATTRACTIVE NATURE OF TEAM CONTACT SPORTS

That team contact sports are sometimes dangerous is beyond dispute, as Askwith in 1991 (p.19), discussing the forthcoming Rugby Union World Cup, points out:

Shortly after 3 pm on Thursday week, 30 of the world's finest athletes, brimming with aggression, will begin to fling themselves at one another with almost comparable brute force. Having 16 stone of solid muscle and bone crash into you at 15mph while you are moving at 15mph in the opposite direction may not quite come into the hammer-and-peach category, but it is not far short of it; especially if the experience is repeated again and again for 80 minutes . . .

Rugby is one of the most violent of all sports, involving a unique combination of legitimate hostile intent and potential for serious injury. Most players, it is true, come through most matches with only the odd bruise or graze to show for their pains. For the unfortunate minority who don't, however, the costs can be much greater.

Even soccer, which has, perhaps, less potential for serious injury than the other sports mentioned earlier, has a strong physical element. Davies (1991, p.114), for example, talking about the then England manager and the nature of soccer, describes this aspect of the game:

Robson had told me I should sit on the bench because 'you see a different game down there. When you are close to the pitch you'll be amazed at the pace of the game and the power, the physical contact. Up there (in the press box) you don't see it all, you can think, oh, it's a game of poetry and space—but down there, it's frenetic. It's frightening.

One of the major reasons people expose themselves to unnecessary risks in sports is for the rewarding feelings of excitement. Team contact sports (like the risk sports of parachuting and downhill ski racing discussed in Chapter 4) provide the participants with the opportunity to experience high levels of felt arousal as pleasant excitement. The characteristics of rugby that Brink (1995) described, the fluid motion, rapid changes of tempo, unexpected switches of direction, and the creation of moving patterns and changing rhythms are common, not only to rugby, but to many other team sports as well. In addition however, team contact sports have the added element of physical confrontation which contributes an extra dimension to the players' pleasant paratelic experience.

There are numerous quotes suggesting that, in spite of the associated risks, these sports are attractive and enjoyable precisely because of the physical contact involved. For example, the position of *hooker* in the middle of the scrum in rugby union, is one playing position where physical confrontation is ever-present. Graham Dawe and Brian Moore, both hookers who have played international rugby for England, appear to be in no doubt about what it is about rugby that they enjoy. "But I think it's the best position on the pitch because it's probably the only one where you're physically confronting your opposite number all through the game. In fact that's what attracted me to rugby in the early days." (Dawe, 1994, p.48.) "A hooker has a direct battle with his opposite number in a way that a winger, for example, cannot. I enjoy that, he said. I know that the All Blacks at Twickenham, the French away, will be huge battles and I look forward to them. That's the good thing about the front row." (Brian Moore quoted in Longmore, 1994, p.44.)

One reversal theory study (Kerr, 1988) provided evidence of consistency in the motivational styles of rugby players adding some support to these anecdotal comments. Kerr (1988) showed that the telic and paratelic dominance patterns of rugby players from four different cultures were similar. The TDS was administered to 106 male rugby players from Canada, Wales, England, and Australia. In spite of the fact that distinct cultural differences had previously been found between general subject populations from three of these countries (Murgatroyd, 1985), no cultural differences (on all three subscales and total telic dominance) were apparent amongst the rugby players. These results suggested that it is the nature of the game, rather than the particular culture in which it is played, that allows the motivation of rugby players to be satisfied.

As Apter (1992) has pointed out, virtually all sports take place within paratelic protective frames. These protective or safety frames are often (though not necessarily) tied in with physical structures and institutionalised playing areas. Soccer, Aussie rules, and rugby football stadia and ice-hockey rinks are all examples of literal spaces that come into this category. Apter (1992) has argued that the rules and laws that regulate what takes place during play in these literal spaces can be thought of in terms of psychological spaces. Both types of spaces are necessary to allow sports to take place in a non-real world setting within a kind of bubble or fish-bowl.

The safety frames associated with team contact sports take on a hybrid or combined form. They are not exactly the same as those necessary to climb mountains or sky dive (see Chapter 4), but neither are they the sort of safety frames that exist in non-contact sports. In non-contact sports, the biggest danger is probably of losing or playing badly, thus damaging one's self-esteem and pride. Players of team contact sports must develop protective frames that allow them to deal not only with the same features of play as non-contact sport performers, but also with the added ingredients of aggression, hard play, and physical violence, and the fact that they face the danger of possible serious injury.

Different sports performers need to psychologically construct protective frames to suit their own idiosyncratic needs within their particular sports. In this way, as long as the protective frame remains intact they can obtain the maximum enjoyment from their sports activities. In the case of team contact sports, the element of physical confrontation (linked to the mastery state and associated feelings of felt toughness—the degree to which individuals feel themselves to be tough, strong, or in control at a given time) adds to the excitement as long as it remains within what is acceptable behaviour in the game.

Acceptability may be prescribed by the actual written laws or rules of the game with the possible addendum of the unwritten rules of the players themselves. Apter (1993, p.34) has rightly indicated that, even within sport, the breaking of some rules is sanctioned. He gives the example of the *professional foul* in soccer (e.g. where a player from one team who has beaten the defence of the other, and has a clear run at goal and a very good chance of scoring, is deliberately brought down by a chasing defender to prevent a goal) which is really a part of the game, and the fighting that takes place in ice hockey which is also sanctioned (players reputedly receive extra payments for fighting). As will be shown later, such incidents may be used as part of a team's tactics. Thus, there are often two sets of rules operating in these games; one the game's official rules administered by referees and umpires, and another set accepted by, and administered by, the players themselves. For example, in a rugby union lineout or league or union scrum, many actions take place that are technically in breach of the laws, but the players accept what takes place up to a certain point. If a player goes too far, retaliatory action (to keep the offending player in line) will usually occur. These player rules have, of course, never been discussed or agreed on, they are just something that players learn through experience. However, they do exist in a grey area and do sometimes change, which can lead to problems if, and when, misunderstandings do arise (Apter, 1993). If behaviour falls outside what is acceptable, the protective frame comes under threat and may, under certain circumstances, be broken.

PHYSICAL PROWESS, HOSTILITY, TOUGHNESS, AND SANCTIONED VIOLENCE

Players and coaches in team contact sports are well aware that, to win against other teams, more often than not they must dominate the other team physically. In real terms, this means that players, or at least some players within any particular team, must be able to exert their physical prowess, hostility, and toughness in order to subjugate the opposing players (these descriptors exemplify the mastery state in reversal theory). In fact, the physical aspect is so important it often outweighs other factors. Tatum and Kushner (1979, p.29) put it like this:

> There are passive teams in the NFL that try to win with pure execution rather than aggressive and violent play. Execution has a place in the NFL, but unfortunately passive teams usually lose while physical teams usually win. That is simply the basic rule of football or any contact sport. In any contact sport it behooves the athlete to be physical.

Examples of this need for hard physical players are readily found in all team contact sports. One only has to think of mid-field players in soccer. There are few soccer teams, certainly in English soccer, that do not give priority to aggressive ball winning, especially among their mid-field players, sometimes at the expense of creativity and effective play-making. In fact, the rest of the team may be structured around one or two really aggressive physical players. Often, the best option for a coach is to find a balance of mid-field players combining both aggressive ball-winners and accomplished play-makers. English soccer, for example, has a whole history of players who fit this aggressive mould. Some like Bruce Rioch (who, in the 1970s, won an English First Division Championship medal with an excellent Derby team and went on to captain Scotland) was a feared opponent known for his ball-winning ability. Incidentally, Rioch also felt no compunction about tackling *over the top* (going in studs first, aimed above the ball at an opponent's shins) as a method of intimidation (Barclay, 1995). However, tackling over the top is, in terms of the soccer rulebook, illegal and Rioch's use of this type of tackle is a form of unsanctioned violence in sport which will be examined in a later section of this chapter.

Some teams may develop strategies and tactics that take advantage of their team's physical superiority. In Australia, for example, rugby league matches between Queensland (Maroons) and New South Wales (Blues), known as the State of Origin Series, are particularly competitive. Take the 1995 series opener for example (Burke, 1995, p.44):

> And Maroons coach Paul 'Fatty' Vautin and rookie prop Tony Hearn both predicted the Maroons forwards would 'stand up and be counted'.
>
> 'We're going to have to get stuck into them that's for sure. We've got to bash them up front,' said Hearn the North Sydney prop who will make his Origin debut.
>
> While Vautin was not predicting any on-field violence, he acknowledged the Maroons would adopt a physical approach.
>
> 'You look at our pack and it is a physical one. It's going to be a physical game and we won't be taking a backward step,' he said.
>
> Queensland forwards Gavin Allen, Hearn and Gillmeister were the hard men of league and they would lead from the front, Vautin said.

Although Burke's (1995) article could be seen merely as pre-game newspaper hype, clearly Queensland's coach and players were hoping to win the game by physically confronting and subduing the Blues' forwards. The language used in the quotes (like *stand up and be counted, get stuck in, lead from the front*, and the more sinister *take no prisoners* and *get your retaliation in first*, from rugby union [see Atyeo, 1979, p.12]), is typical of pre-game and half-time pep talk language common enough amongst players and coaches. What is apparent from this piece and the rest of Burke's (1995) article is that the players concerned (in this case the Maroons) were looking forward to the match and the physical confrontation with considerable relish. Why is it that some individuals find this aspect of team contact sports so rewarding and how can it be explained?

It has already been established earlier in the chapter that sports, including team contact sports, take place within a paratelic protective frame under conditions of high arousal. Within this frame, aggression and violent plays, and counter aggression and violent plays from the other team, increase levels of felt arousal, felt transactional outcome, and felt toughness to even higher levels. Violent plays could, for example, take the form of individual hits in American football and body checks in ice hockey or team plays like an all-out blitz in American football and driving rucks and mauls in rugby union, all of which are permitted under the rules. Some violent and aggressive plays are an intrinsic and acceptable feature of team contact sports.

Another important element in this process seems to be that these plays also have to be carried out successfully in order for the participants to gain the maximum amount of pleasure. For instance, no matter how hard a player goes in, a missed or even mistimed tackle in soccer or rugby is not very satisfying. In rugby league, for example, maximum pleasure from an individual violent play is obtained if a player can line up an opponent and tackle him or her as hard as possible before he or she can off-load the ball. Team or team-unit violent plays in rugby union can also provide maximum pleasure when performed well. New Zealand teams are particularly adept at rucking. This involves the forwards in twos and threes driving forward, often in a very hostile manner, over prostrate players and the ball and using their shoulders (and if necessary feet) to knock opposing players back and/or away from the ball. It would appear that the *success* element adds to feelings associated with the mastery metamotivational state. Successful performance and mastery of personal skills and team or team-unit techniques may well add to feelings of pleasure related to mastering the opposing team. However, pleasure in the mastery state can be obtained not only from success in dominance and control, but also from experiencing high levels of felt toughness, irrespective of success.

Within this scheme of things, players from both teams are liable to have a metamotivational state combination operative comprised of paratelic–conformist–alloic–mastery during play (individuals with the alloic state operative are primarily concerned with what happens to others). Nevertheless, reversal theory research has shown that the motivational styles of professional and Masters sports performers is more telic-oriented than the styles of those participating at lower performance levels (Kerr, 1987; Kerr & van Lienden, 1987). Specifically, these groups were found to be significantly more seriousminded and planning-oriented than serious amateur or recreational sports performers. For groups such as these, performing at a high level, it may be that the likely predominant metamotivational state combination during play is one of telic–conformist–alloic–mastery.

From what has been said in the previous paragraph, it may seem that all the pleasure is only gained by the person who successfully carries out the violent tackle, body check, or hit. There is however, another side to the coin. For players who play these games regularly there is a kind of perverse pleasure to be had in getting the ball or the puck away just before or, in some cases, just after being hit or tackled. In other words, the fact that your opponent(s) are doing their level best to hit you with all they have got and you have outwitted them by managing to pass to a colleague and keep the play going can be a source of tremendous satisfaction. This is especially true if your pass is part of a scoring movement which helps to set up a goal or a try. For the players concerned, knowing that you are going to be tackled or body checked and still managing to successfully pass the ball or puck takes a fair degree of courage. The pleasant feelings concerned may also include feelings of pride arising from a short-lived operative metamotivational combination involving autic–mastery.

It would also seem that the most pleasurable games are those when the competing teams are at about the same playing level or standard. In one-sided games where one team is very much on top and the other team can match neither the skills of their opponents, nor their physical prowess, the end result is that the game is thoroughly dissatisfying for both winning and losing teams and, for that matter, the spectators. Close games, where the members of both teams have the opportunity to carry out a high proportion of permissible aggressive and violent plays (both team and individual) successfully, are the most pleasurable to all concerned.

ADDICTED TO PHYSICAL CONFRONTATION

Again, it may seem surprising to suggest that, like soccer hooligan "super thugs" (see Kerr, 1994), experienced team contact sports players may become addicted to aggressive confrontation and violent plays. However, that is exactly what will be argued here. Kerr's (1994) model of soccer hooligan addiction (based on an adaptation of the work of Brown at the University of Glasgow; see e.g. Brown, 1997) will also be used to explain players' psychological dependence on team contact sports. In more precise terms, of course, it is the overall high levels of positive affect (associated with high levels of felt arousal, felt transactional outcome, and felt toughness that emanate from competitive play and that are added to by physical confrontation) to which team contact sport players are addicted.

The Hedonic Tone Management Model of Addictions has been proposed by Brown (1997) following work on a number of different addictions (see e.g. Brown, 1988, 1991, 1997). Brown has been a prominent writer on applications of reversal theory, and reversal theory plays a major role in the Hedonic Tone Management Model. The model is a flexible one which postulates that addictive behaviours, for example, gambling, alcohol abuse, and even criminal behaviour, all follow a series of similar developmental stages. Although stages 1 and 2 may not be appropriate in this instance, parts of the rest of the model can also be usefully applied to an explanation of why young people enjoy playing hard physical team contact sports and why they may continue to play as adults (see Fig. 7.1). The process begins when young players first try one or other of these sports.

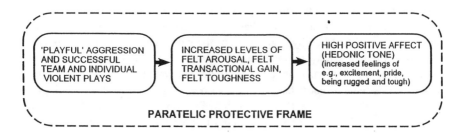

FIG. 7.1.   A graphical representation of the development of high positive hedonic tone within the paratelic protective frame that encapsulates team contact sports.

Through schools and sports clubs, many young people, perhaps in early adolescence sometimes sooner, have the opportunity to sample a number of sports and physical activities. Quite often they will keep trying different sports until they find one that suits them. At this stage, the most important feature of team contact sports activities is that they should, like many other non-contact sports, produce the pleasant playful feelings that reversal theorists have linked to the paratelic state (e.g. Kerr, 1988). Maintaining this approach is one of the keys to keeping beginners' interest and motivation high in any particular sport. For those beginners for whom the telic state is operative during team contact sports, their experience of the intrinsic moderate or high arousal associated with the activity is liable to be anxiety-filled and distinctly unpleasant. For beginners where the telic state is both operative and maintained for relatively long periods, it seems likely that, before long, they will drop out and perhaps move on to another type of sports activity. Those beginners who are enjoying contact team sports have already begun the first stage of addiction development, for they have already discovered the thrill of pleasant high arousal (see Fig. 7.2, point 3). This comes from the excitement provoked by the nature of the play itself and also from discovering the pleasures of being (playfully) aggressive during particular aspects of play (Geen, 1990).

As they progress, they are likely to begin spending more time practising and playing their sport and, as they become more competent and their team and individual skills improve, transactional emotions begin to play a bigger role in their feelings of pleasure. Young players achieve satisfaction through their improving mastery of skills and, for some, mastery of opponents. They are rewarded for their efforts by coaches, parents, their team-mates, and, for example, their own subjective feelings of excitement, pride, and gratitude (Fig. 7.2, point 4). During these early stages, aggression and violence may not be a major feature of their experience, but players are gradually being weaned onto a diet of physicality that will later develop into something much stronger.

By the time the athletes are young adults, they are becoming established players. They have made a strong commitment to their sport in terms of attending practice sessions and playing matches regularly. They typically do extra fitness training by themselves and are probably also concerned about developing healthy eating and sleeping habits. Everyday life for them is now increasingly being taken over by their sports involvement and they may have few other interests. The physical aspect of the game and the need to physically dominate opposing players and teams becomes increasingly salient. Coaches will already be admonishing players to hit and tackle hard and, for some players, this will already be a major source of pleasure. In psychological terminology, the players will have developed powerful positive feedback loops (Fig. 7.2, point 5), which serve to strongly reinforce their behaviour.

The playing schedules for team contact sports usually comprise a series of regular matches, often taking place at weekends throughout the season. In

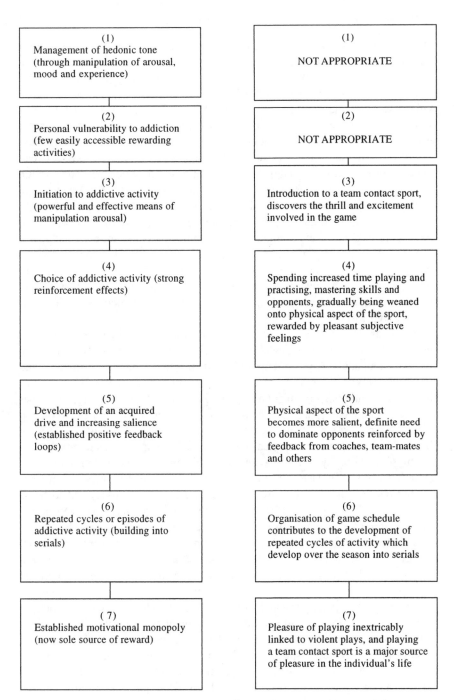

FIG. 7.2. Stages 3–7 of Brown's (1997) model applied to team contact sports. The left-hand panel shows the stages of development of addictive behaviour in general. The right-hand panel shows the addiction to physical and violent plays in team contact sports (adapted from Kerr, 1994).

addition, coaches usually organise two or three coaching and practice sessions per week. The playing structure is organised by others, but it means that the players themselves (unlike other addicts) have an officially approved method of developing what Brown (1997) has termed repeated *cycles* or *episodes,* which eventually accumulate into a *series* (Fig. 7.2, point 6). In simple terms, players can achieve emotional highs on a regular basis through their regular weekend games (cycles or episodes). Practice and coaching sessions may help to add to or maintain these positive emotional states in the periods between games over the season (serials). The injection of extra games, perhaps through extra cup matches, may also mean that even more emotional highs are available to players. If, towards the end of a playing season, a team manages to qualify for the final play-offs against the other top teams, the emotional rewards for players are likely to become higher as they come closer to and, eventually, win a trophy. The majority of teams, however, do not win trophies and, although they may receive some short-lived success in the early rounds and therefore extra psychological reward, partial success also brings with it defeat and an inevitable negative affect reaction (see Chapter 5 on the emotional effects of winning and losing).

As far as the physical component is concerned, this will have taken on a much bigger role in individuals' experience as they mature fully as players. Survival at an adult level is not possible for teams that cannot at least match and preferably outweigh the hostility and violence of their opponents. The result of this is that, while players must be skilful, extremely fit, extra strong, and super fast, only the toughest, hardest, and most durable players will proceed to the top of the playing pyramid. Consequently, it is at this stage that most players are likely to receive maximum pleasure from individual and team hostile and violent plays of the type described earlier. This physical and violent part of the game has become inextricably linked to the pleasures that players obtain from playing. Games that are not close, tough, hard battles are likely not to be as satisfying as those that are. Playing team contact sports may now well be the major source of emotional reward for many players (Fig. 7.2, point 7).

As it has been described here, the model may seem overly simplistic. If so, this may be because it has been described as a one-off, single through-put model. In reality, nothing could be further from the truth. Even though the process may be a relatively slow one, building up over the period of a player's involvement, it is an ongoing and a dynamic one. In addition, there are thought to be feedback loops operating which, as was mentioned in relation to stage 3, link between the different stages of the addiction process. The addiction process in team contact sports may be thought of as similar to the type of addiction associated with exercise addiction, which has been described by some as a *positive* addiction (see Glasser, 1976). Hard physical training and the associated high arousal is an integral part of team contact sports and it is known that exercise can be addictive. Therefore, it seems likely that the exercise element in team contact sports works as another ingredient (along with violent plays) in the addictive process, contributing to the situational highs of the players. Exercise addiction will be discussed more in the next chapter and it will be sufficient here to make the link in passing.

Until now the discussion in this chapter has been about sanctioned or permissible (within the rules) aggression, hostility, and violence in the context of team contact sports. This aggression and violence has a paratelic flavour because sports are generally played with a paratelic protective frame. However, all participants and observers of these sports know that unsanctioned or impermissible violence can also be a feature of these sports. The following section examines how the protective frame may become broken or disturbed, and why unsanctioned or impermissible violence sometimes takes place.

UNSANCTIONED VIOLENCE IN TEAM CONTACT SPORTS

The paratelic form of aggression and sanctioned violence, described earlier, takes place in the absence of real anger and is essentially playful. In any game, the players in one team presume or hope that the players in the other will meet their aggression and sanctioned violence with like kind and a highly competitive game will be the outcome. Where anger or provocativeness exists here, it is likely to be in a parapathic form, which adds to the excitement and pleasant feelings of the situation (see also Chapters 2 & 4).

It has already been mentioned that the predominant operative meta-motivational state combination for team contact sports is one likely to be paratelic–conformist–alloic–mastery. On occasions however, reversals from the paratelic to telic (professionals and some other groups of performers may already have the telic state operative, see earlier) and from the conformist to the negativistic state may take place in players or groups of players. This means that the actions being carried out are then taking place in the presence of real anger. Typically, this is the cause of flare-ups which sometimes occur in sport (see also Geen, 1990, pp.46 & 52). Note also that in the Kerr and Svebak (1994) study of running, basketball, and rugby with relatively inexperienced players, anger was found to increase pre- to post-participation in rugby, but not with the other two sports. In rugby, for example, a player may take exception to a late hit or tackle and induced by this contingent factor (which is outside the official and players' rules and therefore not within the protective frame of the game) reverses to telic and negativistic states, and retaliates accordingly (at the same time also breaking the official rules of the game).

For example, returning to the rucking technique in rugby union. If given a chance in a ruck situation, players from the defending team will try and prevent the attacking team from winning the ball by falling over and lying on or beyond the ball with their bodies (known in the game as *killing the ball*). This is against the laws of the game and those offending players should be penalised by the referee. However, referees do not always penalise the offending players and often the players take the laws into their own hands by raking the bodies of the players on the ground with their boot studs. This raking often leaves long, painful, but not dangerous, scrapemarks down an offending players' back which remind the player that he should not have been killing the ball. What is more, offending players are well aware of what they are doing and fully expect the treatment that they receive. All this can still take place within the protective frame, but if the referee continues not to penalise the offending players then frustration is very likely to prompt a reversal to the telic–negativistic states (at least in some players). Feelings of anger are the result of the reversal and the presence of anger now means that serious unsanctioned violence may take place. In the rugby union rucking situation, this often takes the form of stamping on the head rather than raking players' backs and has led to some terrible injuries. Some of these incidents have resulted in court cases and prosecutions which Young (1993), in his review of recent liability claims in sport, suggests have been increasing in recent years. What these legal interventions show is that, if the protective frame in which the games are played is ruptured or broken, players' impermissible actions are also illegal in the eyes of the law and no longer subject to the absolution normally granted to incidents within sport. Some commentators (e.g. Blanchard & Cheska, 1985; Young, 1993) are convinced that the apparent increases in unsanctioned violence and the subsequent increases in litigation have been brought about by increasing professionalisation, and the need to win in the light of the huge available financial rewards. Litigation may well be increasing, but whether unsanctioned violent actions are also increasing is open to question.

Anger-based unsanctioned violent acts do not always occur as a result of the scenario just described. There are violent acts that are of a more malicious and vindictive nature, and fall outside the rules of both the particular sport and those of the players. There are the individuals who, at the sign of the slightest fracas, and even though they were not involved directly, will take the chance to violently attack opponents. Alternatively, these individuals attempt to provoke trouble or injure players by carrying out vicious acts like eye-gouging, ear biting, head butting, and "bag snatching" (individuals who grab and squeeze a player's scrotum and testicles in rugby), helmet-to-helmet blows in American football, and a whole variety of stick offences in ice hockey. This type of player has been given the name *athletic psychopath* (see Askwith, 1991; also Atyeo, 1979, p.290; McIntosh, 1979, pp.102–103), and they form the subject of the next section.

ATHLETIC PSYCHOPATHS?

Within all of the sports that have been bracketed here as team contact sports there are some players, the *assassins, hatchetmen*, *policemen,* or *enforcers*, as they have sometimes been called, whose job it is to prevent the key opposition players from scoring or setting up plays. These players are usually well known to those who play and follow these sports and often have a deserved reputation. When necessary, they rely on physical intimidation and illegal violence rather than skilful play to take out and stop opponents. A quote from Faulkner (1976, p.98), about ice hockey illustrates the point well:

> Sure you go in and really rap him hard with the elbow and let him have it in the head maybe and the next time you won't have any problem with the guy. Maybe he'll come in the corner but not as hard as he did the first time, he's taking a chance of getting another elbow in the mouth. Maybe you get a penalty but you take him out of the play, that's a good penalty . . .

One of the most infamous incidents in Australian sport took place in the 1989 AFL Grand Final when Hawthorn played Geelong. The incident took place right at the beginning of the game and involved Hawthorn's Dermott Brereton, himself a rugged and uncompromising player, and Geelong player Mark Yeates. In a move that was apparently pre-planned by the Geelong Coach (Stocks, 1995), at the first bounce, right at the start of the game, Yeates cut through the centre square and took Brereton out with a deliberate shoulder charge below the ribs. Brereton, badly hurt, refused to leave the field in spite of being in obvious distress. Although shaken, he played on and later in the game Brereton (along with Geelong's Gary Ablett) turned out to be a scoring hero in a game considered by many to be one of the best AFL Grand Finals ever. The offending player Yeates remained unpunished, but the AFL later made a rule change to prevent this type of incident recurring. Although a rule change in Aussie rules football might prevent deliberate centre square incidents, there are still plenty of other places where they can and do happen and, as in other team contact sports, this type of incident is not uncommon.

It is conceivable that some players, especially those who are given the hitman role by coaches, may become addicted to unsanctioned violence. Given the arguments in Brown's Hedonic Tone Management Model approach to addiction, the processes involved would not appear to be very different from those involved in the model described earlier, where the aggressive and violent plays were all permissible.

The term *athletic psychopaths* has been used to describe these individuals, but are they true psychopaths in the psychological sense? Psychopathic disorder is defined as "a persistent disorder of the mind which results in abnormally aggressive or seriously irresponsible conduct on the part of the patient" and is considered a form of mental illness (see e.g. 1983 UK Mental Health Act; Gregory, 1987). To this author's knowledge, there has been no research work that has examined this topic in sport. Initial reversal theory work on psychopathy has been undertaken (see e.g. Thomas-Peter, 1988, 1993), but again none of the work has examined sport. However, given the criminal records of some of the players, use of the label *athletic psychopaths* may well be correct. Certainly, team contact sports might easily provide the setting for psychopathic behaviour. However, traditionally, psychology has considered that psychopaths have some form of personality trait defect which exhibits itself in antisocial psychopathic behaviour. This view suggests a permanent psychopathic disposition which will permeate the everyday life of the psychopath and has been known to reveal itself through other forms of violent behaviour. Reversal theory's dominance and metamotivational state approach offers a different view of psychopathy in which it is possible for the individual to exhibit psychopathic behaviour only on certain occasions. This was the argument put forward to explain soccer hooligans' regular and periodic, but soccer-specific violent behaviour (Kerr, 1994, pp.98–101). This argument seems equally appropriate for explaining possible regular and sports-specific violent psychopathic behaviour. In other words, some sports performers, if they were so inclined, could satisfy their psychopathic needs through violence on game days, by being a kind of temporary sports psychopath for the day.

CONCLUDING COMMENTS

This chapter has attempted to go where most other sport psychology books have feared to tread. It has examined the motivation and emotion of participants in sports activities that are rife with aggression and violence. Specifically, it has examined the nature of team contact sports and shown why, even though they are dangerous, they are attractive to many people. It has also argued that a major part of this attraction is tied up with the brute force and violence that are intrinsic to these sports and shown how, for some, it may become an established motivational monopoly. Finally, it has explained why unsanctioned violent acts can occur and addressed the topic of whether this type of behaviour can be classified as truly psychopathic .

Throughout, the discussion has avoided any ethical considerations that may be associated with sports aggression and violence. Whether certain types of violent actions are right or wrong is not at issue in this type of psychological text. The point is that these actions do occur in team contact sports and it is the task of sport psychologists to attempt to explain why they happen. There are some sports enthusiasts and administrators who would like to remove, or at the very least water-down considerably, the aggression, hostility, and violence from sports like rugby, Australian rules, and ice hockey. Although there may be just cause for eliminating some of the unsanctioned, malicious acts of violence, to make calls for removal of the legitimate elements of physical confrontation in team contact sports is to seriously misunderstand the nature of the sport. As Apter (1990, p.52) has stated:

> It is a widespread assumption these days that behaviors which display competitiveness, time urgency, hostility and aggression, and experiences which involve confrontation and threat, are stressful and likely to be damaging to the

health of those who indulge in them. And yet these kinds of behaviors and experiences are exactly what sport is all about. A game without confrontation would be no game at all. A contest with no competition would be no contest. It would therefore seem to follow that engaging in sport would be the worst thing anyone could do if they wished to remain happy and sane. And yet clearly sport is not stressful in this sense; it is paradoxically, a form of 'stress' which helps us to avoid stress.

Apter's (1990) quote links the argument back to Brown's (1997) idea of the individual managing his or her hedonic tone through sport, but also forward to the subject matter of the next chapter. Improving psychological well-being through participation in sport and exercise is a topic that is currently receiving more attention in the psychological literature. Like most other areas of sport psychology, reversal theory has a number of unique viewpoints which need to be added to those from other perspectives. These viewpoints on psychological well-being, sport and exercise are presented in the next chapter.

FURTHER READING

1. Kerr, J.H. (1994). *Understanding soccer hooliganism.* Milton Keynes, UK: Open University Press. Chapters 6 & 7.
2. Apter, M.J. (1982). *The experience of motivation: The theory of psychological reversals.* London: Academic Press. Chapter 5, pp.112–117.
3. Geen, R.G. (1990). *Human aggression.* Milton Keynes, UK: Open University Press.

REFERENCES

Apter, M.J. (1990). Sport and mental health: A new psychological perspective. In G.P.H. Hermans & W.L. Mosterd (Eds.), *Sports, medicine and health* (pp.47–56). [Excerpta Medica International Congress Series.] Amsterdam: Elsevier Science Publishers.

Apter, M.J. (1992). *The dangerous edge.* New York: The Free Press.

Apter, M.J. (1993). Phenomenological frames and the paradoxes of experience. In J.H. Kerr, S. Murgatroyd, & M.J. Apter, (Eds.), *Advances in reversal theory* (pp.189–204). Amsterdam: Swets & Zeitlinger.

Askwith, R. (1991, 22 September). Blood sport. *The Observer Magazine,* p.19.

Atyeo, D. (1979). *Blood and guts: Violence in sports.* Melbourne: Cassell.

Bandura, A. (1973). *Aggression: A social learning analysis.* Englewood Cliffs, NJ: Prentice Hall.

Barclay, P. (1995, 25 March). Virtue pays off for Dr. Feelgood. *The Observer,* pp.14–15.

Blanchard, K., & Cheska, A.T. (1985). *The anthropology of sport.* Massachusetts: Bergin & Garvey Publishers.

Brink, A. (1995, 24 June). Dirty old habits die hard. *The Guardian,* p.29.

Brown, R.I.F. (1988). Reversal theory and subjective experience in the explanation of addiction and relapse. In M.J. Apter, J.H. Kerr, & M.P. Cowles (Eds.), *Progress in reversal theory* (pp.191–211). [Advances in psychology series, 51.] Amsterdam: North-Holland/Elsevier.

Brown, R.I.F. (1991). Gambling, gaming and other addictive play. In J.H. Kerr & M.J. Apter (Eds.), *Adult play* (pp.101–118). Amsterdam: Swets & Zeitlinger.

Brown, R.I.F. (1997, in press). A theoretical model of the behavioural addictions—applied to criminal offending. In J. Hodge, M. McMurran, & C. Hollins (Eds.), *Addicted to crime?* Chichester, UK & New York: Wiley.

Burke, B. (1995, 10 May). Rookie Maroons 'will stand up and be counted'. *The Australian*, p.44.

Davies, P. (1991). *All played out. The full story of Italia '90*. London: Mandarin.

Dawe, G. (1994, October). Coaching masterclass. *Rugby World*, p.48.

Faulkner, R.R. (1976). Making violence by doing work: Selves situations and the world of professional hockey. In D.M. Landers (Ed.), *Social problems in athletics*. Illinois: University of Illinois Press.

Geen, R.G. (1990). *Human aggression*. Milton Keynes, UK: Open University Press.

Glasser, W. (1976). *Positive addiction*. New York: Harper & Row.

Gregory, R.L. (1987). *The Oxford companion to the mind*. Oxford: Oxford University Press.

Kerr, J.H. (1987). Differences in the motivational characteristics of "professional", "serious amateur" and "recreational" sports performers. *Perceptual and Motor Skills, 64*, 379–382.

Kerr, J.H. (1988). Play, sport and the paratelic state. In M.J. Apter, J.H. Kerr, & M.P. Cowles (Eds.), *Progress in reversal theory*.[Advances in psychology series, 51.] Amsterdam: North-Holland/Elsevier.

Kerr, J.H. (1994). *Understanding soccer hooliganism*. Milton Keynes, UK: Open University Press.

Kerr, J.H., & Svebak, S. (1994). The acute effects of participation in sport on mood: The importance of level of antagonistic physical interaction. *Personality and Individual Differences, 16*, 159–166.

Kerr, J.H., & van Lienden, H.J. (1987). Telic dominance in masters swimmers. *Scandinavian Journal of Sports Sciences, 9 (3)*, 85–88.

Longmore, A. (1994, 3 December) England's leader of the pack spurred on by careless whispers. *The Times*, p.44.

McIntosh, P. (1979). *Fair play: Ethics in sport and education*. London: Heinemann.

Murgatroyd, S. (1985). The nature of telic dominance. In M.J. Apter, D. Fontana, & S. Murgatroyd (Eds.), *Reversal theory: Applications and developments* (pp.20–41). Cardiff: University College Cardiff Press, and New York: Lawrence Erlbaum Associates Inc.

Russell, G.W. (1993) *The social psychology of sport*. New York: Springer-Verlag.

Smith, M.D. (1983). *Violence and sport*. Toronto: Butterworths.

Stocks, G. (1995, 21 November). Class act left his stamp on Hawks. *The West Australian*, p.83.

Tatum, J., & Kushner, B. (1979). *They call me assassin*. New York: Everest House.

Thomas-Peter, B.A. (1988). Psychopathy and telic dominance. In M.J. Apter, J.H. Kerr, & M.P. Cowles (Eds.), *Progress in reversal theory* (pp.235–244). [Advances in psychology series, 51.] Amsterdam: North-Holland/Elsevier.

Thomas-Peter, B.A. (1993). Negativism and the classification of psychopathy. In J.H. Kerr, S. Murgatroyd, & M.J. Apter, (Eds.), *Advances in reversal theory* (pp.189–204). Amsterdam: Swets & Zeitlinger.

Young, K. (1993). Violence, risk, and liability in male sports culture. *Sociology of Sport Journal, 10*, 373–396.

Zillman, D. (1979). *Hostility and aggression*. Hillsdale, NJ: Lawrence Erlbaum Associates Inc.

8 The Feel Good Factor: Sport, Exercise, and Psychological Well-being

The effect of exercise (especially running) and sports participation on mood or emotion and their potential for improving psychological well-being has generated considerable interest in sports and exercise research in recent years (see e.g. Dishman, 1994; Kerr, Cox, & Griffiths, 1996; McDonald & Hodgdon, 1991; Morgan & Goldston, 1987; Ross & Hayes, 1988; Seraganian, 1993; Stephens, 1988; Sutherland & Cooper, 1990; Willis & Campbell, 1992). In general, the results of research studies reviewed in these publications have supported a positive relationship between exercise and improved physical and psychological well-being. For example, exercise has been found to decrease anxiety and depression and improve self-esteem, mood profiles, and sleep patterns (see e.g. Härmä, 1996; Kerr & Vlaswinkel, 1990).

The effect of exercise on psychological mood and well-being has also been the subject of a number of reversal theory studies (e.g. Kerr & van den Wollenberg, 1997; Kerr & Vlaswinkel 1993, 1995). Before describing the findings of these reversal theory studies, I would like to take a brief look at my own running experience in order to highlight how an activity can be used to increase arousal and, in my case, provoke a reversal to the paratelic state.

As a runner, I have been extremely fortunate to have run in some of the most beautiful places one could find anywhere in the world. For example, in Canada, I have run through the incredible mountains and alongside the raging Bow river at Banff, along the picturesque seawall in Vancouver, and through the beautiful Endowment Lands at the University of British Columbia. In Australia, my routes have taken me through Sydney's fascinating harbour area, past the spectacular Opera House and included the natural parkland at Noosa Heads in Queensland and the surfing beaches of Cottesloe near Perth. In the US, I have run on the spongy wood chips of the Prefontaine trails in Eugene, Oregon and through the breathtaking canyons at Colorado Springs. Now in Japan, not two minutes from my house, I run along narrow roads that traverse the rice fields and by-pass incredible traditional style farmhouses, some with thatched roofs and well-groomed gardens. There are probably few runners in the world who have the good fortune to have experienced such a variety of magnificent running environments.

In spite of all this, I do not really enjoy running. Running for its own sake has never attracted me and I usually have to force myself to do it. As I run, I can hear my breathing rasping and wheezing into reluctant lungs that feel as if they are trapped by a steel band tightening around my ribcage. Every muscle, ligament, and joint in my legs seems to ache and invariably it seems that I have to go through the marathon runner's *wall* every five minutes. Believe it or not, running in the spectacular locations just mentioned did not do much to reduce any of these unpleasant feelings. If my running experience is so unpleasant, why do I continue to do it? In my case, it is really not for health reasons and, if it was to improve my fitness level, I would prefer to involve myself in other more interesting sports activities such as playing ball games.

The primary reason that I go running is because of the pleasant feeling I can enjoy when the run is over, a phenomenon that has been noted by others (e.g. Johnsgard, 1989). To use a phrase currently in vogue in British political circles, I run because of the post-run *feel good factor*. This seems to arise from a combination of psychological and physiological feelings which result in high levels of positive hedonic tone. When I have finished running, my lungs feel flushed out, oxygen-rich blood is coursing through my veins, and a pleasantly tired feeling begins to pervade my whole body. More importantly, my mind also seems to have been flushed out and refreshed and I generally feel good.

For this reason I usually run at about midday, after a morning of telic-oriented work. This is quite deliberate and the after-effects of my run form a part of my "personal planning to optimise mood" (Thayer, 1989, p.174). My arousal level, which increases to high levels during the run (and is associated with unpleasant anxious feelings about bodily aches and pains or whether I can make it up the next hill or to my next "objective", marked by features along the route like the bridge, the bamboo plantation, or the pond), remains high for a period post-run before slowly reducing to more moderate levels. However, running provides an opportunity not only to experience high arousal, but also to induce a reversal to the paratelic state, so that high arousal can be enjoyed to the full. This telic to paratelic reversal usually takes place after I have stopped running or, occasionally, in the latter stages of the run. This means that for most, if not all, of the run I am in the telic state and, it seems, prepared to tolerate high levels of arousal in this state (low levels of felt arousal are usually preferred in the telic state) prior to reversal and the subsequent emotional pay-off.

In fact, in terms of my post-run metamotivational state combination, most of the time my experience of the paratelic state is combined with the conformist, autic, and mastery states (I usually stick to the same route, run alone, feel pleased to have mastered the reluctance of my body during the run, and to have completed the route without stopping). After a midday run, I can return to work in the afternoon feeling good, and (usually) content to continue working, sometimes more efficiently than before. Over the last few years, this routine has become part of my own personal everyday mood management. However, what evidence is there from reversal theory research to support the notion that exercise can be used to modulate felt arousal levels and/or induce reversals?

RESEARCH ON EXERCISE, SPORT, AND WELL-BEING

The purpose of Kerr and Vlaswinkel's (1993) research study was to monitor possible changes in arousal levels and metamotivational state brought about by running amongst regular runners who were running in their usual natural environment. Two field studies were carried out, using male and female runners. In each study, subjects were categorised into equal groups of fast or slow runners, based on their times for running 5.0km (females) and 6.6km (males). It was thought that the experience of running might vary according to an individual's ability in, or success at running. In both studies, runners completed the Telic State Measure (TSM; Svebak & Murgatroyd, 1985) and the Stress–Arousal Checklist (SACL; Mackay, Cox, Burrows, & Lazzerini, 1978) before and after running. In study 1, 32 runners took part in seven 40-minute running sessions, part of a physical education course aimed at improving physical fitness through a programme of varied and increasingly demanding running. In study 2, 67 male and female runners took part in a single running session (females, 5.0km and males, 6.6km). In study 2, arousal preference, as indicated by colour choice (red = indicative of a preference for high arousal in the paratelic state; light blue = indicative of a preference for low arousal in the telic state; see Walters, Apter, & Svebak, 1982) was also measured on several occasions during the run.

The most interesting results from study 1 were related to subjects' experience of arousal across sessions; fast male runners started their running sessions with significantly lower, and ended with significantly higher levels of felt arousal (TSM) than slower male runners. Also, fast female runners' group scores on felt arousal (TSM) were significantly higher than those of slow runners. Study 2 produced results in line with those from study 1: differences in arousal scores between fast and slow runners were also found (see Fig. 8.1a). Fast male subjects scored significantly higher on both felt arousal (TSM) and

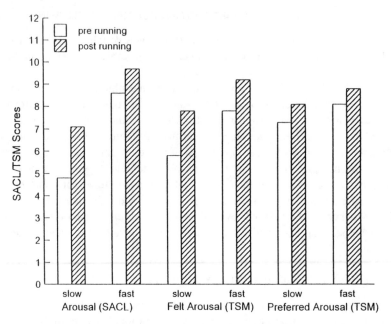

FIG. 8.1a. Pre- and post-running mean arousal scores (SACL and TSM [doubled]) for fast and slow males (from Kerr & Vlaswinkel, 1993).

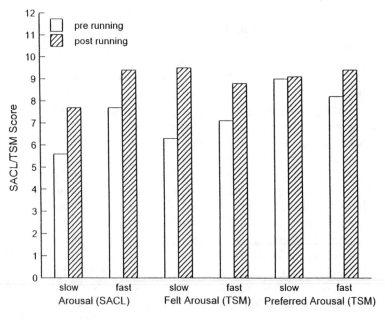

FIG. 8.1b. Pre- and post-running mean arousal scores (SACL and TSM [doubled]) for fast and slow females (from Kerr & Vlaswinkel, 1993).

arousal (SACL) items. In addition, fast male and fast female runners scored significantly lower than the equivalent groups of slow runners on arousal discrepancy (TSM) suggesting, perhaps, that fast runners were more adroit at attaining levels of arousal similar to the levels that they preferred. The slow female running group recorded significantly higher stress (SACL) scores than the fast female group, indicating that their running experience was probably less pleasant than that experienced by fast female runners (see Fig. 8.1b).

Colour choice results indicated that, as the run progressed, most fast male runners changed from a preference for low arousal to a preference for high arousal (i.e. reversed from the telic to the paratelic state) while slower male runners were more evenly distributed, in terms of arousal preference, during running (see Figs. 8.2a & b). The pattern was slightly different for fast female runners. They maintained their preference for low arousal for longer than fast male runners. By the end of the run, however, the majority had also changed to a preference for high arousal and thus reversed to the paratelic state. In contrast, the majority of slow female runners started with a preference for high arousal (i.e. were in the paratelic state), a pattern that remained to the end of the run (see Figs. 8.3a & b). In this part of the analysis, group data tended to mask individual profiles. A few individual runners, for example, consistently chose one colour, thus indicating that, for them, arousal preference and meta-motivational state did not change during the run.

These results provide some support for the notion that exercise has potential for improving psychological well-being. For example, the results have important implications for offsetting the harmful psychological effects that may be associated with certain kinds of repetitive work. As Kerr and Vlaswinkel (1993, p.175) pointed out:

> If exercise, in this case running, allows regularly exercising individuals to compensate for non-preferred arousal levels, it may be possible for exercise at work to be used by employees as a feasible means of modulating levels of arousal (Kerr 1993a). This may be particularly important for workers who are exposed to ill-health as a result of exposure to repetitive work and long periods of decreased arousal (Cox et al., 1982).

The majority of subjects experienced psychological reversals (as indicated by changes in colour choice). Thus, as will be explained next, exercise may also contribute to psychological health by facilitating psychological reversals.

A further study by Kerr and Vlaswinkel (1995) confirmed the role that sports or exercise participation can play in promoting psychological well-being. Data was collected from 42 international MBA student subjects on five occasions during a typical working day comprising of an intensive lecture session in the morning, followed by an optional sport session and another intensive lecture session in the afternoon. All students completed the mood

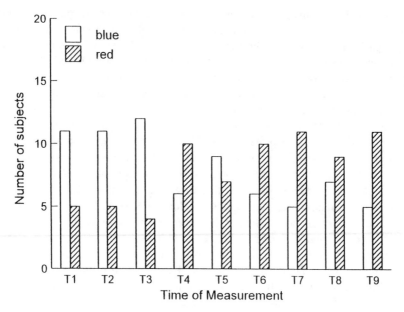

FIG. 8.2a. Fast male runners' colour choice on nine occasions during the run (from Kerr & Vlaswinkel, 1993).

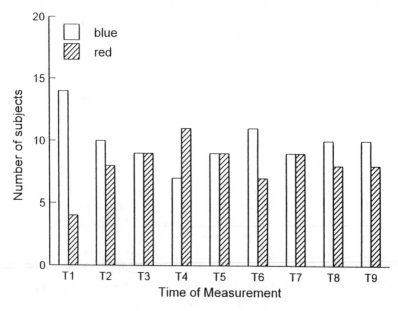

FIG. 8.2b. Slow male runners' colour choice on nine occasions during the run (from Kerr & Vlaswinkel, 1993).

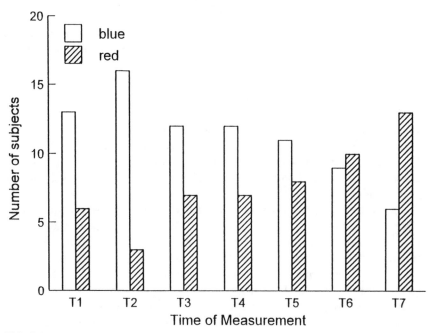

FIG. 8.3a. Fast female runners' colour choice on seven occasions during the run (from Kerr & Vlaswinkel, 1993).

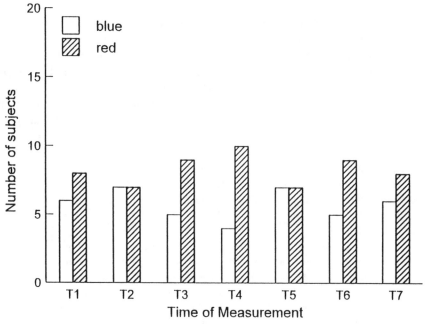

FIG. 8.3b. Slow female runners' colour choice on seven occasions during the run (from Kerr & Vlaswinkel, 1993).

measures on five occasions throughout the day including just prior to and just after the sports session. Of the subjects, 26 actually participated in the sport session, but the remaining 16 preferred to engage in activities related to their course of study. A between-groups comparison of the mood measure item scores revealed that sports participants were significantly less serious before and after the sports session than non-participants. In addition, using a Chi-square analysis, a significantly higher number of participants (60%) indicated that they were in the paratelic state post-sport than non-participants (25%). Differences in felt arousal levels between participant and non-participant groups were also found post-participation, but these failed to reach significance in this study.

As the results of the early reversal theory studies reviewed earlier show, taking part in running, exercise, and sports may allow some people to increase important emotional variables like felt arousal and also induce reversals between particular pairs of states. These reversals may, in turn, bring about changes in overall metamotivational state combinations and the associated emotions. Kerr (1993a, 1996) has argued that these changes in arousal level and/or metamotivational state may be responsible for the *feeling better* or *feel good factor* that some people (including the author) experience after participation (Johnsgard, 1989; Morgan, 1987). In reversal theory, meta-motivational versatility, or the ability to experience the full range of meta-motivational state combinations and emotions, is considered essential to the maintenance of psychological health and well-being (see e.g. Apter, 1990). As a result, exercise and sports activities may be used by some individuals to achieve this type of versatility. Such activities are likely to be less damaging to health in general than other methods of achieving the same end, such as alcohol, tobacco, caffeine, or more extreme substance abuse. At the very least, participation in exercise and sports activities may offset some of the harmful effects of these other methods for manipulating, modulating, and managing arousal levels and hedonic tone (Morris & Reilly, 1987; Thayer, 1989).

Reversal theory focuses on the individual and it is important to keep in mind that, although sports and exercise activities can induce reversals and allow arousal modulation, individual motivation for participation in sport or exercise differs widely. For example, Frey (1993, pp.157–158) in his reversal theory analysis of distance running, stated that:

> Runners have different motives for running. They run for fitness (to lose weight, tone muscles, lower blood pressure), to prepare for an upcoming race (a local all-comers track meet or the Boston marathon), to achieve a personal running goal (a 35-minute 10K or first place in an age division), to escape the pressures and responsibilities of life (a jaunt away from work at lunch hour or away from the kids at home at the weekend), to relish the beauty of nature (a nearby park on a spring morning or an old logging trail on an autumn afternoon), to promote a

positive lifestyle change (quit a drug habit), to make decisions and solve problems, to stimulate creative thinking, to cope with depression or anxiety, to acquire a sense of self-mastery or invincibility, to experience passion and intensity, to engage in fantasy, to show off one's body, or to meet a friend or lover.

Frey (1993) argued that, not only do runners differ in their motivation for running, but their motives may be different for each individual run and these motives are likely to be linked to particular metamotivational states. Taking Frey's (1993) description a stage further, it is easy to see how individual motives could become linked together. For example, a person may run because he or she wants to acquire a sense of self-mastery and discipline (autic–mastery), but chooses a favourite time and a regular route for running in a nearby wood on a spring morning which allows the beauty of nature to be relished (paratelic–conformity). In this example, the motives concerned would appear to be based on a constellation of metamotivational states comprised of paratelic–conformist–autic–mastery. Of course, during specific runs, a certain state or states within any metamotivational state combination might be more prominent than others. In any event, being able to satisfy the needs of particular states or state combinations through running or other forms of exercise, may provide powerful reinforcement for continued participation in the activity. In summary, in thinking about reversal theory and the exercise-linked feel good factor, a number of points need to be considered:

1. Motivation for participation in exercise and sports activities is likely to differ for each individual.

2. An individual's motives may be different on different occasions.

3. Reversals may occur throughout an activity, so an individual's operative metamotivational state combination may vary across each occurrence of the activity.

4. The prominence of particular metamotivational state(s) within any state combination (and the intensity of the resultant emotions) can vary on different occasions.

Although there is a positive side to participation in sports and exercise activities, in terms of satisfying the needs of particular states (or state combinations) and contributing to the maintenance of an individual's meta-motivational and emotional equilibrium, there is another side to the coin. Some individuals may use exercise to replace and improve on other types of arousal and mood modulation strategies. These individuals appear to have discovered that continuous use of excessive levels of exercise and sport activities can provide a relatively reliable and effective means of manipulating hedonic tone in the directions they desire (see Brown, 1997). However, these individuals run the risk of becoming dependent on, or addicted to, sports and exercise activities in what Glasser (1976) has called a *positive addiction.*

TOO MUCH OF A GOOD THING: EXERCISE DEPENDENCE

For some time now, sport psychology texts have included sections on exercise dependence (e.g. Kremer & Scully, 1994; Willis & Campbell, 1992) and it is not unusual to find research papers (Chapman & De Castro, 1990; de Coverly Veale, 1987; Hailey & Bailey, 1982; Sachs & Pargman, 1979) and reviews (Pierce, 1994) in psychological journals on this topic. Individuals who are thought to be exercise dependent generally follow punishing daily schedules of exercise activity. They may continue to exercise in spite of injury or illness, and relationships with family members and friends may be adversely affected. As a result of the excessive amount of time spent exercising, individuals often report feeling persistently tired and only feeling alive when exercising. They also often report feeling depressed, irritable, and tense if, for any reason, they are forced to withdraw from exercise.

There may well be two distinct groups of exercise dependent people: Those who engage in regular, sometimes excessive exercise as a reliable, effective, and healthy means of manipulating hedonic tone in the desired direction, and those who carry exercise to absolute extremes, to the point where it becomes an unhealthy addiction. It is thought that the numbers of truly exercise dependent individuals (in the clinical sense of the term; see later) amongst the general population are relatively small (Veale, 1995).

With respect to the former group of exercisers, a number of studies have examined exercise withdrawal effects amongst regular runners (e.g. Carmack & Martens, 1979; Conboy, 1994; Morris, Steinberg, Sykes, & Salmon, 1990; Thaxton, 1982). These studies have shown that even regular runners who are not necessarily extreme cases, experience withdrawal effects when an effective form of hedonic tone management has been withdrawn. Typical of these studies was one by Conboy (1994) who investigated whether the amount of dysphoria experienced by regular runners would be greater on days when they did not run than days on which they ran. He asked 61 runners to complete the Profile of Mood States (POMS; McNair, Lorr, & Droppleman, 1971) on 10 days on which they ran and 2–5 days on which they did not run. Significantly higher levels of dysphoria were found on all seven of the POMS mood states on days on which the runners did not run. Another study by Morris et al. (1990) studied two matched groups of 20 runners over a six-week period. One group continued normal running activity during the six-week period, the other group stopped running for weeks 3 and 4. The General Health Questionnaire (GHQ: Goldberg & Hillier, 1979) and a short form of the Zung Anxiety and Depression Scales (Zung, 1974) were completed by the subjects on Sunday evenings at the end of each of the six weeks. At the end of the second week of withdrawal, scores on the *severe depression* subscale (GHQ) were significantly greater in the group that withdrew from exercise than the control group. Also, after both the first and second weeks of withdrawal, scores on GHQ subscales *somatic symptoms, anxiety, insomnia,* and *feelings of being under strain* were all significantly greater in the group that withdrew from exercise than in the control group. Results from the Zung scales (1974) confirmed those obtained from the GHQ. This evidence suggests that any occurrence that prevents the regularly exercising person from exercising will produce a stressful experience of unpleasant emotions.

With respect to the latter group, the truly exercise dependent people, it might be useful to construct a reversal theory profile of their likely metamotivational *modus operandi.*

The types of sports activities frequently quoted in the literature as being associated with exercise dependence (running, cycling, swimming, aerobics, and weight training) are of the *endurance* and *safe* type. As was pointed out in Chapter 3, participants in endurance sports (characterised by repetitive movements and enduring activity) and safe sports (little danger of injury or death) have been found to be significantly more telic dominant than participants in *explosive* or *risk* sports (Kerr & Svebak, 1989; Svebak & Kerr, 1989). Exercise activities of the endurance type suit the telic dominant motivational style quite nicely. Remember, the individual in the telic state enjoys the anticipation and satisfaction of achieving goals which are often considered essential and unavoidable. Consequently, exercise activities that involve attaining certain time or distance goals are attractive to the telic dominant person who frequently has the telic state operative, so much so that he or she may be prepared to tolerate high levels of arousal, common to some types of endurance activity, in order to achieve the desired goals.

A good illustration of the motivation of telic dominant athletes and the lengths that they are prepared to go to achieve their goals was provided by the interview responses of a triathlete who scored very high on telic dominance (as measured by the Telic Dominance Scale; Murgatroyd, Rushton, Apter, & Ray, 1978), and who competed in the Ironman triathlon competition in Hawaii (Kerr, 1991, p.87). Asked to describe how he felt after finishing the event, he said:

> I could hardly walk. I got a massage afterwards. People had to help me to stand up—not one person, but three or four. When I stood up, I couldn't walk for let's say 4 or 500 metres to reach my room. My muscles just refused to make the movement of standing up . . . It was all worth it. There were three objectives that I wanted to reach: finish the job, a certain time, a certain position. I said to myself that I had to finish somewhere between number 50 and number 150 out of 900 and I had to finish in the top 10 of the swimming [event]. I was satisfied... [The subject actually finished in 101st position overall].

Telic dominant individuals also like to plan activities carefully, and these types of exercise activities tend to involve a large time commitment which, in the initial stages at least, often has to be planned into a tight daily schedule. For example, the training undertaken by one person addicted to exercise and sports involved repetitive weekly patterns in which weight training, aerobics, cycling, and step aerobics were alternated with running. These activities amounted to an average of three hours of activity per day, on top of which an additional four hours per week were spent playing and training for soccer (Cohen, 1995). This type of training regime undoubtedly involved considerable planning.

For the exercise dependent individual, endurance type sports and exercise activities may become merely an extension of their telic dominant lifestyle and, as Kerr (1993b) has argued, exercise dependence is probably linked to telic dominance. Exercise dependent individuals often become obsessional about aspects of their exercise, for example, carefully checking times and distances in swimming or cycling, measuring heart rate every time they exercise, and/or keeping detailed personal training logs or diaries. Fontana (1981) has linked obsessional personality traits with telic dominance and Kagan and Squires (1985), in a study of regularly exercising students, found that compulsiveness and rigidity are personality features of those male subjects who exercised the most. This is not to say that all telic dominant exercisers will necessarily become exercise dependent, but some are obsessional to the point where their whole life revolves around exercise.

The excessive regimes of the addicted exerciser undoubtedly also require high levels of conformity in order to be completed. Undertaking long hours of running or completing repeated lengths in a swimming pool would not fit well with the negativistic state and the experience of felt negativism. By its very nature, exercise dependence would appear to be associated with the conformity state. At times, the conformist motive to complete sports and exercise schedules may become extreme, with individuals attempting to carry on exercising even when injured, sometimes causing long-term damage to their physical health.

In the vast majority of cases of exercise dependence (especially where it may be linked to anorexia nervosa or bulimia nervosa) individuals become focused totally on themselves. For example, Morgan (1979) observed a tendency to *turn inward* amongst serious runners when they were running about 100 miles a week. The individual's preoccupation with exercise activities and the increasing demands on his or her time, just to complete the desired amount of exercise, will affect other aspects of daily life, including relationships with family and colleagues at work, and as a result cause even greater distress in the long term. (That is unless, as Veale, 1995, suggested, dependent exercisers have organised their lifestyles by including relationships or lack of relationships and occupations that accommodate their preoccupation.) The person may thus also spend a disproportionate amount of time with the autic state operative at the expense of the alloic state.

There are several reports in the research literature from exercise dependent individuals which emphasise the sense of mastery and control that exercise brings (e.g. Robbins & Joseph, 1985; Yates, Leehey, & Shisslak, 1983). It would appear that exercise provides these individuals with the possibility for control within a pattern of daily living that may otherwise contain a large degree of uncertainty. For example, Willis and Campbell (1992, p.72) (in drawing attention to explanations of exercise withdrawal effects in runners suggested by Robbins and Joseph, 1985) stated that:

> A second behavioral explanation, called a mastery hypothesis, is related to the possible dependence of some runners on the daily reinforcement of competence and self-worth that running provides. Running may be so central to the identity of some runners that they experience distress when forced to miss a workout.

This points to the mastery state making up the fourth part of addicted exerciser's likely predominant metamotivational state combination, which is telic–conformist–autic–mastery (see Figs. 2.5 & 2.6).

EXCESSIVE EXERCISE AND REVERSAL PROBLEMS

Excessive exercise is liable to occur when the individual concerned has problems reversing in everyday life. There would appear to be three possible reversal theory explanations of how the metamotivational processes associated with excessive exercise work. Within this scheme, particular states, such as the telic and mastery states, may play a more prominent role than other meta-motivational states.

As with some other psychological problems (see Apter, 1989; Kerr, Frank-Regan, & Brown, 1993; Murgatroyd & Apter, 1984), the exercise dependent individual may be *stuck* or *trapped* in a particular combination of states most of the time (telic–conformist–autic–mastery), with only very occasional reversals to other states. Apter (1989) pointed out that an inability to reverse and experience the full range of metamotivational states and state combinations can be a major source of psychological disturbance. In this case, the need for extreme levels of frequent and regular exercise is necessary to maintain emotional equilibrium. *Reversal inhibition* (i.e. when individuals become locked in particular metamotivational states or state combinations) may have developed to a similar degree as with other pathological conditions (e.g. vandalism or violent crime) described by Murgatroyd and Apter (1984).

1. Although the individual may often be stuck in particular states or state combinations in everyday life (e.g. telic–conformist–autic–mastery), in sport he or she may be able to behave in a way that enables him or her to achieve the pleasure of satisfaction within that specific state or state combination (Apter, 1989, p.145). In other words, excessive exercise with, for example, the completion of schedules and exercise plans, along with the achievement of

personal goals and the domination of mind over body, provides the individual with tremendous satisfaction within the operative telic–conformist–autic–mastery state combination. The experience of high arousal within this state combination (in which the telic state is likely to be especially salient) may even be tolerated in order to achieve the other goals that form the basis of the individual's high levels of hedonic tone.

2. It may be that, for some individuals who are experiencing reversal inhibition, excessive exercise helps to facilitate reversal, for example, from the telic to the paratelic state. This may be the only means or opportunity for these individuals, who often suffer from chronic anxiety, to reverse to the paratelic state and experience high arousal (intrinsic to sport and exercise activities) as pleasant excitement rather than as unpleasant anxiety (Apter 1989, p.151). For these individuals, excessive exercise may be the only source of telic to paratelic reversals, occurring during exercise and enduring perhaps for a short time afterwards, before reversals recur. It may be that, over time, reversal induction becomes more difficult and individuals may have to engage in increasingly harder and more frequent exercise activities to provoke reversals.

3. Reductions in anxiety levels are often experienced post-exercise (see e.g. Morgan, 1987) and it could be that some individuals have found that exercise is one way of forcing a decrease in unpleasant high felt arousal (anxiety) to lower levels which can then be experienced as pleasant relaxation, (Kerr, 1996). In addition, felt transactional outcome can be increased through feelings of net gain associated with completing the exercise activity in the mastery state and experienced as pride. However, as time goes on the person may find it more difficult to manage unpleasant levels of felt arousal and felt transactional outcome and, again, individuals may have to engage in increasingly harder and more frequent exercise activities to generate the same changes post-exercise.

The three alternatives offered here appear to be the most likely reversal theory explanations of the motivational mechanics of how and why exercise dependence may occur.

EXERCISE DEPENDENCE AND EATING DISORDERS

De Coverly Veale (1987) made a distinction between clinical exercise dependence, which was secondary to some form of eating disorder, and primary exercise dependence, where there is a stereotyped and routine preoccupation with exercise, existing independently. He proposed a list of diagnostic criteria for use as a basis for assessing whether or not individuals are primary exercise dependent. Some eight years later, Veale (1995) pointed out that neither the World Health Organization (WHO: 1994; ICD-10) nor the American Psychiatric Association (APA: 1994; DSM-IV) has recognised primary exercise dependence as a diagnostic category, and that there was no existing clinically validated syndrome of primary exercise dependence. He developed an updated operational list of diagnostic criteria in the same style as the WHO and APA instruments (Veale, 1995) (see Fig. 8.4).

Veale (1995)	*Brown (1997)*
	5. *Development of an acquired drive and increasing salience.* An addiction is developed through a positive feedback loop involving a series of cognitive failures which lead to an acquired drive for particular feeling states as goals
A. Preoccupation with exercise which has become stereotyped and routine.	and to the salience of a single activity as a source of reward. Deficient self-awareness (vigilance), short-term planning and crisis management, faulty decision making all
B. Significant withdrawal symptoms in the absence of exercise (for example, mood swings, irritability, insomnia).	contribute to the development of salience and consequent conflict leading to narrowing of easily accessible alternative rewarding activities. Increasing salience leads to increasing tolerance, withdrawals and relief action which in turn lead to yet greater salience.
	6. *Cycles.* During the latter stages of its development the engagement in the addictive activity comes in repeated cycles or in episodes which make up a serial.
	7. *Established motivational monopoly.* At the point of full development of a motivational monopoly or reward specialism a single addictive activity so dominates thinking, feeling, and behaviour (i.e. has such salience) that it becomes virtually the sole source of reward and is used to
C. The preoccupation causes clinically significant distress or impairment in their physical, social, occupational or other important areas of functioning.	maintain a near continuous subjective mood or feeling state producing mounting conflict within and without and leading to relief action to avoid withdrawals. Decisions are now made solely on a basis of extremely short-term reward or relief as mere crisis management.
D. The preoccupation with exercise is not better accounted for by another mental disorder (e.g. as a means of losing weight or controlling calorie intake as in an eating disorder).	

FIG. 8.4.   Showing the operational diagnostic criteria for "primary" exercise dependence (Veale, 1995) and stages 5 to 7 of Brown's (1997) Hedonic Management Model of Addictions.

Based on his clinical experience, Veale (1995) was of the opinion that, although rare, primary exercise dependence does exist, though it is much less common than secondary exercise dependence. However, most people with minor problems arising from primary exercise dependence do not seek help from clinicians, but simply adapt their lives to fit in with their dependence. Such individuals may not be sufficiently distressed in their physical health, family, social, or occupational functioning. They may however, as mentioned earlier, overtrain and experience chronic fatigue and may remain vulnerable to any withdrawal from exercise (Veale, 1995).

On close examination, it becomes obvious that Veale's (1995) operational diagnostic criteria are closely related to some of the stages in the Hedonic Tone Management Model of Addictions (Brown, 1991, 1997) described in Chapter 7 (see Fig. 8.4).

Exercise and sports activities are, by comparison with the requirements of some other addictions, almost always available and easily accessible. From the point of view of the Hedonic Tone Management Model of Addictions (Brown, 1991, 1997), via the manipulation of arousal and reversals, exercise can provide consistent, regular, reliable, and immediate pleasurable and rewarding experiences. Thus, it becomes possible to account for both the addictive behaviour of primary exercise dependent individuals (who do not exhibit any specific emotional distress) and that of secondary exercise dependent individuals (who do exhibit some form of chronic emotional dysphoria; Veale, 1995).

Exercise addictions have been shown to be related to other compulsive behaviours such as anorexia or bulimia nervosa (e.g. Epling & Pierce, 1988; Epling, Pierce, & Stefan, 1983). Anorexics and bulimics may seek the assistance of exercise to help reduce their weight. Some exercise dependent individuals can develop an exaggerated concern about the shape of their body and their weight which gives a powerful additional push to their extreme behaviour. There have already been a number of studies that have linked extreme exercise dependence with eating problems in, for example, general athletic populations (Black & Burckes-Miller, 1988; Sundgot-Borgen, 1994), long-distance running (Katz, 1986; Yates et al., 1983), and adolescent boxing (Lovett, 1990). However, Taub and Benson (1992) found no evidence of eating disorders in male and female adolescent swimmers.

As far as reversal theory is concerned, this link between exercise dependence and anorexia and bulimia nervosa is not surprising. Anorexics are also thought to experience persistent telic and mastery metamotivational states (Kerr et al., 1993) and may be trapped in a particular state combination in a similar way to exercise dependent individuals. It seems likely that the processes that lead to exercise dependence combined with anorexia and/or bulimia nervosa appear to work in a similar way to the development of other dependent behaviour, for example, smoking, gambling, and alcoholism (Brown, 1991, 1997; O'Connell, 1988).

EXERCISE AND SPORTS ACTIVITIES AS INTERVENTIONS

A main theme of this chapter has been that participation in sports and exercise activities can play a useful role in maintaining psychological health and well-being. Kerr (e.g. 1996) has also argued that sports and exercise activities could be useful as stress management techniques. In both cases, the effectiveness of the activities are tied into achieving metamotivational state versatility, in the sense of experiencing the complete range of metamotivational state combinations and relatively frequent reversals between them.

However, there is another less positive, potentially harmful aspect of interventions based on the use of exercise or sports activities. The danger is that running or other sports and exercise activities may merely become an alternative or an additional problem for the addicted individual to try and deal with. Johnsgard (1989, p.47), in considering the results of the use of running to help people with smoking and drinking addictions, described how one subject proved to be the exception in the group of subjects:

> The significant drop in addictions suggests that those men who began to run in order to give up or control tobacco and alcohol dependencies were no longer concerned about them. I received autobiographical statements from all of the men and women in this group, and it appears that of the entire group, only a single woman had failed to give up the addiction (to tobacco) which had motivated her to take up running. Her story was a strange one. She began to run in her late 50s and discovered that she had harbored a great athletic potential. Before long she became an ultramarathoner, regularly competing in races longer than the standard 26.2 mile marathon. But she complained that instead of losing her cigarette addiction, she now had two addictions. She related that she carried cigarettes in a fannypack during 50-mile mountain races, and that when she stopped for a break she would light two cigarettes at once in order to save time when inhaling an energizing hit. I sometimes wonder if she is still alive, what with subjecting her heart to such peril. At any rate she was an anomaly.

As illustrated by the experience of this single subject, although exercise may be used as a form of coping (perhaps to control feelings of anxiety and panic in other cases) it may prove to be an inappropriate strategy if the underlying problems are not resolved. Therapists need to be sure, in recommending sports and exercise activities, that they are not leading clients into the development of inappropriate strategies for reversal, especially those that Murgatroyd and Apter (1984) have termed *temporally inappropriate strategies*. According to Apter (1989, p.147) these are reversal strategies that:

> . . . are immediately effective in reducing distress, or obtaining gratification, and in this sense they are functional, but they have unfortunate long-term

consequences. What this comes to is that the distress which individuals using these strategies are currently avoiding by means of them will become even more difficult for them to avoid as time passes, or their chance of pleasure will be much diminished. In this way they are storing up problems for themselves in the future.

CONCLUDING COMMENTS

In terms of reversal theory research, the topics covered in this chapter have received only minimal attention. Those results that have been mentioned are merely the tip of the iceberg and there is a whole range of research topics and questions waiting to be investigated and answered. For example, with the exception of the studies reviewed here, little is known about how reversals and manipulations of felt arousal and felt transactional outcome through sport can contribute to general psychological health and well-being. It would be beneficial to engage in studies of individuals over extended time periods to find out how their participation in sport and exercise activities contributed to their metamotivational versatility and equilibrium over the long term.

In addition, attempting to identify and rectify metamotivational patterns associated with poor metamotivational versatility and equilibrium are equally of interest. For example, it would be interesting to test the hypothesised relationship between primary exercise dependence and metamotivational dominance, described earlier, by carrying out a study that included reversal theory measures of dominance and measures of exercise dependence (e.g. Ogden, Veale, & Summers, 1994). In addition, if other measures, such as the Eating Attitudes Test (Garner & Garfinkel, 1979), were also included, a start could be made on unravelling the links between dominance, eating problems, and secondary exercise dependence. Furthermore, going on beyond dominance, it would be interesting to identify the metamotivational state combinations associated with excessive exercise and examine how these fitted in with the everyday metamotivational patterns of the individuals concerned. Perhaps most interesting of all would be to develop a methodology that would allow The Hedonic Tone Management Model of Addictions (Brown, 1991, 1997) to be tested in an exercise and sports context.

The penultimate chapter in this book deals with stress in sport. On the one hand it will be shown that experiencing and confronting stress is an integral part of sport, on the other hand it will also be shown that sometimes things can become unbalanced, the effects of stress can build up, and may force some athletes to drop out.

FURTHER READING

1. Kerr, J.H., & Vlaswinkel, E.H. (1993). Self-reported mood and running. *Work & Stress, 7*(3), 161–177.

2. Kerr, J.H. (1993). An eclectic approach to psychological interventions in sport: Reversal theory. *The Sport Psychologist, 7,* 400–418.
3. Apter, M.J. (1989). *Reversal theory: Motivation, emotion and personality.* London: Routledge. Chapter 9.
4. Annett, J., Cripps, B., & Steinberg, H. (Eds.) (1995). *Exercise addiction: Motivation for participation in sport and exercise. Proceedings of a British Psychological Society, Sport and Exercise Psychology Section Workshop.* Leicester: The British Psychological Society.

REFERENCES

American Psychiatric Association (1994). *Diagnostic and statistical manual of mental disorders.* Washington, DC: American Psychiatric Association.

Apter, M.J. (1989). *Reversal theory: Motivation, emotion and personality.* London: Routledge.

Apter, M.J. (1990). Sport and mental health: A new psychological perspective. In G.P.H. Hermans & W.L. Mosterd (Eds.), *Sports, medicine and health* (pp.47–56). [Excerpta Medica International Congress Series]. Amsterdam: Elsevier Science Publishers.

Black, D.R., & Burckes-Miller, M.E. (1988). Male and female college athletes: Use of anorexia nervosa and bulimia nervosa weight loss methods. *Research Quarterly, 59,* 252–256.

Brown, R.I.F. (1991). Gambling, gaming and other addictive play. In J.H. Kerr & M.J. Apter (Eds.), *Adult play: A reversal theory approach* (pp.101-118). Amsterdam: Swets & Zeitlinger.

Brown, R.I.F. (1997, in press). A theoretical model of the behavioural addictions—applied to criminal offending. In J. Hodge, M. McMurran, & C. Hollins (Eds.), *Addicted to crime?* Chichester, UK, & New York: Wiley.

Carmack, M.A., & Martens, R. (1979). Measuring commitment to running: A survey of runners' attitudes and mental states. *Journal of Sport Psychology, 1,* 25–42.

Chapman, C.L., & De Castro, J.M. (1990). Running addiction: Measurement and associated psychological characteristics. *Journal of Sports Medicine and Physical Fitness, 30,* 283–290.

Cohen, R. (1995). Video interviews: 'Hooked' on exercise. In J. Annett, B. Cripps, & H. Steinberg (Eds.), *Exercise addiction: Motivation for participation in sport and exercise. Proceedings of a British Psychological Society, Sport and Exercise Psychology Section Workshop.* (pp. 54–59). Leicester: The British Psychological Society.

Conboy, J.K. (1994). The effects of exercise withdrawal on mood states in runners. *Journal of Sport Behavior, 17,* 188–203.

Cox, T., Thirlaway, M., & Cox, S. (1982). Repetitive work, wellbeing and arousal. In H. Ursin & R. Murison (Eds.), *Biological and psychological basis of psychosomatic disease,* (pp.71–77). New York: Pergamon.

de Coverly Veale, D.M.W. (1987). Exercise dependence. *British Journal of Addiction, 82,* 735–740.

Dishman, R.K. (1994). *Advances in exercise adherence.* Champaign, IL: Human Kinetics.

Epling, W.F., & Pierce, W.D. (1988). Activity based anorexia nervosa. *International Journal of Eating Disorders, 7,* 475–485.

Epling, W.F., Pierce, W.D., & Stefan, L. (1983). A theory of activity based anorexia. *International Journal of Eating Disorders, 3,* 27–46.

Fontana, D. (1981). Obsessionality and reversal theory. *British Journal of Clinical Psychology, 20,* 299–300.

Frey, K. (1993). Distance running: A reversal theory analysis. In J.H. Kerr, S. Murgatroyd & M.J. Apter (Eds.), *Advances in reversal theory* (pp.157–164). Lisse: Swets & Zeitlinger.

Garner, D.M., & Garfinkel, P.E. (1979). The Eating Attitudes Test: An index of the symptoms of anorexia nervosa. *Psychological Medicine, 9*, 273–279.

Glasser, W. (1976). *Positive addiction.* New York: Harper & Row.

Goldberg, D., & Hillier, V.F. (1979). A scaled version of the General Health Questionnaire. *Psychology and Medicine, 9*, 139–145.

Hailey, B.J., & Bailey, L.A. (1982). Negative addiction in runners: A qualitative approach. *Journal of Sport Behavior, 5*, 150–154.

Härmä, M. (1996). Exercise, shiftwork and sleep. In J.H. Kerr, T. Cox, & A. Griffiths (Eds.), *Workplace health, employee fitness and exercise* (pp.129–144). London: Taylor & Francis.

Johnsgard, K.W. (1989). *The exercise prescription for depression and anxiety.* New York: Plenum Press.

Kagan, D.M., & Squires, R.L. (1985). Addictive aspects of physical exercise. *Journal of Sports Medicine, 25*, 227–237.

Katz, J. (1986). Long-distance running, anorexia nervosa and bulimia: A report of two cases. *Comprehensive Psychiatry, 27*, 74–78.

Kerr, J.H. (1991). Sport: Work or play? In J.H. Kerr & M.J. Apter (Eds.), *Adult play: A reversal theory approach* (pp.43–53). Lisse: Swets & Zeitlinger.

Kerr, J.H. (1993a). Inducing reversals: Employee exercise breaks. In J.H. Kerr, S. Murgatroyd, & M.J. Apter (Eds.), *Advances in reversal theory* (pp.247–256). Lisse: Swets & Zeitlinger.

Kerr, J.H. (1993b, September). *Reversal theory explanations of exercise dependence.* Paper presented at the 23rd European Congress of Behaviour and Cognitive Therapies, London, UK.

Kerr, J.H. (1996). Stress, exercise and sport. In S. Svebak & M.J. Apter (Eds.), *Stress and health: A reversal theory perspective.* London: Taylor & Francis.

Kerr, J.H., Cox, T., & Griffiths, A. (1996). *Workplace health, employee fitness and exercise.* London: Taylor & Francis.

Kerr, J.H., Frank-Regan, E., & Brown, R.I.F. (1993). Taking risks with health. [Special Edition]. *Patient Education and Counselling, 22*, 73–80.

Kerr, J.H., & Svebak, S. (1989). Motivational aspects of preference for and participation in risk sports. *Personality and Individual Differences, 10*, 797–800.

Kerr, J.H., & van den Wollenberg, A.E. (1997). High and low intensity exercise and psychological mood states. *Psychology & Health, 12*(4).

Kerr, J.H., & Vlaswinkel, L. (1990). Exercise and anxiety: A review of literature. *Anxiety Research, 2*(4), 309–321.

Kerr, J.H., & Vlaswinkel, E.H. (1993). Self-reported mood and running. *Work & Stress, 7*(3), 161–177.

Kerr, J.H., & Vlaswinkel, E.H. (1995). Sport participation at work: An aid to stress management? *International Journal of Stress Management, 2*(2), 87–96.

Kremer, J., & Scully, D. (1994). *Psychology in sport.* London: Taylor & Francis.

Lovett, J.W.T. (1990). Bulimia nervosa in an adolescent boy boxer. *Journal of Adolescence, 13*, 79–83

Mackay, C.J., Cox, T., Burrows, G.C., & Lazzerini, A.J. (1978). An inventory for the measurement of self-reported stress and arousal. *British Journal of Social and Clinical Psychology, 17*, 283–284.

McDonald, D.G., & Hodgdon, J.A. (1991). *Psychological effects of aerobic fitness training.* New York: Springer-Verlag.

McNair, D.M., Lorr, M., & Droppleman, L.F. (1971). *Manual for the Profile of Mood States.* San Diego, CA: Educational and Industrial Testing Service.

Morgan, W.P. (1979). Negative addiction in runners. *The Physician and Sports Medicine, 7*(2) 57–70.

Morgan, W.P. (1987). Reduction of state anxiety following acute physical activity. In W.P.

Morgan, & S.E. Goldston (Eds.), *Exercise and mental health* (pp.105–109). Washington: Hemisphere Publishing.

Morgan, W.P., & Goldston, S.E. (Eds.) (1987). *Exercise and mental health.* Washington: Hemisphere Publishing.

Morris, W.N., & Reilly, N.P. (1987). Toward the self-regulation of mood: Theory and research. *Motivation and Emotion, 11,* 215–249.

Morris, M., Steinberg, H., Sykes, E.A., & Salmon, P. (1990). Effects of temporary withdrawal from regular running. *Journal of Psychosomatic Research, 34,* 493–500.

Murgatroyd, S., & Apter, M.J. (1984). Eclectic psychotherapy: A structural phenomenological approach. In W. Dryden (Ed.), *Individual psychotherapy in Britain.* London: Harper & Row.

Murgatroyd, S., Rushton, C., Apter, M.J., & Ray, C. (1978). The development of the Telic Dominance Scale. *Journal of Personality Assessment, 42,* 519–528.

O'Connell, K.A. (1988). Reversal theory and smoking cessation. In M.J.Apter, J.H. Kerr, & M.P. Cowles (Eds.), *Progress in reversal theory,* (pp.181–190). Amsterdam: North Holland/ Elsevier.

Ogden, J., Veale, D.M.W., & Summers, Z. (1994). *The Exercise Dependence Questionnaire.* Paper presented at the 23rd European Congress of Behaviour and Cognitive Therapies, London, UK.

Pierce, E.F. (1994). Exercise dependence syndrome in runners. *Sports Medicine, 18,* 149–155.

Robbins, J.M., & Joseph, P. (1985). Experiencing exercise withdrawal: Possible consequences of therapeutic and mastery running. *Journal of Sport Psychology, 7,* 23–39.

Ross, C.E., & Hayes, D. (1988). Exercise and psychological well-being in the community. *American Journal of Epidemiology, 127*(4), 762–771.

Sachs, M.L., & Pargman, D. (1979). Running addiction: A depth interview examination. *Journal of Sport Behavior, 2,* 143–155.

Seraganian, P. (1993). *Exercise psychology: The influence of physical exercise on psychological processes.* Chichester, UK: Wiley.

Stephens, T. (1988). Physical activity and mental health in the United States and Canada: Evidence from four population surveys. *Preventive Medicine, 17,* 35–47.

Sundgot-Borgen, J. (1994). Eating disorders in female athletes. *Sports Medicine, 17*(3), 176–188.

Sutherland, V.J., & Cooper, C.L. (1990). Exercise and stress management: Fit employees— healthy organisations? *International Journal of Sport Psychology, 21,* 202–217.

Svebak, S., & Kerr, J.H. (1989). The role of impulsivity in preference for sports. *Personality and Individual Differences, 10*(1), 51–58.

Svebak, S., & Murgatroyd, S. (1985). Metamotivational dominance: A multimethod validation of reversal theory constructs. *Journal of Personality and Social Psychology, 48*(1), 107–116.

Taub, D.E., & Benson, R.A. (1992). Weight concerns, weight control techniques, and eating disorders among adolescent competitive swimmers: The effect of gender. *Sociology of Sport Journal, 9,* 76–86.

Thaxton, L. (1982). Physiological and psychological effects of short-term exercise addiction on habitual runners. *Journal of Sport Psychology, 4,* 73–80.

Thayer, R.E. (1989). *The biopsychology of arousal and mood.* New York: Oxford University Press.

Veale, D.M.W. (1995). Does primary exercise dependence really exist? In J. Annett, B. Cripps, & H. Steinberg (Eds.), *Exercise addiction: Motivation for participation in sport and exercise. Proceedings of a British Psychological Society, Sport and Exercise Psychology Section Workshop.* (pp.1–5). Leicester: The British Psychological Society.

Walters, J., Apter, M.J., & Svebak, S. (1982). Color preference, arousal and the theory of psychological reversals. *Motivation and Emotion, 6,* 193–215.

Willis, J.D., & Campbell, L.F. (1992). *Exercise psychology.* Champaign, IL: Human Kinetics.

World Health Organization (1994). *The ICD-10 classification of mental and behavioral disorders*. Geneva: World Health Organization.

Yates, A., Leehey, K., & Shisslak, M. (1983). Running—An analogue of anorexia. *The New England Journal of Medicine, 308*(5), 251–255.

Zung, W.W.K. (1974). The measurement of affects: Depression and anxiety. In P. Pichot & R. Olivier-Martin (Eds.), *Psychological measurements in psychopharmacology*. Basel: Karger.

9

Over the Top?: Stress in Competitive Sports

Harold Gimblett, Somerset and England batsman, was no ordinary cricketer. In a 19-year career that began in 1935, he scored 49 centuries, twice scoring over 2000 runs in a single season and, in one match against Sussex, scoring 310. However, Foot's (1982) book, aptly named *Harold Gimblett, tortured genius of cricket*, recorded Gimblett's battles to cope with the pressures of being a top-class cricketer. All through his cricket career and for much of the rest of his life, he endured chronically high levels of anxiety. On 1 March 1976, aged 63, Gimblett committed suicide by taking an overdose of tablets (Roberts, 1982).

From the description in the following quotation McIlvanney (1992, p.24), those who follow soccer might recognise another tortured genius who sought solace in a different way:

> With feet as sensitive as a pick-pocket's hands, his control of the ball under the most violent pressure was hypnotic. The bewildering repertoire of feints and swerves, sudden stops and demoralising spurts, exploited a freakish elasticity of limb and torso, tremendous physical strength and resilience for so slight a figure and balance that would have made Isaac Newton decide he might as well eat the apple.

This was how McIlvanney (1992) described a player who the current manager of Manchester United soccer club, Alex Ferguson, said was "The greatest talent our football has produced—easily" (McIlvanney, 1992). The player concerned was George Best, whose soccer talent was without equal. At the age of 27, he quit first-class soccer prematurely and then suffered for years as an alcoholic.

Why should a player like Best, at the top of his career, drop out? As he said himself in an interview some years later (McIlvanney, 1992, p.30):

> It had nothing to do with women and booze, or car crashes or court cases. It was purely and simply football. Losing wasn't in my vocabulary. I had been conditioned since boyhood to win, to go out and dominate the opposition. When the wonderful players I had been brought up with—Charlton, Law, Crerand, Stiles—went into decline, United made no real attempt to buy the best replacements available . . . It sickened me to the heart that we ended up being just about the worst team in the First division and went on to drop into the Second.

This was a player whose experience of the pressures of being a top performer was different from those of cricketer Gimblett. Best thrived on the competition and being a member of a Manchester United team that was one of the greatest in soccer history. When the team began to break up and Manchester United and Best were no longer winning, it became too much and his attempt at coping centred on alcohol abuse.

Boris Becker, who won the Wimbledon Men's Tennis Championship for the first time in 1985 at age 17 and recently won the 1996 Australian Open Championship, has, at times, also considered dropping out. Becker's reasons for this are also to do with winning, but are entirely different from those given by Best. According to Becker (Atkin, 1990a, p.3), the experience of winning, dominating opponents and beating them can also be stressful:

> My opponents are human beings, not enemies. In order to survive a tournament you have to be some kind of beast. You have to beat your opponent psychologically. After tough tournaments I frequently go through phases of deep depression and see no reason to go on.

One final example illustrates how, for some athletes, victory does not come easily and the demands placed on them drive them to risk their health by taking performance-enhancing drugs like anabolic steroids. Given the risks involved, why do sportsmen and women break the rules over drug use? Rodda (1994, p.23) quotes British shot putter Neil Brunning, after he was caught and banned for using drugs in 1992:

> I didn't get any advice about what I was doing. I just took the tablets. I thought sod it if I get caught, I get caught.
> I did it because I felt others in my event were doing it. It is hard to motivate yourself when you are being beaten by someone who you think is on the stuff.

It would appear that, although Brunning realised he was breaking the rules, the only way he thought he could be successful was to comply with what he perceived was the norm amongst his fellow contestants.

These examples and quotations have been included in the introduction to this chapter to draw attention to some of the different sources and forms of stress associated with sport and the very different perceptions and responses of the individual performers concerned. The fact that the perception of stress and responses to it vary a good deal from person to person is a central element in the reversal theory approach to stress. In Chapter 2, which outlined the basic concepts in reversal theory, the concept of stress was not discussed. Consequently, before moving on to examine reversal theory research on stress effects in sport, it is necessary to clarify briefly the reversal theory approach to stress (see Apter, 1989; Apter & Svebak, 1989; Svebak & Apter, 1996).

REVERSAL THEORY AND STRESS

A number of approaches (other than reversal theory) to understanding the stress process, and not restricted to the sport context, (e.g. Cox & Mackay, 1985; Mackay, Cox, Burrows, & Lazzerini, 1978; McGrath, 1976; Quick, Murphy, & Hurrell, 1992) have emphasised that there are two different possible types of stress. These are stress that develops as a result of "overload" and stress that develops as a result of "underload" on an individual. McGrath (1976, p.4), for example, described stress as being "the result of the interaction of an individual with his or her environment which forces on the person a demand, a constraint, or an opportunity for behavior." In these terms, he concluded that an imbalance or mismatch between environmental demand and the capability of the individual could be stressful in either direction (i.e. overload or underload). In addition, the extent to which a demand on an individual is stressful depends on whether it is perceived as stressful by the individual concerned (e.g. Csikszentmihalyi, 1988; Lazarus, 1966).

The reversal theory approach to stress also takes on board notions about overload or underload and the importance of the subjective interpretation in a person's experience of stress, but develops them beyond the conceptual level of the approaches just mentioned. In reversal theory, stress is thought to arise as a result of tension which has been defined as a discrepancy between the preferred and actual level of a variable. This form of stress is known as *tension-stress* and could, for example, be brought about by a discrepancy between the preferred and actual levels of felt arousal. In the case of arousal discrepancy then, two forms of tension-stress are possible. Stress arising as a result of too high demand (e.g. arousal levels higher than preferred, posing a threat which results in anxiety) is known as *telic tension-stress*. Stress arising as a result of too low demand (e.g. arousal levels lower than preferred, resulting in a lack of stimulation or threat which leads to boredom) is known as *paratelic tension-stress* (Apter, 1989). It is important to emphasise here that there are two possible forms of arousal discrepancy that arise not only because arousal levels can be too high or too low, but because these levels are too high or too low in relation to two different preferred levels of arousal. Other forms of tension-stress are possible and would result from mismatches between preferred and actual levels of other variables such as felt negativism, felt toughness, or felt transactional outcome. These forms of tension-stress will be examined in more detail later in this chapter.

In addition, any effort expended by an individual to compensate for the unpleasant feelings associated with tension-stress is known as *effort-stress*. In the case of telic tension-stress, effort-stress takes the form of effortful attempts at coping with the stressors, while effort-stress associated with paratelic tension-stress is concerned with the active setting up of challenges (Apter & Svebak, 1989). Paratelic effort-stress is an interesting concept because it allows for the fact that some people may actually enjoy having to cope with stressful conditions. In other words, what would otherwise be stressful, and is conventionally regarded as stressful, becomes instead something that is pleasant and joyful. In this sense, paratelic effort-stress is not really stressful at all.

To summarise, reversal theory has two distinct forms of stress. Tension-stress is about the experience of tension caused by a discrepancy between the preferred and experienced level of a variable (like arousal), effort-stress is about coping with that tension (discrepancy) (Apter, 1989; Apter & Svebak, 1989; Kerr, 1990; Svebak & Apter, 1996).

DIFFERENCES IN STRESS RESPONSE:
TELIC/PARATELIC DOMINANCE

Martin and his colleagues at the University of Western Ontario carried out a series of research studies in the mid 1980s which provided important evidence in support of reversal theory arguments about motivational style and the experience of stress. The results showed that there were clear differences in the way that telic and paratelic dominant individuals experienced stress (e.g. Martin, 1985; Martin, Kuiper, Olinger, & Dobbin, 1987).

According to reversal theory, paratelic dominant people, more often than not, prefer and enjoy high arousal. If environmental demands or stressors increase arousal then, for paratelic dominant people, this will usually be a pleasant experience (at least up to a point). If demands or stressors are at too low a level, it is likely that the paratelic dominant person will experience paratelic tension-stress and feelings of boredom. By way of contrast, telic dominant people more often prefer low arousal. For them, if stressors increase arousal, telic tension-stress is induced which usually results in increasingly unpleasant mood disturbance and feelings of anxiety.

Martin et al. (1987), in the first of their experiments, used the Telic Dominance Scale (TDS; Murgatroyd, Rushton, Apter, & Ray, 1978) and the Profile of Mood States (POMS; McNair, Lorr, & Droppleman, 1971) measures to establish that there were no differences between telic and paratelic dominant people in their general experience of moods (i.e. they found no significant differences between the two groups overall with respect to POMS scores). They then used the Daily Hassles Scale (DHS; Kanner, Coyne, Shaefer, & Lazarus, 1981) and the Life Events of College Students (LECS; Sandler & Lakey, 1982) in a single testing session as measures of stress in the life of students. Their results revealed an interaction between dominance (TDS), stress (DHS), and moods (POMS) which confirmed the reversal theory arguments about the experience of stress. For telic dominant subjects, a predicted linear relationship between life events and moods was obtained; as stressful events (LECS) increased, *mood disturbance* (the term given to the total score on the POMS with high scores reflecting more unpleasant moods like anger, anxiety, and depression) increased and moods became increasingly unpleasant. For paratelic dominant subjects, a curvilinear relationship was found, as the frequency of negative life events increased, mood disturbance decreased and moods became increasingly pleasant. After a certain point, however, mood disturbance

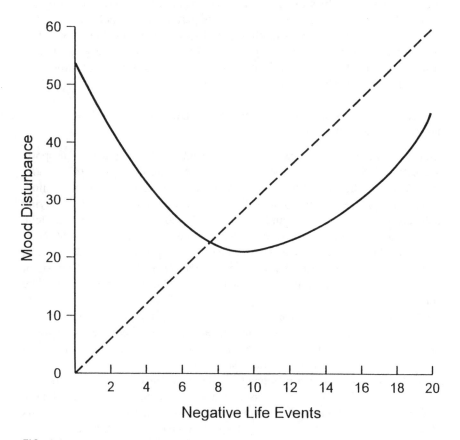

FIG. 9.1. The relationship between Negative Life Events and Mood Disturbance for telic dominant (dashed line) and paratelic dominant (solid line) subjects (from Martin, 1985).

stopped decreasing and then began to increase following a path similar to that of the telic dominant subjects (see Fig. 9.1). It was thought that, at the point where the change occurred, negative life events had built up and become strong enough to switch these individuals to the telic state, whereupon their curve reverted to the same pattern as that for telic dominant subjects. Similar results were found for subjects' experience of daily hassles (DHS) and provided further support for differences in the telic/paratelic dominant individuals' stress response (Martin et al., 1987; see also Martin, 1985).

REVERSAL THEORY RESEARCH ON STRESS IN THE SPORTS CONTEXT

In general, the intrinsic qualities of sport, its physical and psychological demands, competitiveness and confrontation and, in some cases, hostility, aggression, and violence, mean that when people engage in sport activities they are exposing themselves to what would be considered, in conventional terms, potential sources of stress. For many sports participants, it is because of the element of stress and its stimulating and challenging qualities that they participate willingly and with enthusiasm in sport. Some reversal theory research studies have examined sports participants' experience of stress and some interesting findings have come to light.

Dominance-based Differences in the Stress Response in Sport

Summers and Stewart (1993) undertook a study with a population of sports subjects which confirmed the findings of Martin et al.'s (1987) study, described earlier, that utilised subjects from a general student population. Using a simple median split of total TDS scores, two groups of baseball playing subjects (semi-professional and university, N=50) were divided into telic (N=23) and paratelic groups (N=27). Subjects completed the POMS (McNair, et al., 1971), the Hassles and Uplifts Scale (Delongis, Folkman, & Lazarus, 1988) and the Athletic Life Events Scale (Passer & Seese, 1983). Analysis of the data indicated that telic dominant baseball subjects exhibited a positive linear relationship between severity of stressors (both life events and weekly hassles) and mood disturbance. By way of contrast, paratelic dominant baseball subjects were found to exhibit a curvilinear relationship between severity of stress and mood disturbance. These results confirm the different response to stress by telic and paratelic dominant sports subjects.

These dominance-based differences in the experience of stress also help to explain some of the differences associated with telic and paratelic dominance and participation in particular sports activities, discussed in previous chapters (e.g. Chirivella & Martinez, 1994; Kerr & Svebak, 1989; Svebak & Kerr, 1989). Individual perceptions of and responses to the level of stress generated by particular sports activities are very likely to be related to participation in those activities.

Group Differences in Stress Response with Different Sports

Kerr and Svebak (1994) undertook a study to examine the stress response and possible changes in emotions that resulted from participating in three sports activities: easy running in small groups, basketball, and rugby. The sports activities were chosen on the basis of whether they involved a low, medium, or high level of "antagonistic physical interaction" (API), the term the experimenters used to represent certain aspects of the individual's perception of the cognitive and social consequences that occur naturally in competitive sport settings, including the inter- and intra-team interaction, competitiveness, and confrontation (physical contact), elements that are common in most team sports. The level of API was also manipulated between sports. For instance, in rugby, the highest level of API condition, subjects participated in a warm up, intensive tackle practice, and a period of full-contact competitive play. In the basketball session (medium-level API), subjects completed periods of warming up, skills practice, and competitive play. In the easy running condition, small groups of subjects were asked to run at a comfortable pace in a non-competitive way.

The subjects were volunteer male students (N = 109) randomly allocated to the experimental conditions within their regular university physical education classes. Subjects completed the Tension and Effort Stress Inventory (TESI; e.g. Svebak, 1993; Svebak et al., 1991) instrument pre- and post-sport sessions. The TESI has two items that are concerned with bodily or "internal" stress, and "external" stress that arises from the individual's interaction with the external situation (both items relate to tension-stress), and two items concerned with "internal" and "external" effort (both items relate to effort-stress), in addition to 16 items concerned with specific pleasant and unpleasant emotions (see Chapter 5).

The results indicated that there was a significant relationship between level of API and stress, with participation in the three sports provoking different stress responses in the participants. The smallest pre- to post-activity changes were associated with running (low API) and the largest with rugby (high API) (see Fig. 9.2a). For example, a significant group by time of testing interaction was obtained which reflected reduced external stress scores after running and increased scores on external stress after rugby (see Fig. 9.2b). Also with respect to internal or bodily stress, highly significant changes pre- to post-activity were revealed. External and internal effort scores mirrored the external and internal stress scores. Similarly, external effort scores (a consequence of interaction with the external situation) were reduced after running and increased after rugby, with basketball providing only a minor change. Significant group

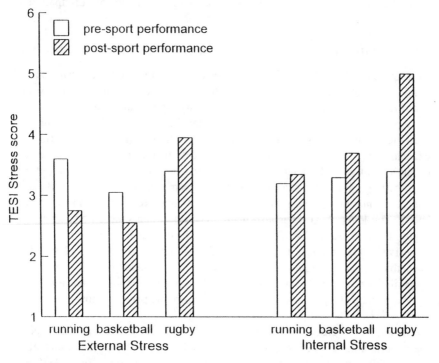

FIG. 9.2a.   Changes in TESI stress (external and internal) pre- and post-sport performance (from Kerr & Svebak, 1994).

differences in internal effort scores pre-to post-activity were again found to be greatest with rugby (high API) and least with running (low API).

The data on emotions indicated that positive affect outweighed negative affect, with mean pleasant emotion scores for all three conditions (low, medium, and high API) approximately double unpleasant emotion scores. Overall, hedonic tone remained pleasant. Changes in emotions were linked to level of API and the stress and effort results just outlined. The strongest changes in emotions were found with rugby; pleasant emotions were reduced and unpleasant emotions were increased (Kerr & Svebak, 1994). These changes appear to be associated with the high level of API in the rugby session which, in contrast to running and basketball, involved tackle practice and full-contact competitive play. The results of this study show that levels of tension and effort-stress in sport depend on the type of sport and the nature of the activity within a sport (e.g. different levels of API). Although sport can be stressful and may induce changes in pleasant and unpleasant emotions, subjects in this study generally experienced participation as pleasant.

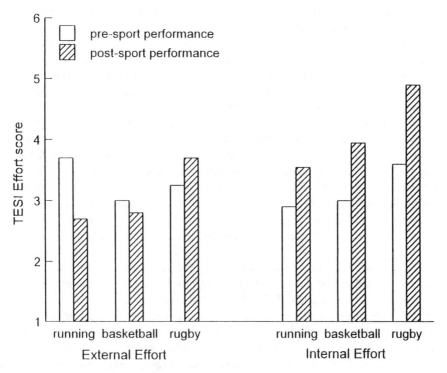

FIG. 9.2b.   Changes in TESI effort (external and internal) pre- and post-sport performances (from Kerr & Svebal, 1994).

Individual Differences in Efforts to Cope With Stress

The results of a canoeing study by Males and Kerr (1996) discussed in Chapter 5 provide an interesting illustration of individual differences in responses to stress. In Chapter 5 the relationship between affect and performance was reviewed and the results of two particular subjects (G & F) were highlighted. The two canoeists' TESI stress and effort scores (not discussed in Chapter 5) provide an interesting contrast, especially in terms of efforts to cope with tension-stress, and they are discussed here.

Canoeist G achieved his season's best performance at the World Championships, where he also reported the season's highest levels of internal and external stress (tension-stress) prior to competing. However, his individual response (effort-stress) to those high levels of internal and external stress differed. Scores on internal effort were greater than internal stress scores, whereas scores on external effort were considerably less than external stress scores (see Fig. 9.3a). The researchers suggested that, at least on this occasion, G's bodily state may have been more important to him than external considerations. As a result, his efforts to cope (effort-stress) were directed towards dealing with bodily stress.

Canoeist F's best performance took place at a local event in front of his home crowd, just after his selection for the national team. His internal stress score was matched by his internal effort score, but was below his mean score for the season. His external stress score was higher than his mean score for the season and his external effort scores higher still. At the World Championships, his worst performance, his stress scores were similar to his scores at the local event, but both internal and external effort scores were higher than the stress scores (see Fig. 9.3b). Males and Kerr (1996) proposed that this may have reflected a desire to *try harder* on the part of canoeist F and may have been related to his desire for a higher than average arousal level at the same event. As a result, coping efforts (effort-stress), as reflected by TESI scores, exceeded tension-stress. A discrepancy between stress levels and coping efforts was thought to be important because this preceded this subject's worst performance.

The three reversal theory studies just outlined represent the first steps in attempts to understand the stress and coping processes in sport. Summers and Stewart (1993) investigated differences in the response to stress by telic and paratelic dominant sports subjects. Kerr and Svebak (1994) examined the stress experience of student performers at the recreational level in sports with different levels of API, and Males and Kerr (1996) observed stress and coping in top-level performers. There are many other stress-related topics in sport which are ripe for reversal theory-based studies. For example, future studies might examine tension-stress effects in sport which arise as a result of mismatches in levels of preferred and felt negativism, felt toughness (or control), or felt transactional outcome. Studies could also examine the role of different forms of tension-stress in drop-out from children's and youth sport and burnout in top-level sport. A discussion of some of the important aspects of burnout follows in the latter sections of this chapter.

BURNOUT AND OTHER STRESS-RELATED PROBLEMS IN SPORT

Sport psychology research on stress has primarily been concerned, at one level, with the drop-out of young performers from sport (e.g. Gould, Feltz, Horn, & Weiss, 1982; Robinson & Carron, 1982; Scanlan, 1985; Whitehead, 1993) and at another level with stress and burnout amongst coaches and professional athletes (e.g. Caccese & Mayerberg, 1984; Capel, Sisley, & Desertrain, 1987; Dale & Weinberg, 1990; Henschen, 1986; Rotella & Heyman, 1986). Much of the interest in sport psychology has concentrated on identifying stress effects due to over-stimulation or overload (telic tension-stress in reversal theory). Less attention appears to have been directed to stress effects in athletes due to under-stimulation or underload (paratelic tension-stress in reversal theory),

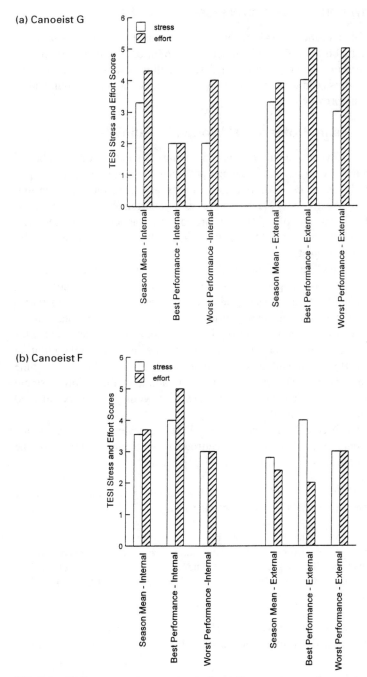

FIG. 9.3. TESI stress (tension-stress) and effort (effort-stress) scores for canoeists G (a) and F (b) (from Males & Kerr, 1996).

although Smith's (1986) theory paper, which outlined a cognitive–affective model of athletic burnout, did include both types of stress. By concentrating on elite performers in women's professional tennis, illustrations of how both of these forms of stress can contribute to athletic burnout or athletic withdrawal or drop-out will be provided.

Tension-stress in Professional Women's Tennis

During the last 20 years, female professional tennis has had a large number of young competitors who began as teenage prodigies and subsequently dropped out prematurely as a result of overuse injuries and psychological burnout problems. Tracy Austin, who played on the centre court at Wimbledon as a 14-year-old in 1977, was one of the first, Andrea Jaeger was another. Jaeger, who was ranked 6th, 5th and 3rd in the world in 1980, 1982 and 1983 respectively, retired at age 20 (August, 1994; Keating, 1990).

Jennifer Capriati, another top-level player, appears destined to follow players like Austin and Jaeger. Having started her professional career at just under 14 years old, at age 18 she had already taken a year off from tennis reputedly because of burnout and injuries.[1] During her time off, she was in trouble with the police over a shoplifting incident and, in 1994, was arrested for possession of marijuana, after which she spent time in a drug rehabilitation clinic (August, 1994). Her subsequent attempts at a tennis comeback at the time of writing have been unsuccessful. What is it about women's professional tennis in recent times that has caused these very young and very talented players to abandon their sport?

For Martina Navratilova, whose incredible achievements in women's professional tennis were featured in the introductory chapter of this book, the answer to this question is clear (Irvine, 1990, p.3):

> 'I feel very lucky that I'm still here competing and giving the youngsters a run for their money,' she said. 'And I'm playing pain free, which at my age is a bonus.'
>
> It would not be so, she feels, had she been subjected to the workload, surface changes and pressure from the media and public which young players must endure nowadays. 'If they get things right they shouldn't suffer burnout but I really don't think any of today's players will last as long as either Chris [Evert] or I have'.

In the same interview conducted in 1990 (p.3), Navratilova said of Capriati, "She's so innocent and happy-go-lucky. She really enjoys her game. If I were to

---

[1]"Capriati suffers loss on return to tennis" (1994, 11 November). *The Japan Times*, p.19.

"Tennis disproved critics with hot new talent, record attendance and purses" (1994, 27 December). *The Japan Times*.

give her any advice it would be to keep it that way. Don't do it for any other reason."

Similar statements are currently being made about Martina Hingis who became a professional player two years ago, at the age of 13 and who, in spite of playing a restricted tournament schedule, is currently ranked in the top 20 players in the world. At the 1996 Australian Open Tennis Championships, Hingis, now 15, defeated 25-year-old Brenda Schultz-McCarthy to advance to the quarter-finals of a Grand Slam event for the first time. Her opponent, Brenda Schultz-McCarthy, when interviewed after their match and asked about Hingis' approach said[2]:

> That's typical Martina, . . . For her, it's just a game, which is great, I think. I wish I could see it like that. I'm 25. You fight for every point, and then this little girl just hits an underhand serve.
>
> She's 15 years old, what can you expect? She enjoys it out there, and plays a very quick game. We are very good friends; she's a very nice girl. For her it's an exhibition, it's fun.

Dr Ken Smith, one of the originators of reversal theory has pointed out (Roberts, 1982) that:

> A sportsman enjoys the game up until the point when it becomes a matter of great importance. Then he comes under pressure. His game becomes his work, and this can produce an anxiety-avoiding state.
>
> Bjorn Borg and Steve Davis got to the top and then went off the boil. It was as if what they were doing became more of a job, less a matter of fun.
>
> Great sportsmen are the ones who enjoy the challenges. Others get knocked down and stay down.

The pressure and demand that comes with success is likely to bring about a change from a playful paratelic approach to playing (typical of Capriati in her early career and Hingis now), to play in the anxiety-avoiding telic state. The telic influence on their tennis activity means that the high arousal associated with top-level play, which previously was enjoyed in the paratelic state, becomes re-interpreted as unpleasant anxiety, and mismatches in preferred and actual arousal levels result in the experience of telic tension-stress. If the individual's efforts to cope prove ineffectual and telic tension-stress (in addition to other forms of tension-stress; see later) is endured for long periods, psychological burnout is a probable outcome. An interesting point to note in this connection is that burnout has been associated with somatic problems (e.g. Apter, 1996; see also Svebak et al., 1991). In many of the cases mentioned

---

[2] " 'Little Martina' has some fun with 'Big Brenda' " (1996, 27 December). *The Japan Times*, p.20.

earlier, the reasons given for withdrawing from tennis frequently include a recurrent injury as well as motivational problems. Other recent examples include the premature retirements of Gabriela Sabatini (stomach injury) and Kimiko Date ("limits of her strength"), both aged 26.

There are, of course exceptions, as not all young female professional tennis players burn out. Steffi Graf and Monica Seles were also tennis champions at a very early age, and both have survived and are still playing in their twenties. In the case of Seles, this is in spite of a being stabbed with a knife by a spectator when she was 19 years old, which prevented her from playing for two years. In the case of Graf, her standard of play has been consistently high over the years, with only occasional problems. However, in contrast to the telic tension-stress described earlier, some of Graf's problems, when they did occur, would appear to have been primarily of the paratelic tension-stress variety. For example, prior to the Wimbledon Championships in 1990, Graf was beating all her opponents with considerable ease and had completed a string of 66 victories which began with the French Open in 1989. Writing about Graf, Atkin (1990b, p.2) said:

> The biggest enemy, it seems, is the one within. All year, even when winning her ninth Grand Slam title, the Australian Open last January, Steffi has looked distracted and played, by her supreme standards, indifferently. Some athletes thrive on domination of their field, others eventually get bored. This, many felt, was what was happening. Winning, and the rewards associated with it, had become meaningless when compared with the pressure on private life that was involved.

It seems that, at this time, victory for Graf had become too easy and the challenge, which is important to many sports performer's motivation, had disappeared. Graf had been unbelievably successful during this period, but for other less successful players the lifestyle associated with being a professional player may also be a source of paratelic tension-stress. The gruelling nature of the tennis tournament circuit means that they have little time for paratelic-oriented enjoyment and there is a danger that their whole tennis experience may become just a boring grind. If prolonged, this type of paratelic tension-stress is likely to lead to the player dropping out from tennis and seeking other ways to spend their time.

The explanations of telic and paratelic stress given here are simplifications of the stress process. There are other facets to the build-up of tension-stress in sport and often, where burnout occurs, it is as a result of a complex interaction of factors. Tension-stress may not just be of the telic or paratelic variety, but may arise from a number of other metamotivational sources. As mentioned earlier, mismatches between preferred and experienced levels of felt negativism, felt toughness (or control), or felt transactional outcome may also contribute to a build-up of negativistic or mastery tension-stress. For example, young female tennis players are often pushed by family members, who act as managers and sometimes coaches, to conform to rigorous training and playing regimes. In some cases, such as Capriati, they may be the sole financial support for the whole family (August, 1994).

Sabatini, Graf, and Pierce are other examples of young players who have experienced problems as a result of difficulties with family members, but have managed to cope. For example, Pierce's father, who has on occasion verbally and reputedly physically assaulted his daughter and disrupted her matches (Atkin, 1993a, b), was eventually banned at the 1993 French Open for rowdy behaviour by the women's authorities. As Pierce has stated (Atkin, 1993a, p.45):

> His behaviour doesn't help me at all. I talk to him about it all the time. He says he gets so consumed in the match that he can't help it. He's trying to be helpful but he's not. He has to realise that I can figure it out for myself on the court. Steffi Graf went through it with her father and Jennifer Capriati has had to make changes with her parents. It happens with a lot of the girls on the circuit.

Players may be forced to spend long periods of time in a telic–conformist metamotivational state combination, at a time when many other adolescents typically enjoy the pleasures of the paratelic and negativistic states. As in any family relationship, parental pressure usually exacerbates adolescent reaction and under the extreme conditions required to play professional tennis, will almost inevitably lead to difficulties. Like most individual sports performers, young female tennis players will also spend a good deal of time in the mastery and autic states. This can also be a source of stress if parents continue to try to control their child's tennis career and daily life at a time when young people want to exert independence and be masters of their own lives.

Such constraints may lead young female tennis players to engage in (often purposeless) rebellions or negativistic behaviour. As Braman (1996, p.7) stated:

> ... burnout could be postulated as due to the satiation of sets of generalized goal-directed behaviors organized around the telic-conformity state ... As satiation of the behavioral sets associated with the telic–conformist state builds up, there begin to occur involuntary reversals to a purposeless negativistic state (reversals not unlike the "involuntary rest pauses" which occur as a result of satiation in all types of work).

Tension-stress can also arise if individuals have little opportunity to experience the sympathy and alloic states. Much of their time in tennis is oriented to autic–mastery. For example, they must constantly master higher and higher levels of skill as they have to deal with technological developments in racquet design. In addition, as they attempt to climb up the rankings, they must dominate their opponents and, as was evident from the quote by Becker at the beginning of the chapter, this can lead to difficulties associated with the mastery–sympathy and autic–alloic states.

In female professional tennis, a likely predominant operative state combination for players might be telic–conformist–autic–mastery. In addition to telic and paratelic considerations, tension-stress may also arise from spending prolonged periods of time in the conformity, mastery, or autic states. Having particular metamotivational state combinations operative for long periods is likely to affect the metamotivational equilibrium and versatility of young athletes at a time in their maturational development when they are, perhaps, least able to tolerate the tension-stress that is the outcome. As Braman (1996, p.8) pointed out:

> As burnout develops, the person discovers much to his chagrin that he can no longer reliably behave in ways which previously gained him crucial rewards. His confidence and self-esteem suffer, and often all he wants to do is to get totally away from the situation. Burnout, which is the product of rewarded behavior carried to extreme, therefore ends by taking the rewards out of the situation, ultimately causing the person to abandon what he is doing . . . When burnout happens to athletes, more often than not, it is to the best, most motivated and serious that it happens . . . Most sports behavior satiates rapidly because of the large expenditure of energy involved, and because the range of responses practiced are usually circumscribed. Repeating over and over precise and energetic sets of movements, as one does in training for most sports, makes satiation almost a certainty. The dedicated, highly motivated athlete, therefore, always faces the risk of training too much.

The following section examines in more detail what sports psychologists, coaches and performers can do to counter the effects of stress.

COUNTERACTING STRESS EFFECTS IN SPORT

The reversal theory analysis of problems associated with stress in sport in this chapter will almost certainly lead interested practising sport psychologists, coaches, and athletes to ask: "How can the effects of tension-stress in sport be counteracted? What, for example, could have been done in the tennis examples just described?"

As far as women's professional tennis is concerned, substantial changes made recently in the player age eligibility rules by the Women's Tennis Council may help young competitors to offset the stressful effects of practising for and playing top-level tennis. The rule changes came about as a result of the high incidence of medical problems in young female players and followed a report by an independent task force of sports medicine professionals. The task force reported that, amongst other things, female tennis players are at special risk for acute and chronic problems, including depression, anxiety, low self-esteem, eating disorders, and menstrual disturbances. The essence of the rule change is a gradual phasing in for players between the ages of 14 and 18 which limits number of tournaments in which they can participate (Howard, 1995).

For reasons outlined earlier, this rule change makes good sense from the reversal theory point of view. A more gradual introduction and phasing in to professional tennis might allow players to avoid burnout, at the same time building up a tolerance to, or a means of coping with, any stressful effects that arise from playing professional tennis at a young age. Other female sports in which top-level performers tend to be very young, like swimming and gymnastics, might be forced to make similar rule changes in the future. Any sport that involves very young athletes in heavy training and performing regimes may, as a result of spending extended periods in particular meta-motivational state combinations, precipitate a kind of metamotivational imbalance that will lead to the experience of stress. Young elite performers in other sports may well be subject to the same types of problems as young professional female tennis players.

One way of dealing with stress in sport is to consider the possibility of using some form of psychological intervention. Briefly, any form of reversal theory-based intervention in sport (see Kerr, 1993, 1996) first needs to take into account a performers' metamotivational dominance characteristics. For example, in the case of a paratelic dominant personality, stress management strategies need to address the need for new and different challenges. Stress management strategies are also likely to prove effective if, where appropriate, they can prevent prolonged discrepancies in preferred and felt levels of metamotivational variables, like felt arousal or felt negativism.

Within the tennis context, for example, paratelic tension-stress might be reduced by allowing the player to follow a less regimented, more flexible approach to training and playing. Such an approach could perhaps be combined with the inclusion of new and different activities in training or the flexibility to occasionally engage in another type of demanding sport. Also, encouraging the player to engage in other activities outside the tennis context, which allow high levels of felt arousal to be achieved and enjoyed, might prove successful in offsetting stress effects arising from boredom. This may mean, for example, that coaches should attempt to set up and develop situations, specific to tennis, in which players can experience the full range of metamotivational states. The crux of the matter in counteracting tension-stress will be to try and avoid similar situations and repeated practices where players may become psycho-logically restricted by a kind of metamotivational straitjacket.

In this context, a study on swimming by Curry (1992) is of interest. Curry's (1992) study is included here as an example of how small changes in training and practice programmes could be used to alter the motivational experience of performers. The study experimented with off-season training programmes to improve motivation. The coach of a US university swimming team managed his team with what is known as a *Theory X* style of management (McGregor, 1960). Briefly, this is an autocratic style of management: swimmers were carefully monitored and directed, training activities were compulsory and no input from swimmers in the design of training programmes or practices was allowed. In the off-season, when swimmers were geographically dispersed and unsupervised, this style of management was not successful. It tended to generate negativism and resentment in the swimmers, who returned to university for the next season in poor physical condition.

The researcher (Curry, 1992), in cooperation with the coach, decided to experiment with a different approach, known as the *Theory Y* management style (McGregor, 1960): the coach was less autocratic, helping swimmers to set goals and suggesting training strategies. The actual implementation of the off-season training was left to the ingenuity and creativity of the swimmers themselves. With this approach, it was assumed that swimmers would want to maintain their physical fitness because it was important to them as swimmers and not because the coach demanded it. In a nutshell, the new approach proved to be much more successful, in that the majority of the team trained and tried to improve their condition during the off-season (confirmed by a number of pre- and post-off-season physical comparisons).

Analysing the two approaches from a reversal theory perspective, reversal theorists would recognise that one major difference was in terms of the negativism–conformity pair of states. Rather than feeling negativistic towards the coach's autocratic demands as they had in the past, there was now nothing to be rebellious about and the majority completed the training because they wanted to. Another difference can be attributed to the mastery–sympathy and autic–alloic pairs of states. Rather than feeling resentment (and perhaps guilt), the new approach gave the swimmers the opportunity to experience pride and virtue along with improved felt transactional outcome and overall hedonic tone.

CONCLUDING COMMENTS

It should not be forgotten that, for many sports performers, subjecting themselves to the challenging demands of sport is a tremendous source of pleasure and reward. The majority of those who reach the highest levels possess the necessary resources to meet the demands of high-level competition and come through unscathed, thoroughly enjoying their time at the top. It is true that, from time to time, some do experience periods of temporary staleness or burnout, but these tend to be short-lived. In comparative terms, a few top-level athletes may develop chronic psychological problems and some specific groups of athletes, like young female tennis professionals, may be at particular risk for burning themselves out.

One of the purposes of this chapter has been to show that stress in sport can arise from a number of different metamotivational sources. Thinking back to the four performers (Gimblett, Best, Becker, and Brunning) who were highlighted in the introduction to the chapter, the source of stress in each case would appear to have been different. The source of cricketer Harold Gimblett's telic tension-stress would, according to Foot (1982), appear to have been chronically high levels of anxiety. Although Gimblett managed to more or less cope through his cricket career and for most of his life, the stress eventually became so severe that he committed suicide.

For soccer player George Best, alcoholism was his way of dealing with the stress that arose from no longer being part of a highly successful winning team. It seems likely that Best's stress could be categorised as autic–mastery tension-stress. All the feelings of pride and triumph experienced as a result of domination over players and teams seem to have evaporated and been replaced by feelings of humiliation and loss of face when his team Manchester United was relegated to the second division.

Unlike Best, tennis player Boris Becker appears to have been able to cope with his stress and continue playing relatively effectively. It is interesting to note that his stress also appeared to be linked to the mastery state, but in a different way. For him, there appears to have been a conflict between the desire to defeat opponents and win matches and at the same time maintain some feeling for the opponent as a person. The source of Becker's tension-stress would appear to be his occasional reversals from a state combination of autic–mastery to alloic–sympathy. In the latter case, tension–stress occurs because he perceives what he is doing as self-centred and about toughness rather than sensitivity.

Finally, shot-putter Neil Brunning resorted to taking performance-enhancing drugs because he wanted to be successful. (Once again, his motivation is influenced by the autic and mastery states.) In addition, his decision to take drugs appears to have been taken while he was in the negativistic state and feeling rebellious towards the sport's authorities, but perceiving himself to be conforming to the drug-taking behaviour of his opponents. It appears that a major source of his tension-stress was a discrepancy in preferred and felt negativism experienced as negativistic tension-stress. However, in Brunning's case, autic and mastery tension-stress may also have played a role.

Without having access to the individual sports performers involved at the time they were having problems, interpretation of the different forms of tension-stress unfortunately remains as post hoc speculation. However, this is still useful in the sense that it allows different forms of tension-stress to be isolated and categorised. It seems very likely that athletes are currently (and may have in the past) presented problems to sport psychologists that reversal theorists would recognise as different forms of tension-stress.

The next and final chapter in this book looks to the future. It examines the role that reversal theory ideas and concepts can play in maximising the effectiveness of sports coaching and sport psychology practice. In addition, it discusses the direction that reversal theory research in sport might take in the next few years.

FURTHER READING

1. Kerr, J.H. (1996). Stress, exercise and sport. In S. Svebak & M.J. Apter (Eds.), *Stress and health: A reversal theory perspective*. Washington, DC: Taylor & Francis.
2. Kerr, J.H. (1993). An eclectic approach to psychological interventions in sport: Reversal theory. *The Sport Psychologist, 7,* 400–418.
3. Svebak, S., & Apter, M.J. (Eds.) (1996). *Stress and health: A reversal theory perspective*. Washington, DC: Taylor & Francis.
4. Smith, R.E. (1986). Toward a cognitive–affective model of athletic burnout. *Journal of Sport Psychology, 8,* 36–50.

REFERENCES

Apter, M.J. (1989). *Reversal theory: Motivation, emotion and personality*. London: Routledge.

Apter, M.J. (1996). Reversal theory, stress and health. In S. Svebak & M.J. Apter (Eds.), *Stress and health: A reversal theory perspective*. Washington, DC: Taylor & Francis.

Apter, M.J., & Svebak, S. (1989). Stress from the reversal theory perspective. In C.D. Spielberger, I. G. Sarason, & J. Strelau (Eds.), *Stress and emotion* (pp.39–52). Washington, DC: Hemisphere-McGraw Hill.

Atkin, R. (1990a, 24 June). Boris banks on bouncing back. *Observer Wimbledon Special*, p.3.

Atkin, R. (1990b, 24 June). Hard Graf for odds-on Steffi. *Observer Wimbledon Special*, p.2.

Atkin, R. (1993a, 30 May). Tennis father banned. *Observer*, p.45.

Atkin, R. (1993b, 4 July). Crying shame for the girls. *Observer*, p.44.

August, M. (1994, 19 May). Too much too soon for Jenny. *The West Australian*, p.3.

Braman, O.R. (1996). *The role of response satiation in overtraining and burnout in sports*. Paper presented at the 1st International Workshop on Motivation and Emotion in Sport: Reversal Theory, Tsukuba, Japan, 1–4 October.

Caccese, T.M., & Mayerberg, C.K. (1984). Gender differences in perceived burnout of college coaches. *Journal of Sport Psychology, 6,* 279–288.

Capel, S.A., Sisley, B.L., & Desertrain, G.S. (1987). The relationship of role conflict and role ambiguity to burnout in high school basketball coaches. *Journal of Sport Psychology, 9,* 106–117.

Chirivella, E.C., & Martinez, L.M. (1994). The sensation of risk and motivational tendencies in sports: An empirical study. *Personality and Individual Differences, 16,* 777–786.

Cox, T., & Mackay, C.J. (1985). The measurement of self-reported stress and arousal. *British Journal of Psychology, 76,* 183–186.

Csikszentmihalyi, M. (1988). The flow experience and its significance for human psychology. In M. Csikszentmihalyi & I.S. Csikszentmihalyi (Eds.), *Optimal experience: Psychological studies of flow in consciousness* (pp.15–35).Cambridge: Cambridge University Press.

Curry, T.J. (1992). Applying theory Y in sport sociology: Redesigning the off-season conditioning program of a big ten swim team. In A. Yiannakis & S.L. Greendorfer (Eds.), *Applied sociology of sport* (pp.151–165). Champaign, IL: Human Kinetics.

Dale, J., & Weinberg, R. (1990). Burnout in sport: A review and critique. *Journal of Applied Sport Psychology, 2,* 67–83.

Delongis, A., Folkman, S., & Lazarus, R.S. (1988). The impact of daily life on health and mood: Psychological and social resources as mediators. *Journal of Social Psychology and Personality, 54,* 486–495.

Foot , D. (1982). *Harold Gimblett, tortured genius of cricket*. London: Heineman.

Gould, D., Feltz, D., Horn, T., & Weiss, M. (1982). Reasons for attrition in competitive youth swimming. *Journal of Sport Behavior*, *5*, 155–165.

Henschen, K.P. (1986). Athletic staleness and burnout: Diagnosis, prevention and treatment. In J.M. Williams (Ed.), *Applied sport psychology* (pp.327–342). Palo Alto, CA: Mayfield Publishing Company.

Howard, R.R. (1995). Rule changes in women's tennis target medical issues. *The Physician and Sports Medicine*, *23*, 25–26.

Irvine, D. (1990, June 23). Navratilova bridges the generation gap. *The Guardian*, p.19.

Kanner, A.D., Coyne, J.C., Shaefer, C., & Lazarus, R.S. (1981). Comparison of two modes of stress management: Daily hassles and uplifts versus major life events. *Journal of Behavioural Medicine*, *4*, 1–39.

Keating, F. (1990, June 23). Younger still and younger the women champions come. *The Guardian*, p.19.

Kerr, J.H. (1990). Stress and sport: Reversal theory. In G. Jones & L. Hardy (Eds.), *Stress and performance in sport* (pp.107–131). Chichester, England: J. Wiley and Sons.

Kerr, J.H. (1993). An eclectic approach to psychological interventions in sport: Reversal theory. *The Sport Psychologist*, *7*, 400–418.

Kerr, J.H. (1996). Stress, exercise and sport. In S. Svebak & M.J. Apter (Eds.), *Stress and health: A reversal theory perspective*. Washington, DC: Taylor & Francis.

Kerr, J.H., & Svebak, S. (1989). Motivational aspects of preferences for, and participation in, "risk" and "safe" sports. *Personality and Individual Differences*, *10*, 799–800.

Kerr, J.H., & Svebak, S. (1994). The acute effects of participation in sports on mood. *Personality and Individual Differences, 16(1)*, 159–166.

Lazarus, R.S. (1966). *Psychological stress and the coping process*, New York: McGraw-Hill.

Males, J.R., & Kerr, J.H. (1996). Stress, emotion and performance in elite slalom canoeists. *The Sport Psychologist, 10*, 17–36.

Martin, R.A. (1985). Telic dominance, stress and moods. In M.J. Apter, D. Fontana, & S. Murgatroyd (Eds.), *Reversal theory: Applications and developments*. Cardiff: University College Cardiff Press and New York: Lawrence Erlbaum.

Martin, R.A., Kuiper, N.A., Olinger, L.J., & Dobbin, J. (1987). Is stress always bad? Telic versus paratelic dominance as a stress moderating variable. *Journal of Personality and Social Psychology, 53*, 970–982.

Mackay, C.J., Cox, T., Burrows, G.C., & Lazzerini, A.J. (1978). An inventory for the measurement of self-reported stress and arousal. *British Journal of Social and Clinical Psychology, 17*, 283–284.

McGrath, J.E. (1976). Stress and behavior in organizations. In M. Dunette (Ed.), *Handbook of industrial and organizational psychology*. Chicago: Rand McNally.

McGregor, D. (1960). *The human side of enterprise*. New York: McGraw-Hill.

McIlvanney, H. (1992). The Best years of our lives. *The Observer Magazine*, p.24.

McNair, D.M., Lorr, M., & Droppleman, L.F. (1971). *The Profile of Mood States*. San Diego, CA: Educational and Industrial Testing Service.

Murgatroyd, S., Rushton, C., Apter, M.J., & Ray, C. (1978). The development of the Telic Dominance Scale. *Journal of Personality Assessment, 42*, 519–528.

Passer, M.W., & Seese, M.D. (1983). Life stress and athletic injuries. Examination of positive and negative life events and three moderator variables. *Journal of Human Stress, 9*, 11–16.

Quick, J.C., Murphy, L.R., & Hurrell, J.J. (1992). *Stress and well-being at work*. Washington, DC: American Psychological Association.

Roberts, J. (1982, December 9). On cricket's tragic genius. *Daily Mail*.

Robinson, T.T., & Carron, A.V. (1982). Personal and situational factors associated with dropping out versus maintaining participation in competitive sport. *Journal of Sport Psychology, 4*, 364–372.

Rodda, J. (1994, November 3). BAF to name steroid dealers. *Guardian*, p.23.

Rotella, R.J., & Heyman, S.R. (1986). Stress, injury, and the psychological rehabilitation of athletes. In J. M. Williams (Ed.), *Applied sport psychology* (pp.343–364). Palo Alto, CA: Mayfield Publishing Company.

Sandler, I.N., & Lakey, B. (1982). Locus of control as a stress moderator: The role of control perceptions and social support. *American Journal of Community Psychology, 10,* 65–80.

Scanlan, T.K. (1985). Sources of stress in youth sport athletes. In M. Weiss & D. Gould (Eds.), *Sports for children and youth* (pp.75–89). Champaign, IL: Human Kinetics.

Smith, R.E., (1986). Toward a cognitive-affective model of athletic burnout. *Journal of Sport Psychology, 8,* 36–50.

Summers, J., & Stewart, E. (1993). The arousal performance relationship: Examining different conceptions. In S. Serpa, J. Alves, V. Ferriera, & A. Paula-Brito (Eds.), *Proceedings of the VIII World Congress of Sport Psychology* (pp.229–232). Lisbon, Portugal: International Society of Sport Psychology.

Svebak, S. (1993). The development of the Tension and Effort Stress Inventory (TESI). In J.H. Kerr, S. Murgatroyd, & M.J. Apter (Eds.), *Advances in reversal theory.* Amsterdam: Swets and Zeitlinger.

Svebak, S., & Apter, M.J. (1996). *Stress and health: A reversal theory perspective.* Washington, DC: Taylor & Francis.

Svebak, S., & Kerr, J.H. (1989). The role of impulsivity in preference for sports. *Personality and Individual Differences, 10*(1) 51–58.

Svebak, S., Ursin, H., Endresen, I., Hjelmen, A.M., & Apter, M.J. (1991). Back pain and the experience of stress, efforts and moods. *Psychology and Health, 5,* 307–314.

Whitehead, J. (1993). Why children might choose to do sport—or stop. In M.J. Lee (Ed.), *Coaching young people* (pp.109–121). London: E. and F. Spon.

10 Rethinking the Script: Future Directions in Reversal Theory Sports Research and Practice

The final chapter in this book will concentrate on possibilities for future developments in the application of reversal theory to sport and exercise activity. To date, most effort has been invested in research and a promising start has been made in sport psychology practice, but the potential of reversal theory in coaching is, as yet, largely untapped. This chapter will examine reversal theory sports research, practice, and coaching in turn and set out some of the directions that future developments within each area might take.

REVERSAL THEORY SPORTS RESEARCH

Reversal theory investigators in general, as well as those specifically involved in sports research, have adopted a flexible approach to the use of different research techniques. Examples include the combination of psychophysiological measurement and rating scales used in several of Svebak's studies (see e.g. Rimehaug & Svebak, 1987) and the multimethod approach of Svebak and Murgatroyd (1985), who utilised a combination of psychometric scales, psychophysiological measurement, and interview material in their study of metamotivational dominance. Similarly, in sports research, investigators have been willing to use different techniques to gain access to information about the psychological processes at work when people participate in sports and exercise activities (e.g. white-water slalom canoeing: Males & Kerr, 1996; Males, Kerr, & Gerkovich, 1997). One innovative technique that may well prove to be of tremendous value in this task in the future was described by McLennan and

Omodei (1995) at the 7th International Conference on Reversal Theory held in Melbourne.

The technique involves the use of a lightweight head-mounted video camera which records the sports person's visual field while actual performance is taking place. This visual record is then used to assist the individual in recalling important psychological aspects of complex decision making after an event. Omodei and McLennan (1994) undertook an experiment in which video-assisted recall was used to examine complex decision-making in orienteering. In the experiment, the equipment was not generally considered intrusive by the majority of orienteering subjects. Compared to free-recall procedures, orienteers were found to be able to recall and describe two to four times more detail about their experiences while completing the orienteering course. In addition, orienteers' recollections, based on video-assisted recall, often included features of psychological affect like anxiety, anger, and confusion, which the comparatively dispassionate free-recall accounts did not.

Although perhaps not suitable for all sports events, this technique could be used effectively in future reversal theory studies. For example, monitoring mental states during performance has proved difficult for sport psychologists, but this technique might allow detailed information to be collected post-event. Video-assisted recall could be used to glean additional information about psychological states and reversals in competitors during sports performance. In addition to the possibilities of including techniques like video-assisted recall in reversal theory research, there are examples of ongoing studies that have already produced impressive results and which will undoubtedly help to map the future direction of reversal theory sports research. Several of these typify the innovative and eclectic approach that is becoming a feature of reversal theory sports research. The white-water slalom canoeing research studies (Males & Kerr, 1996; Males et al., 1997) have already been reviewed extensively elsewhere in this book. Two other examples are outlined next.

One line of reversal theory research, pioneered by Sven Svebak in Norway, has undoubted potential for the future. Svebak has been responsible for a remarkable series of psychophysiological studies which have identified differences in physiological response tendency and biological characteristics associated with telic and paratelic dominance and states. A summary of the results of these studies is shown in Table 10.1.

In all but one of these studies, subjects were not recruited on the basis of their involvement in sports, but the results have very important implications in the sports context. These results also form the basic rationale for a number of more recent sport-specific studies which have been exploring the links between motivational characteristics, biological characteristics, and a person's prefer-ence for and participation in different types of sports. (e.g. Braathen & Svebak, 1990; Kerr & Svebak, 1989; Svebak, 1990; Svebak et al., 1993; Svebak & Kerr, 1989). Svebak is convinced (see e.g. Svebak, 1990) that there is a three-way relationship between these three components. Some of the research evidence

TABLE 10.1
Summary of Svebak's Findings

Dependent Measures	Metamotivation	
	Telic	Paratelic
1. *Skeletal muscles*		
(a) Tonic changes (passive)[1,2,3,4,5,6,13]	High	Low
(b) Phasic changes (active)[2,3,13]	Low	High
(c) Fibre composition[12]	Type I	Type II
2. *Cardiovascular measures*		
(a) Tonic heart rate changes (threat)[1,3,7]	High	Low
(b) Phasic heart rate changes (comedy)[8]	Low	High
(c) Pulse transit time[7]	Short	Long
3. *Respiration rate (threat)*[1,9]	High	Low
4. *Respiration amplitude*		
(a) Tonic changes (threat)[1,4,9]	High	Low
(b) Phasic changes (comedy)[8]	Low	High
5. *Cortical activity*		
(a) Area in synchrony[10]	Small	Large
(b) P300 amplitude[11]	Large	Small

1	Svebak, Storfjell, & Dalen (1982).	8.	Svebak & Apter (1987).
2	Svebak (1984).	9.	Svebak (1986b).
3	Svebak (1986a).	10.	Svebak (1985a).
4	Svebak & Murgatroyd (1985).	11.	Svebak, Howard, & Rimehaug (1987).
5	Apter & Svebak (1986).	12.	Svebak et al. (1990).
6	Rimehaug & Svebak (1987).	13.	Braathen & Svebak (1990).
7	Svebak, Nordby, & Ohman (1987).		

Summary of findings that indicate response tendencies and biological characteristics in some physiological systems in relation to telic/paratelic characteristics (state or state-dominance) (from Apter & Svebak, 1992).

supporting this link has already been reviewed in this book. The results of studies on the role that impulsivity plays in sports preference (Kerr & Svebak, 1989) were summarised in Chapter 3 and motivational aspects of preference for and participation in risk sports (Svebak & Kerr, 1989) were described in Chapter 4. Both of these studies showed that preference for and participation in certain types of sport were associated with telic or paratelic dominant lifestyles and therefore support the proposed link between motivational characteristics and sport preferences.

However, Svebak (1990) further hypothesised a more specific three-way link between muscle fibre type (type 1, "slow twitch" or type 2 "fast twitch"), endurance (anaerobic) or explosive (aerobic) sports, and telic or paratelic

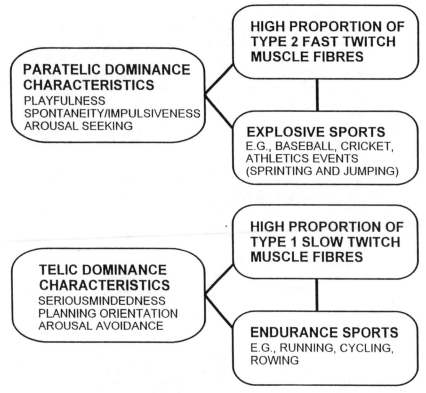

FIG. 10.1. Showing Svebak's hypothesised 3-way link between telic/paratelic dominance, type of sport and muscle fibre type in participants.

metamotivational characteristics (see Fig. 10.1, also Svebak et al., 1990). He stated (1990, p.91):

> It is assumed that a person who is motivationally dominated by serious-mindedness, planning orientation, and arousal avoidance, and who is also biologically 'dominated' by endurance fibers in his or her striate muscles, is in balance with motor demands when performing some kind of endurance sport. Conversely, the individual who is dominantly playful, impulsive and arousal seeking, and who is thus motivationally 'prepared' for explosive sports, is in balance with motor demands when performing some kind of explosive sport with high demands on explosive skeletal muscle discharges.

In testing Svebak's proposal, Braathen and Svebak (1990), for example, used electromyographic (EMG) techniques to investigate differences between elite performers of explosive sports, endurance sports, and sports involving a mix of explosive and endurance qualities. In the laboratory, they examined EMG recordings from striate muscles while subjects performed a perceptual motor task involving the operation of a joystick with one arm. Previous work (e.g. Rimehaug & Svebak, 1987; Svebak & Murgatroyd, 1985) had shown the importance of readings from the passive (non-operating) forearm when the joystick was being operated. On the basis of this earlier work, the researchers anticipated finding important differences in the passive forearm in the so-called "EMG gradient" (a measure of the increase and decrease of muscle tension over time) between elite performers of endurance and explosive sports. As predicted, they found that EMG gradients were relatively steep in elite performers of endurance sports (with a high proportion of type 1 muscle fibres), but extremely shallow, almost non-existent in elite explosive sports performers (with a high proportion of type 2 muscle fibres). This important finding adds further support to the existence of a connection between sports performers' motivational characteristics, their preference for and participation in exercise and sports activities, and their biological characteristics.

There are a number of obvious practical implications if this triangular relationship can be established. For instance, in terms of exercise participation, a good match between the three features increases the chance of enjoyment or satisfaction, and of a person adhering to a specific exercise or sports activity. Conversely, a mismatch may produce dissatisfaction with the activity and the likelihood that the person will opt out. Mismatches may be of different types. Svebak (1990) has indicated that mismatches may, for example, involve (1) a person participating in an exercise or sports activity which is at odds with his or her biological make-up; (2) a person participating in an exercise or sports activity which elicits levels of a variable (e.g. felt arousal, felt toughness) that is different from those preferred by the individual concerned; (3) a mismatch between particular motivational characteristics (e.g. cognitive impulsivity) and biological characteristics (rather than choice of activity) in any one person. Avoiding mismatches and achieving the appropriate balance between motivational characteristics, biological characteristics, and a person's preference and participation may be especially important for success in sport at the elite level (Apter & Svebak, 1992; Braathen & Svebak, 1990; Svebak, 1990).

A good deal more research on this topic will be necessary before the three-way relationship is definitely confirmed, but over the next few years other reversal theory researchers will have the opportunity to expand and develop the useful beginning made by Svebak and his co-workers.

Svebak's work, which tests reversal theory concepts through psychophysiological investigation, challenges the common practice in psychophysiology which traditionally has tended to ignore the role of subjective feelings in experimental subjects. Another reversal theory researcher, Ian Purcell in Perth, Australia, is also challenging accepted practice, but in the area of skilled performance, rather than psychophysiology. Generally, the practice of workers in this area, and especially those who have developed theoretical models of skilled performance, has been to avoid examining the influence of factors such as personality, cognition, and emotion on skilled performance. Glencross

(1993, p.252) summed up the situation well, after reviewing several of the important models of skilled performance, when he stated:

> One further comment should be made, and this relates to the inadequacies of all the models reviewed in addressing issues of motivation and the impact that personality and affective factors can have upon performance. Indeed, the sport psychologist usually sees these factors as his or her major concern, the single major issue in an applied setting. It is timely that models of human skill and performance address these factors as an integral part of skill learning and performance, not as separate factors, too often ignored or assumed not to be relevant by those studying human skill.

Purcell is attempting to break new ground in this area by including reversal theory dominance and state measuring instruments, as well as "think aloud" protocols and interview techniques, in a series of field studies on strategic planning and decision-making in golf (see e.g. Purcell & Kerr, 1995).

There are, of course some other topics that have received little previous attention from reversal theory researchers. One only has to think of topics like group dynamics, group cohesion, and teamwork; effective leadership; aggression and violence; aspects of children's sport; or sports career retirement problems, and a whole range of new and interesting research possibilities present themselves.

REVERSAL THEORY IN PRACTICE

Although it may not be their intention, sport psychologists who act as consultants to individuals or teams, or who regularly deal with athletes experiencing difficulties may lose sight of the fact that many sports people cope effectively with the demands of performance (Kerr, 1993). For example, sport psychologists may inadvertently give the impression that all performers will suffer from acute anxiety and stress prior to an important competitive occasions (see also Chapter 6). The truth is, however, that many athletes look forward with relish to big events and do not experience unpleasant feelings. A good example is provided by international rugby union player Rory Underwood who was interviewed shortly before a crucial 1996 championship match between England and France in Paris (Keating, 1996, p.22):

> 'The match atmosphere in Paris is said to scare visiting sides,' Underwood said, 'but I've always found it can gee you up wonderfully. I remember watching Paris games on television when I was at school and being thrilled by the din and general commotion of whistles and brass bands. When I actually ran out to play there in 1984, it was exactly the same. I love it.'

It would be wrong to deny that some sports performers do sometimes develop quite severe psychological problems. Indeed, some good examples were provided in the previous chapter. Such cases require careful clinical treatment which may well fall outside the expertise of a sport psychologist. Other athletes, however, may wish to develop their psychological skills with the aim of enhancing performance during competition, or may seek the assistance of a sport psychologist to deal with a temporary setback in performance. How can reversal theory help in these situations and what form will reversal theory-based consultancy work in sport take in the future?

Teaching performers about arousal modulation has been to the forefront in sport psychology for some time. This has involved informing athletes about techniques for increasing and/or decreasing arousal prior to or, in some cases, while competing (Loehr, 1982; Orlick, 1986). The recent emphasis, however, has been on teaching arousal reduction techniques, such as progressive relaxation (Jacobson, 1938) and autogenic training (Schultz & Luthe, 1969). Kerr (1989, 1990, 1993) has argued that reversal theory-based cognitive intervention in sport offers more possibilities for affecting arousal and how it is interpreted by the individual than the conventional approach to arousal modulation offered in most sport psychology texts (e.g. Weinberg & Gould, 1995). Kerr's (1989, 1990, 1993) arguments are based on the X-shaped curve (representing the relationship between arousal and hedonic tone) first hypothesised by Apter (1982) and discussed in Chapter 6. Remember that in this X-shaped relationship, there are thought to be unpleasant and pleasant forms of low arousal (boredom and relaxation) and unpleasant and pleasant forms of high arousal (anxiety and excitement). The experience of high or low arousal as pleasant or unpleasant is tied in with whether an individual is in the telic or paratelic state at the particular time.

Consequently, in addition to teaching the performer to engage in some form of arousal modulation, performers could perhaps be taught how to create the environmental conditions that would induce reversals to the opposite meta-motivational state(s). As shown in Fig. 10.2, athletes with the telic state operative and experiencing unpleasantly high levels of arousal as anxiety, could either reduce arousal or induce a reversal to the paratelic state where high levels of arousal would be reinterpreted as pleasant. Athletes with the paratelic state operative and experiencing unpleasantly low levels of arousal as boredom, could either increase arousal or induce a reversal to the telic state where low levels of arousal would be reinterpreted as pleasant. For further details about ideas and techniques for inducing reversals and modulating arousal for athletes see Kerr (1993).

A good example of how reversals (in this case together with arousal modulation) could work in practice in and around slalom canoeing was described in subject C's interview transcript (Males et al., 1997) in Chapter 5.

The point is that, given the inherent inconsistency of human behaviour, athletes may find themselves in an inappropriate state of mind when competing. From the reversal theory point of view, performers should become

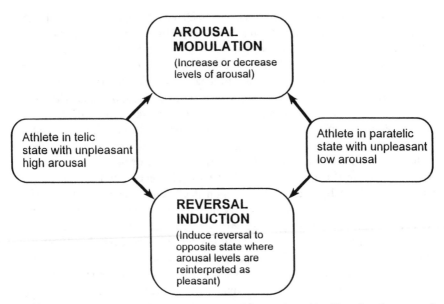

FIG. 10.2. Showing additional options for cognitive intervention with athletes based on reversal induction.

adept at recognising when their operative metamotivational pattern is not appropriate for performance. In general, athletes' planning should remain flexible enough to optimise competitive mood by inducing reversals or modulating levels of motivational variables (like felt arousal) should it be necessary.

It is through the work of Jonathan Males (see e.g. Males, 1995) as a consultant sport psychologist in England, that real progress is being made in reversal theory-based consultancy with sports people. The case example, described next, provides a good illustration of the intervention possibilities summarised in Fig. 10.2. In therapeutic work, reversal theory is often used in combination with other techniques (see e.g. Murgatroyd & Apter, 1984). This allows the conceptual framework of the theory to be used to understand the athlete's problem and provide a sound basis from which a suitable therapeutic technique, chosen by consultant and client, can be used to deal with the problem (Kerr, 1993; Murgatroyd & Apter, 1984).

This was the approach that Males (1995) used in one example with a professional pool player who, in spite of starting well in matches and establishing substantial leads, would often lose concentration, and the matches, as a result of intrusive negative self-talk. Males (1995) employed ideas from psychosynthesis (Assagoli, 1969/1990), including the idea of sub-personalities, along with the notion of reversals between states from reversal theory, in his sessions with the pool player. Very briefly, after the use of chair dialogues and imagery (see Males, 1995) careful consideration suggested that the source of the negative self-talk problem was one of inappropriate reversals during play between telic and paratelic states. Over a series of further sessions, the pool player was able to reduce the level of negative self talk by learning to recognise when a reversal was necessary and, using therapeutic techniques from psychosynthesis, to facilitate the appropriate reversal.

It should be stated at this point that further study is required to work out the possibilities for cognitive intervention with respect to the other pairs of states in reversal theory. In previous chapters, the important role that the mastery–sympathy, autic–alloic, and negativism–conformity pairs play in certain sports situations has been outlined. In the same way that it is possible to modulate levels of felt arousal and induce reversals between the telic and paratelic states, it should be possible to modulate levels of felt toughness, felt transactional outcome, and felt negativism, and spark reversals between the other pairs of states where this is deemed necessary or appropriate for maximising performance.

As the applications of reversal theory in sport continue to develop, the challenge to sport psychologists will be to diagnose sports performers' problems correctly and recommend appropriate reversal theory-based therapy or counselling (see Kerr, 1993). If sport psychologists can meet this challenge, perhaps the unfortunate and extreme actions taken by performers like Gimblett, Best, and Brunning (described in Chapter 9) can be pinpointed earlier and perhaps prevented.

REVERSAL THEORY AND COACHING

Reversal theory publications on sport outnumber those on any other topic yet, to date, there has not been a single publication on the implications of reversal theory for coaches and coaching. In spite of this, there is plenty of evidence in the coaching literature that some of the elements of coaching practice (which are largely based on coaches' experience of what works well) bear a close resemblance to concepts from reversal theory. This section will highlight some examples of coaching practice and draw parallels with reversal theory formulations.

Some readers may be familiar with the *Inner Game* (Gallwey, 1976) which is based on the principles of Zen Buddhism. The fundamentals of the inner game approach were first applied to tennis, but are applicable to many sports activities. In order to understand the inner game approach in tennis it is necessary to understand the distinction that Gallwey (1976) makes between what he calls *Self 1* and *Self 2* and the ongoing internal dialogue that, he claims, goes on between them. Self 1 is controlled by conscious thought and characterised by recurring self-instruction. In tennis, for example, it is often concerned with carrying out every detail of coaching points correctly, and evaluating the outcome, a process that often results in the person "trying too hard". Self 2, on the other hand, can be thought of as being concerned with natural learning and "just letting things happen". Gallwey (1976, p.8) described a typical Self 1 scenario in tennis:

> With most players, the self doing the talking seems to know all about how to play tennis because it is telling the other self—the part that actually has to hit the ball—how to do it.
> ... Then, having told it how, Self 1 doesn't trust that the arm will do it right because it is a 'bad' arm, with a 'bad' habit, so it makes the arm do it correctly, tightening most of the muscles in the arm (and face!) as it tries to force it into Self 1's idea of the right position. Being too tight to make a smooth and accurate connection with the ball, the arm misguides the racket, the ball is mishit . . .

Many people who have played tennis will be able to recognise this sequence of events. Many will also be able to remember occasions when Self 2 was apparently at work (Gallwey, 1976, p.9):

> When it [Self 2] produces a shot that flies off the racket, undistorted by our own 'trying', we stand amazed and call it lucky. Sometimes we feel as if someone else hit the shot. Yet if we don't immediately become self-conscious about this phenomenon, we can repeat it over and over—until Self 1 comes rushing back to try and analyze what's causing us to play so well, so that it can make it happen some more. When it starts trying, you start missing, the magic is broken, . . .

Gallwey (1976) favours the Self 2 approach to learning tennis and includes in his book a number of coaching practices, techniques, and tips that encourage the tennis player, and especially the beginner, to shift from Self 1 to Self 2. In other words, by concentrating on Self 2, which is process-oriented rather than outcome-oriented (like Self 1), learning and performance will be more effective. There is an obvious link here to the telic and paratelic concepts in reversal theory (and incidentally also to the controlled–automatic processing distinction in cognitive psychology, see e.g. Schmidt, 1991, pp.32–34). The serious, goal-oriented approach of Self 1 is easily recognisable as characteristic of behaviour in the telic state, as is the "just let it happen", spontaneous approach of Self 2 as reflecting behaviour in the paratelic state. Indeed, Fontana (1981, 1991) has written about the telic and paratelic concepts from reversal theory and Zen Buddhism, and also evident are links between the Inner Game approach (Gallwey, 1976) and the strategy employed by Males (1995) with the pool player described earlier.

There are many sports that involve large body movements or swinging a racquet, club, or bat where the telic approach to learning may actually hinder the progress of the participant. As Greg Norman, the Australian golfer said, after playing a nine shots under par first round at the 1996 Augusta

Masters tournament (a new first round Masters record), "The Japanese have a phrase for it—'Let it happen, let it flow'—and that's just what I did. I let it, flow."[1]

Norman's play in the second and third rounds was also outstanding. He went into the final round with a six-stroke lead over second-placed Nick Faldo. However, in the fi0nal round Norman's shots went amiss, he squandered his lead, and the Augusta Masters' title went to Faldo by five strokes. Golf experts (including David Leadbetter, Faldo's coach) noted some variation in Norman's pre-shot routine in the final round and that he appeared to have speeded up his club swing (I.P. Purcell, personal communication, April 16–17, 1996). In addition, Purcell (1996) speculated that: "There was variability in Norman's preshot routine on the final day and I would be very surprised if he didn't start focusing on the future outcome rather than being task-oriented and present centred."

Given these observations, it may have been that Norman's poor performance in the final round was because he lost the "let it happen, let it flow approach" that he said was important to his first-round play. It would appear that when hitting his shots in the final round, in Inner Game terms he allowed Self 1 to take over from Self 2 and, in reversal theory terms, the telic state rather than the paratelic state was operative.

Certainly, in the beginning stages of learning a new sport or sports skill, the paratelic approach has distinct benefits. This is especially true with young children. An impressive literature now exists on the motivation of children in sport (see e.g. Roberts & Treasure, 1992; Weiss & Chaumerton, 1992, for reviews), and texts that deal with coaching children (e.g. Lee, 1993) are now including chapters or sections on the motivation of young learners. It is here that the common ground between good coaching practice and reversal theory ideas and concepts is perhaps most apparent. The clear message from the published material on children's motivation is that a coaching approach to learning sports and skills based on that usually used with adults is totally inappropriate for children. An example from Thorpe (1993, p.285), provides a good illustration. Referring to short tennis, a game based on the full game, but designed especially for young children, he states:

> I welcomed the advent of short tennis in that it seemed to provide a medium in which children could show ability and task mastery, and gain social approval. In that a variety of new tactics and skills are possible (in direct contrast to tennis), breakthrough might seem to occur more often, games could be structured quickly, with simple scoring that satisfied the victory goal, and the pleasure of seeing lots of youngsters having fun together seemed to suggest that teamwork was a real possibility.

---

[1]"Norman masters Augusta" (1996, 13 April). *The Japan Times*, p.22.

... It was unfortunate, therefore, that a game designed for young children became structured in a way which exaggerated the 'showing ability' 'victory' or 'outcome' goals. One has to question (and indeed sensitive people in the LTA have) the wisdom of allowing club, county, regional and national short tennis competitions to dominate the sport ...

From this quote, it can be seen how the initiative of short tennis, a move away from the telic-oriented adult game to a paratelic-oriented fun activity, was so successful that it was eventually undermined and re-invented by the telic influence of misguided adults. However, this example goes beyond telic–paratelic considerations. Indeed, it is in the widespread development of modified games, like short tennis, where equipment, playing area, and rules have been adapted to the needs of children, that other metamotivational considerations are brought into the discussion.

It is interesting that Thorpe (1993) should mention task mastery as being an important element in the development of young players. Sport psychology research (e.g. Roberts & Treasure, 1992) has shown that a mastery-oriented learning climate geared towards individual achievement goals, rather than outcome goals, is important in maintaining the motivation and involvement of young sports participants. Mastery at a young age should be about mastering skills and techniques instead of mastering people. Winning should be played down, where possible (although it seems that it will always be present to some degree in sports), by using small-side games with ample changes of teams or players and numerous opportunities for scoring. For young children, autic–mastery motives can more usefully be satisfied by personal skill and technique acquisition. The results of research on motivation in young sport performers reported by Roberts and Treasure (1992) and Weiss and Chaumerton (1992), interpreted in reversal theory terms, tend to support this view.

It is also noticeable that young children often show a concern for their opponents. The origins of their feelings towards opponents lie in the alloic–sympathy metamotivational pair. In this respect, for insightful coaches, it would seem that having the alloic–sympathy state combination frequently operative in participants during coaching sessions might be conducive to enjoyment at this level.

Equally, children's games and sports do not require the fixed rules or techniques of the adult version. Again, by using small-side activities, the rules can be modified easily and frequently to suit the coaches' needs in assisting the children to learn. Having children constrained in some way, by having to conform to strict rules, and in some cases sports etiquette (e.g. dress, or being told that there is only one correct way to hold a cricket bat or a tennis racquet), may not be beneficial to their development as it may invoke the negativistic state in an unproductive way. From the reversal theory point of view, the most effective approach to coaching young children is one that will allow the participants to engage in the full range of metamotivational experience. In other words, a coaching regime that is flexible enough to invoke different metamotivational states and state combinations, and which permits relatively frequent reversals as the learning process takes place, is desirable. In this way, young children especially will be liable to stay interested and involved in sport for longer. The absence of such coaching regimes may be one of the reasons why drop out rates from children's sports are currently high (Weiss & Chaumerton, 1992).

CONCLUDING COMMENTS

In discussing methodological issues and measurement problems identified by North American sport psychologists, Schutz (1994) pointed out that there were two global problems evident from the literature. These were lack of theory and excessive adherence to traditional methodologies. He stated (p.39):

> In general, it is perceived that we rely too heavily on theories borrowed from psychology or sociology with the result that there exists a lack of theoretical models specific to sport psychology. Personally, I'm not sure that I agree with this conclusion. Sport psychology, after all, is the study of sport and exercise from a psychological perspective, and thus the utilization of available psychological theories and methodologies is appropriate and necessary . . .

Kerr (e.g. 1993) has argued that reversal theory's comprehensive conceptual basis can contribute substantially to sport psychology. In addition, the open-minded attitude to the use of different methodologies has already been demonstrated numerous times by reversal theory psychologists whose expertise is not limited to sport (see Apter, Kerr, & Cowles, 1988; Kerr, Murgatroyd, & Apter, 1993; Svebak & Apter, 1996). Reversal theory has the potential to make a massive contribution to the understanding of all facets of human behaviour in sports and physical activity. Surely it is time for sport psychologists (especially the younger generation), to *rethink the script* and go beyond the restricting conventionality of much of contemporary sport psychology. By taking on board reversal theory and investigating a wide range of topics using as many relevant methodologies as possible, the opportunities for researchers appear to be limitless.

In many ways, reversal theory sports research is still in its early stages and this book may well have generated more questions than it has answered, but it is the author's hope that it will stimulate new debates, new lines of inquiry, and new directions in the applications of reversal theory to sport.

REFERENCES

Apter, M.J. (1982). *The experience of motivation: The theory of psychological reversals.* London: Academic Press.

Apter, M.J., Kerr, J.H., & Cowles, M.P. (Eds.) (1988). *Progress in reversal theory.* [Advances in Psychology, 51.] Amsterdam: North Holland/Elsevier.

Apter, M.J., & Svebak, S. (1986). The EMG gradient as a reflection of metamotivational state. *Scandinavian Journal of Psychology, 27*, 209–219.

Apter, M.J. & Svebak, S. (1992). Reversal theory as a biological approach to individual differences. In A. Gale & M.W. Eysenck (Eds.), *Handbook of individual differences: Biological perspectives* (pp.323–353). Chichester, UK: Wiley.

Assagoli, R. (1969/1990). *Psychosynthesis: A manual of principles and techniques.* London: Mandala.

Braathen, E.T., & Svebak, S. (1990). Task-induced tonic and phasic EMG response patterns and psychological predictors in elite performers of endurance and explosive sports. *International Journal of Psychophysiology, 8*, 55–64.

Fontana, D. (1981). Reversal theory, the paratelic state, and Zen. *European Journal of Humanistic Psychology, Vol IX*, 229–236.

Fontana, D. (1991). Reversals and the Eastern religious mind. In J.H. Kerr & M.J. Apter (Eds.), *Adult play: A reversal theory approach* (pp.141–150). Amsterdam: Swets & Zeitlinger.

Gallwey, W.T. (1976). *Inner tennis: Playing the game.* New York: Random House.

Glencross, D.J. (1993). Human skill: Ideas, concepts and models. In R.N. Singer, M. Murphey, & L.K. Tennant (Eds.), *Handbook on research on sport psychology* (pp.242–253). New York: Macmillan.

Jacobson, E. (1938). *Progressive relaxation.* Chicago: University of Chicago Press.

Keating, F. (1996, 20 January). A whiff of revolution in the Parc. *Guardian*, p.22.

Kerr, J.H. (1989). Anxiety, arousal and sport performance: An application of reversal theory. In D. Hackfort & C.D. Spielberger (Eds.), *Anxiety in sports: An international perspective* (pp. 137–151). [Series in Health Psychology and Behavioral Medicine]. New York: Hemisphere Publishing.

Kerr, J.H. (1990). Stress and sport: Reversal theory. In G. Jones & L. Hardy (Eds.), *Stress and performance in sport* (pp.107–131). Chichester, UK: J. Wiley & Sons.

Kerr, J.H. (1993). An eclectic approach to psychological interventions in sport: Reversal theory. *The Sport Psychologist, 7*, 400–418.

Kerr, J.H., Murgatroyd, S., & Apter, M.J. (Eds.) (1993). *Advances in reversal theory.* Amsterdam: Swets & Zeitlinger.

Kerr, J.H., & Svebak, S. (1989). Motivational aspects of preference for and participation in risk sports. *Personality and Individual Differences, 10*, 797–800.

Lee, M. (1993). *Coaching children in sport.* London: E. & F.N. Spon.

Loehr, J.E. (1982). *Mental toughness training for sports.* Lexington, MA: Stephen Green Press.

Males, J.R. (1995, July). *Helping athletes perform: Integrating reversal theory and psychosynthesis in applied sport psychology.* Paper presented at the 7th International Conference on Reversal Theory, Melbourne, Australia.

Males, J.R., & Kerr, J.H. (1996). Stress, emotion and performance in elite slalom canoeists. *The Sport Psychologist, 10*, 17–36.

Males, J.R., Kerr, J.H., & Gerkovich, M. (1997). *Metamotivational states during canoe slalom competition: A qualitative analysis using reversal theory.* Manuscript submitted for publication.

McLennan, J., & Omodei, M.M. (1995, July). *Studying dynamic psychological phenomena in real-world settings.* Paper presented at the 7th International Conference on Reversal Theory, Melbourne, Australia.

Murgatroyd, S., & Apter, M.J. (1984). Eclectic psychotherapy: A structural-phenomenological approach. In W. Dryden (Ed.), *Individual psychotherapy in Britain* (pp.392–414). London: Harper & Row.

Omodei, M.M., & McLennan, J. (1994). Studying complex decision-making in natural settings: Using a head-mounted video camera to study competitive orienteering. *Perceptual and Motor Skills, 79*, 1411–1425.

Orlick, T. (1986). *Psyching for sport: Mental training for athletes.* Champaign, IL: Human Kinetics.

Purcell, I., & Kerr, J.H. (1995, July). *Expertise and psychological reversals in sport: Solving the puzzle through golf*. Paper presented at the 7th International Conference on Reversal Theory, Melbourne, Australia.

Rimehaug, T., & Svebak, S. (1987). Psychogenic muscle tension: The significance of motivation and negative affect in perceptual-cognitive task performance. *International Journal of Psychophysiology, 5*, 97–106.

Roberts, G.C., & Treasure, D.C. (1992). Children in sport. *Sport Science Review, 1*(2), 46–64.

Schmidt, R.A. (1991). *Motor learning and performance: From principles to practice*. Champaign, IL: Human Kinetics.

Schultz, J., & Luthe, W. (1969). *Autogenic methods* (Vol.1). New York: McGraw-Hill.

Schutz, R.W. (1994). Methodological issues and measurement problems in sport psychology. In S. Serpa, J. Alves, & V. Pataco (Eds.), *International perspectives on sport and exercise psychology* (pp.35–55). Morgantown, WV: Fitness Information Technology Inc.

Svebak, S. (1984). Active and passive forearm flexor tension patterns in the continuous perceptual motor task paradigm: The significance of motivation. *International Journal of Psychophysiology, 2*, 167–176.

Svebak, S. (1985a). Serious-mindedness and the effect of self-induced respiratory changes upon parietal EEG. *Biofeedback and Self-Regulation, 10*, 49–62.

Svebak, S. (1986a). Cardiac and somatic activation in the continuous perceptual-motor task: The significance of threat and serious-mindedness. *International Journal of Psychophysiology, 3*, 155–162.

Svebak, S. (1986b). Patterns of cardio-somatic respiratory interaction in the continuous perceptual-motor task paradigm. In P. Grossman, K. Jansen, & D. Vaitl (Eds.), *Cardiorespiratory and cardiosomatic psychophysiology* (pp.219–230). New York: Plenum Press.

Svebak, S. (1990). Personality and sports participation. In G.P.H. Hermans & W.L. Mosterd (Eds.), *Sports, medicine and health* (pp.87–96) [Excerpta Medica International Congress Series.] Amsterdam: Elsevier.

Svebak, S., & Apter, M.J. (1987). Laughter: An empirical test of some reversal theory hypotheses. *Scandinavian Journal of Psychology, 28*, 189–198.

Svebak, S., & Apter, M.J. (Eds.) (1996). *Stress and health: A reversal theory perspective*. Washington, DC: Taylor & Francis.

Svebak, S., Braathen, E.T., Sejersted, O.M., Bowim, B., Fauske, S., & Laberg, J.C. (1990). Biopsy assessment of fast and slow twitch muscle fibres: Prediction of tonic EMG activation in perceptual motor task performance. *Psychophysiology, 27*, (suppl.), 568.

Svebak, S., Braathen, E.T., Sejersted, O.M., Bowim, B., Fauske, S., & Laberg, J.C. (1993). Electromyographic activation and proportion of fast versus slow twitch muscle fibers: A genetic disposition for psychogenic muscle tension? *International Journal of Psychophysiology, 15*, 43–49.

Svebak, S., Howard, R., & Rimehaug, T. (1987). P300 and the quality of performance in a forewarned 'Go-' 'Nogo' reaction time task: The significance of goal-directed lifestyle and impulsivity. *Personality and Individual Differences, 8*, 313–319.

Svebak, S., & Kerr, J.H. (1989). The role of impulsivity in preference for sports. *Personality and Individual Differences, 10*(1), 51–58.

Svebak, S., & Murgatroyd, S. (1985). Metamotivational dominance: A multimethod validation of reversal theory constructs. *Journal of Personality and Social Psychology, 48*, 107–116.

Svebak, S., Nordby, H., & Ohman, A. (1987). The personality of the cardiac responder: Interaction of seriousmindedness and Type A behavior. *Biological Psychology, 24*, 1–9.

Svebak, S., Storfjell, O., & Dalen, K. (1982). The effect of a threatening context upon motivation and task-induced physiological changes. *British Journal of Psychology, 73*, 505–512.

Thorpe, R. (1993). Putting theory into practice: A sport example. In M. Lee (Ed.), *Coaching children in sport*. London: E. & F.N. Spon.

Weinberg, R.S., & Gould, D. (1995). *Foundations of sport and exercise psychology*. Champaign, IL: Human Kinetics.

Weiss, M.R., & Chaumerton, N. (1992). Motivational orientations in sport. In T.S. Horn (Ed.), *Advances in sport psychology* (pp.61–99). Champaign IL: Human Kinetics.

APPENDIX A

Summary of studies investigating dominance in sport (Chapter 3)

Study	Population	Sport	Measures	Results
Kerr, 1987	Dutch: 37 professional 38 serious amateur 45 recreational 20 non-sport	– cycling/soccer – field hockey/table tennis/show jumping – range of sports	TDS	– professional sig. higher than other groups on PO, SM, and total TDS score
Kerr & van Lienden, 1987	Dutch: 38 Masters 37 professional* 38 serious amateur* (*from previous study)	– swimming – cycling/soccer – field hockey/table tennis/show jumping	TDS	– Masters sig. higher than serious amateur and recreational on PO, SM, and total TDS score – No sig. diffs. between Masters and professional
Sell, 1991	American: 13 professional (M) 19 professional (F) 15 amateur (M)	elite triathlon	TDS	– amateur (M) sig. higher on AA than professional (M)
Kerr & Cox, 1988	British: 13 skilled 13 average 14 novice	squash	TDS	– no sig. diffs. in subscale and total TDS scores between ability groups
Cox & Kerr, 1989	English: 10 skilled club 10 county 10 England Under 19s	squash	TDS	– no sig. diffs. between winners and losers from three squash tournaments

Study	Population	Sport	Measures	Results
Kerr, 1988	106 English, Welsh, Canadian, Australian players	high-level rugby	TDS	– no sig. diffs. between groups on subscale and subscale and total TDS scores
Svebak & Kerr, 1989	Australian:			
(1)	25 'endurance' 25 'explosive'	– high-level cross-country runners – high-level tennis/field hockey	TDS	– 'endurance' sig. higher on PO, AA and total
(2)	human movement students 24 'paratelic sports'	– e.g. baseball/cricket/touch football/surfing/windsurfing	TDS	– 'non-paratelic sports' sig. higher on PO, SM and total TDS score
	24 'non-paratelic sports' performers	– e.g. long-distance running/ rowing		
(3)	181 general students 'paratelic sports' performed/preferred 'non-paratelic sports' performed/preferred	– e.g. baseball/cricket/touch football/surfing/windsurfing – e.g. long-distance running/ rowing	TDS	– no sig. diffs. between groups but sig. gender diffs. found. Females preferred but did not participate in 'paratelic sports' — attributed to social norms
Vlaswinkel & Kerr, 1990	Dutch:			
(1)	22 professional 22 recreational	soccer	NDS	– no sig. diffs. between groups on NDS subscale or total score
(2)	22 team sport 38 individual sport	– professional soccer – high-level long-distance running	NDS	– team sig. higher on RN

Study	Population		Sport	Measures	Results
Braathen & Svebak, 1992	(1)	Norwegian: talented teenage performers explosive (M=50,F=31)	– e.g. sprinting/jumping/racquet sports	NDS	– M sig. higher than F on RN; – team sig. lower on RN than endurance and explosive;
		endurance (M=106, F=54)	– e.g.rowing/race walking/cross-country skiing		– explosive sig. higher than team on PN
		team (M=47, F=30)	– baseball/soccer/volleyball		
	(2)	high level of excellence (M=97, F=47) moderate level of excellence (M=130, F=77)	across all sports	NDS	– high level sig. higher on PN than moderate level

TDS Telic Dominance Scale   NDS Negativism Dominance Scale
PO   planning orientation   PN   proactive negativism
SM   serious-mindedness   RN   reactive negativism
AA   arousal avoidance

APPENDIX B

Summary of studies investigating dominance in risk sports (Chapter 4)

Study		Population	Sport	Measures	Results
Kerr & Svebak, 1989	(1)	Australian students: 27 risk sport preference 9 safe sport preference	– e.g. caving/canoeing/surfing/ motor sports – e.g. archery/bowling/golf/snooker	TDS	– risk preference sig. lower on AA; – SM and PO approached significance
	(2)	Summer: 14 risk sport performers 8 safe sport performers	– e.g. surfing/caving – e.g. walking/hiking/snooker	TDS	– risk performers sig. lower on AA than safe performers
		Winter: 11 risk sport performers 10 safe sport performers	– e.g. downhill skiing – e.g. walking/hiking/snooker	TDS	– risk performers sig. lower on AA, SM than safe performers
Kerr, 1991	(1)	Australian: 32 skilled 31 skilled 34 skilled	surfing sailboarding weight training	TDS	– surfers and sailboarders sig. lower on AA, SM, PO subscales and total TDS scores than weight trainers
	(2)	Dutch: 21 elite level 18 elite level 17 elite level	parachuting motorcycle racing marathon running	TDS	– parachutists and motorcycle racers sig. lower than marathon runners on AA and total TDS scores
	(3)	British: 25 proficient solo pilots 25 control	gliding non-sport	TDS	– glider pilots sig. lower on AA

196

Study	Population	Sport	Measures	Results
Chirivella & Martinez, 1994	Spanish: 30 low risk 53 intermediate risk 21 high risk	tennis karate parasailing	TDS NDS	– TDS: parasailors sig. lower on AA than karate and tennis and sig. higher on SM than tennis. Gender diffs. found, females least active in tennis – NDS: tennis sig. higher on RN and total NDS score than parasailors and karate
Vlaswinkel & Kerr, 1990 (1)	Dutch students: 10 risk sport performers 27 safe sport performers	– risk e.g. caving/canoeing/ surfing/motor sports – safe e.g. archery/bowling/golf/ snooker	NDS	– risk performers sig. higher on RN than safe performers
(2)	Dutch: 38 high-risk sport performers 25 less risky sport performers 38 safe-sport performers	– elite motorcycle racing – Olympic sailing – high-level long-distance runners	NDS	– no sig. diffs. on NDS subscale or total scores
Summers & Stewart, 1993	Australian: 25 high-risk paratelic sport 25 safe telic sport 25 safe paratelic sport 25 safe paratelic sport non-sport group	– skydivers – rowers – semi-professional baseballers – university baseballers	TDS	– skydivers sig. lower on AA than other groups

TDS	Telic Dominance Scale	NDS	Negativism Dominance Scale
PO	planning orientation	PN	proactive negativism
SM	serious-mindedness	RN	reactive negativism
AA	arousal avoidance		

APPENDIX C

Summary of studies investigating winning and losing in sports (Chapter 5)

Study	Sports & Population	Measures	Successful	Less Successful
Kerr & Van Schaik, 1995	Dutch: 17 top-level rugby players over four games (two won, two lost)	TSM SACL	– TSM: after winning, sig. less serious and more spontaneous – SACL: arousal sig. higher, stress sig. lower than after losing	
Kerr & Pos, 1994	Dutch: elite and sub/elite gymnasts, 7 A-level, 7 B-level at training and competition	TSM SACL	(A-level) – no sig. diffs. in felt and preferred arousal, arousal discrepancy and effort training and competition (TSM) – pre-competition sig. lower felt arousal than B-level (TSM) – sig. lower scores on serious pre- and post-training and planning post-training and planning post-training and B-level (TSM) – stress only sig. higher pre-competition (SACL)	(B-level) – sig. higher effort between competition and training (TSM) – pre-competition arousal discrepancy sig. higher and more negative than A-level (TSM) – post-training sig. higher on arousal discrepancy than A-level (TSM) – stress sig. higher pre- and post-competition than pre- and post-training (SACL)
Kerr & Cox, 1989, 1990	British squash players: 40 males divided into skilled, average and novice groups for performing squash tasks	TSM SACL TDS	(Skilled) high levels of arousal (TSM/SACL) accompanied by low levels of stress (SACL) and arousal discrepancy (TSM) pre–post task TSM: increases in planning (sig.) and serious (approaching sig.) were obtained for all groups pre–post task TDS: no sig. diffs. between groups on telic dominance	(Average/Novice) high levels of arousal (TSM/SACL) accompanied by high levels of stress (SACL) and arousal discrepancy (TSM) pre–post task

Study	Sports & Population	Measures	Successful	Less Successful
Cox & Kerr, 1989, 1990	English squash players: 30 males playing in three different simulated squash tournaments (four games) for club, county, and	TSM SACL TDS	(Winners) – arousal (SACL) sig. higher than losers' games – stress (SACL) decreased sig. across games – majority of winners in telic state (TSM)	(Losers) – arousal (SACL) changed sig. across games – stress (SACL), arousal discrepancy (TSM) decreased sig. and serious scores (TSM) increased sig. after game 2 – majority of loser sin telic state until game 2, then more balanced telic–paratelic (TSM)
			TDS: no sig. diffs. between groups on TDS scores	
Males & Kerr, 1996	English world-class canoeists: 9 canoeists monitored over a season's events	TESI TSM items 3 and 4	– generally, no sig. changes in pleasant, unpleasant emotions, stress, effort (TESI) and felt arousal (TSM) across events	– sig. greater arousal discrepancy (TSM) pre worst performance for one canoeist only
			comparison of two canoeists' (F&G) best and worst performances: only sig. difference was for G on anger (TESI) between best and worst – for G: arousal sig. lower, arousal discrepancy sig. higher before worst than before best (TSM) – for F: pre worst, felt and preferred arousal higher than season's average (TSM)	

Study	Sports & Population	Measures	Successful	Less Successful
Wilson & Phillips, 1995	Australian squash players: 60 males playing in tournament for ABC&D grades	– TSM – MC – aspects of play scales – TDS – NDS	(Winners) – total TSM scores decreased sig. from pre- and during game to post-game (TSM) – in close games, sig. less telic than losers (TSM) – experienced sig. more pleasant than unpleasant somatic and transactional, more conformist than negativistic, more high than low felt transactional outcome and more mastery than sympathy emotions (MC)	(Losers) – sig. higher scores on tension stress (arousal discrepancy) (TSM), more unpleasantness and dissatisfaction than winners – experienced sig. more negativistic than conformist, more telic than paratelic, mastery than sympathy and unpleasant than pleasant transactional emotions (MC) – pre-game, sig. more conformist and pleasant transactional emotions, which changed to more negativistic and unpleasant transactional emotions post-game (MC) – sig. more dissatisfied than winners in not-close games – sig. higher unpleasantness when lost easily to player of same strength – correlation between NDS score and unpleasantness – both winners and losers sig. more dissatisfied after playing stronger opponent than same strength or weaker – no sig. diffs. between groups on TDS scores

TDS	Telic Dominance Scale	NDS	Negativism Dominance Scale	MC	Mood Checklist
PO	planning orientation	PN	proactive negativism	SACL	Stress-Arousal Checklist
SM	serious-mindedness	RN	reactive negativism	TESI	Tension & Effort Stress Inventory
AA	arousal avoidance			TSM	Telic State Measure

APPENDIX D

TELIC DOMINANCE SCALE (TDS)

Murgatroyd, S., Rushton, C., Apter, M.J., & Ray, C. (1978)

The *Telic Dominance Scale (TDS)* is a 42-item personality scale designed for use with adult subjects. It consists of three 14-item subscales which relate to different aspects of telic dominance, although the seriousmindedness subscale is taken as the defining subscale. The subscales are defined as follows:

1. *Seriousmindedness (SM).* This measures the frequency with which a subject sees himself or herself to be engaged in activities whose primary purpose is to achieve a goal beyond these activities, rather than activities which are indulged in for their own sake. In other words, it is about how frequently the subject is in a state of mind that is oriented to what he or she sees as serious ends, rather than a state of mind oriented towards the more playful enjoyment of ongoing sensations, skills, etc.

2. *Planning orientation (PO).* This measures the frequency with which a subject sees himself or herself to be involved in activities that require planning ahead and an orientation to the future, rather than activities that are more unplanned, spontaneous, or oriented to the "here-and-now".

3. *Arousal avoidance (AA).* This measures the frequency with which a subject sees himself or herself to be engaged in activities that might be expected to reduce arousal, rather than activities that might be expected to increase it.

The scale is scored in a telic direction, a telic choice on each item counting 1, and a "not sure" response counting 1/2. The scale therefore yields three separate subscale scores (the maximum score on each being 14) and an overall telic dominance score (the maximum score being 42). Here is the complete scale, including instructions to subjects:

Instructions:

Here are some alternative choices. If you have an open choice, which of the following alternatives would you usually prefer. Please complete *all* the items by putting a cross in the circle corresponding to your choice, making *one* choice for each numbered item. Only if you are not able to make a choice should you put a cross in the circle corresponding to 'Not sure'. Try to answer all of the items by putting a cross in one of the circles for each item, using the 'Not sure' choice as little as you can. Work quickly and do not spend too much time on any one item: it is your first reaction we want.

This is not a test of intelligence or ability and there are no right or wrong answers.

1. Compile a short dictionary for
      financial reward
   Write a short story for fun
   Not sure

2. Going to evening class to improve
      your qualifications
   Going to evening class for fun
   Not sure

3. Leisure activities which are just
      exciting
   Leisure activities which have a
      purpose
   Not sure

4. Improving a sporting skill by
      playing a game
   Improving it through systematic
      practice
   Not sure

5. Spending one's life in many
      different places
   Spending most of one's life in one
      place
   Not sure

6. Work that earns promotion
   Work that you enjoy doing
   Not sure

7. Planning your leisure
   Doing things on the spur of the
      moment
   Not sure

8. Going to formal evening meetings
   Watching television for
      entertainment
   Not sure

9. Having your tasks set for you
   Choosing your own activities
   Not sure

10. Investing money in a long term
       insurance/pension scheme
    Buying an expensive car
    Not sure

11. Staying in one job
    Having many changes of job
    Not sure

12. Seldom doing things "for kicks"
    Often doing things "for kicks"
    Not sure

13. Going to a party
    Going to a meeting
    Not sure

14. Leisure activities
    Work activities
    Not sure

15. Taking holidays in many different places
    Taking holidays always in the same place
    Not sure
16. Going away on holiday for two weeks
    Given two weeks of free time, finishing a needed improvement at home
    Not sure
17. Taking life seriously
    Treating life lightheartedly
    Not sure
18. Frequently trying strange foods
    Always eating familiar foods
    Not sure
19. Recounting an incident accurately
    Exaggerating for effect
    Not sure
20. Spending £100 having an enjoyable weekend
    Spending £100 on repaying a loan
    Not sure
21. Having continuity in the place where you live
    Having frequent moves of house
    Not sure
22. Going to an art gallery to enjoy the exhibits
    To learn about the exhibits
    Not sure
23. Watching a game
    Refereeing a game
    Not sure
24. Eating special things because you enjoy them
    Eating special things because they are good for your health
    Not sure
25. Fixing long-term life ambitions
    Living life as it comes
    Not sure
26. Always trying to finish your work before you enjoy yourself
    Frequently going out for enjoyment before all your work is finished
    Not sure

27. Not needing to explain your behaviour
    Having purposes for your behaviour
    Not sure
28. Climbing a mountain to try to save someone
    Climbing a mountain for pleasure
    Not sure
29. Happy to waste time
    Always having to be busy
    Not sure
30. Taking risks
    Going through life safely
    Not sure
31. Watching a crucial match between two ordinary sides
    Watching an exhibition game with star performers
    Not sure
32. Playing a game
    Organising a game
    Not sure
33. Glancing at pictures in a book
    Reading a biography
    Not sure
34. Winning a game easily
    Playing a game with the scores very close
    Not sure
35. Steady routine in life
    Continual unexpectedness or surprise
    Not sure
36. Working in the garden
    Picking wild fruit
    Not sure
37. Reading for information
    Reading for fun
    Not sure
38. Arguing for fun
    Arguing with others seriously to change their opinions
    Not sure
39. Winning a game
    Playing the game for fun
    Not sure
40. Travelling a great deal in one's job
    Working in one office or workshop
    Not sure

41. Planning ahead
     Taking each day as it comes
     Not sure

42. Planning a holiday
     Being on holiday
     Not sure

The specific items that relate to each subscale, and the telic option for each item (where "a" is the first option as listed and "b" the second option on each item) are as follows:

Seriousmindedness: 13 (b)   17 (a)   24 (b)   31 (a)   38 (b)
                        14 (b)   22 (b)   28 (a)   33 (b)   39 (a)
                        16 (b)   23 (b)   29 (b)   37 (a)

Planning orientation: 1 (a)   6 (a)   10 (a)   26 (a)   41 (a)
                         2 (a)   7 (a)   20 (b)   27 (b)   42 (a)
                         4 (b)   8 (a)   25 (a)   32 (b)

Arousal avoidance: 3 (b)   11 (a)   18 (b)   30 (b)   36 (a)
                         5 (b)   12 (a)   19 (a)   34 (a)   40 (b)
                         9 (a)   15 (b)   21 (a)   35 (a)

Murgatroyd, Rushton, Apter, and Ray (1978) give the alpha coefficients (Cronbach, 1951; N=119) for each subscale as SM=.691, PO=.655, AA=0.734, Total=.837. In addition, test–retest reliability scores of the TDS over different periods of elapsed time are shown in Table 1. All of the test–retest reliabilities were found to be significant at the $P<.01$ level.

Other TDS reliability and validity information is provided in Murgatroyd et al. (1978) and Apter (1989, pp. 55–60). See also Tacon and Abner (1993) for norms and other data on the TDS. A second scale for measuring telic dominance, known as the Paratelic Dominance Scale (PDS), has been developed more recently in the US (Cook & Gerkovich, 1990).

TABLE 1
Test-retest reliability scores of TDS subscales

Group	N	Time Between	Serious-mindedness	Planning Orientation	Arousal Avoidance
Art & Psychology Student & Staff	32	6 hours	.952	.803	.872
Technical College Students	48	6 weeks	.605	.773	.790
Undergraduate Psychology Students	32	6 months	.634	.702	.711
Housewives	15	12 months	.632	.677	.698

REFERENCES

Apter, M.J. (1989). *Reversal theory: Motivation, emotion and personality.* London: Routledge.

Cook, M.R., & Gerkovich, M.M. (1990). Reliability and validity of the Paratelic Dominance Scale. In J.H. Kerr, S. Murgatroyd, & M.J. Apter (Eds.), *Advances in reversal theory* (pp.177–188). Amsterdam: Swets & Zeitlinger.

Cronbach, L.T. (1951). Coefficient alpha and the internal structure of tests. *Psychometrica, 16,* 197–334.

Murgatroyd, S., Rushton, C., Apter, M.J., & Ray, C. (1978). The development of the Telic Dominance Scale. *Journal of Personality Assessment, 42,* 519–528.

Tacon, P., & Abner, B. (1993). Normative and other data for the Telic Dominance and Negativism Dominance Scales. In J.H. Kerr, S. Murgatroyd, & M.J. Apter, (Eds.), *Advances in reversal theory* (pp.165–175). Amsterdam: Swets & Zeitlinger.

APPENDIX E

NEGATIVISM DOMINANCE SCALE (NDS)

McDermott, M.R., & Apter, M.J. (1988)

The *Negativism Dominance Scale (NDS)* is an 18-item personality scale designed for use with adolescent and adult subjects. (On the form that is given to subjects, it is labelled the *Social Reactivity Scale* in order to make the objectives of the test less obvious.) It consists of two 7-item subscales which relate to different types of negativism dominance, and four "filler" items. The two subscales are defined as follows:

    1. *Proactive negativism.* This measures the frequency with which a subject indulges in negativistic or rebellious behaviour in order to provoke situations that are exciting and fun. It is labelled "proactive" because it is about how frequently the subject sets out to cause gratuitous trouble.
    2. *Reactive negativism.* This measures the frequency with which a subject reacts to disappointments and frustrations with feelings of resentment, and/or with vindictive or vengeful behaviour. It is labelled "reactive" because it is about the way in which the subject reacts to certain kinds of situations.

The scale is scored in a negativistic direction, a negativistic choice on each item counting 2, and a "not sure" response counting 1. For scoring purposes, the filler items (included in order to reduce the chance of response sets occurring) are disregarded. The scale therefore yields two separate subscale scores (the maximum score on each being 14) and an overall negativism dominance score (the maximum score being 28). Here is the complete scale, including instructions to subjects:

Instructions:

This is a measure of the way in which you react in certain social situations. For each of the following eighteen items three responses are given. For each item choose the response which is most true of you. These responses do not represent all possible ones but please accept this and make your choice from those which happen to be given. Try to use the 'not sure' response as little as possible. Do not think too long about your answer. It is your first reaction that is important. Put a 'X' in the circle next to the response which is most true of you.

This is not a test of intelligence or ability and there are no right or wrong answers.

Thank you for your help.

1. When you are told that you are breaking a rule (for example, 'No Smoking'), is your first reaction to
   - (a) stop breaking the rule any further
   - or, (b) go ahead and still break the rule?
   - (c) not sure

2. You have been treated badly by someone. Do you
   - (a) try to get back at the person
   - or, (b) hope that things will improve?
   - (c) not sure

3. In trying to complete an exercise routine, you go through some pain. Do you
   - (a) continue
   - or, (b) give up?
   - (c) not sure

4. "I enjoy the thrill I get from being difficult and awkward." Do you
   - (a) agree
   - or, (b) disagree?
   - (c) not sure

5. If people are unkind to you, do you feel you should be
   - (a) unkind back
   - or, (b) understanding?
   - (c) not sure

6. Do you find it exciting to do something "shocking"?
   - (a) yes, often
   - or, (b) no, hardly ever
   - (c) not sure

7. If you are asked particularly NOT to do something, do you feel an urge to do it?
   - (a) no, hardly ever
   - or, (b) yes, often
   - (c) not sure

8. You are in a group of people who are drinking, but you do not like alcohol and are offered a drink. Would you
   - (a) refuse the drink
   - or, (b) accept the drink?
   - (c) not sure

9. Do you tease people unnecessarily just so as to have some fun at their expense?
   - (a) yes, often
   - or, (b) no, hardly ever
   - (c) not sure

10. A parking attendant tells you that you cannot park where you have just put the car. Would you
    - (a) apologise and move it
    - or, (b) argue with the attendant?
    - (c) not sure

11. How often do you do something you shouldn't just to get some excitement?
    (a) not often at all
    or, (b) often
    (c) not sure

12. You are asked to take part in an activity which secretly you dislike. Would you
    (a) say you have something else planned
    or, (b) try hard to avoid an argument?
    (c) not sure

13. If you get yelled at by someone in authority, would you
    (a) get angry and argue back
    or, (b) try hard to avoid an argument
    (c) not sure

14. If a person your age was mean to you, would you
    (a) try to forget it
    or, (b) try to get revenge?
    (c) not sure

15. Can you think of anything you oppose strongly?
    (a) no
    or, (b) yes
    (c) not sure

16. A charity will not accept you as a volunteer. Is your first reaction to
    (a) thank them for considering you
    or, (b) tell them to "go to hell"?
    (c) not sure

17. How often do others say that you are a difficult person?
    (a) rarely
    or, (b) often
    (c) not sure

18. If you ask a person at a party to dance with you who says 'no' without offering any explanation, would you
    (a) get annoyed
    or, (b) accept it?
    (c) not sure

The items in each subscale and the negativistic option for each item are as follows:

Proactive negativism:	1 (b)	4 (a)	6 (a)	7 (b)
	9 (a)	11 (b)	17 (b)	
Reactive negativism:	2 (a)	5 (a)	10 (b)	13 (a)
	14 (b)	16 (b)	18 (a)	

McDermott (1988a) pointed out that the current version of the NDS containing 18 items was derived from ratings and factor analysis of an original pool of 137 items. Following item ratings and analysis on two US student samples, a 30-item NDS was administered to a US sample (N=130) and a British sample (N=136) of high-school students (aged 16–17). Independent factor analysis of the US and British data revealed a two-factor solution for each. The similarity of factor loadings from the separate factor analyses allowed the two data sets to be combined and a further factor analysis was carried out. The final 18-item NDS consisted of the seven items that loaded highest on each of the two factors and four filler items. These two factors were labelled 'proactive' and 'reactive' negativism.

Information on validity testing can be found in McDermott (1988b) and Apter (1989, pp.104–109). Normative and other data for the NDS can be found in Tacon and Abner (1993). Further details regarding the psychometric development, properties and use of the NDS ('rebelliousness' questionnaire) should be addressed to Dr. Mark McDermott, Lecturer and researcher in psychology, Department of Psychology, University of East London, Romford Road, Stratford, London E15 4LZ, UK (e-mail m.r.mcdermott@uel.ac.uk).

REFERENCES

Apter, M.J. (1989). *Reversal theory: Motivation, emotion and personality*. London: Routledge.

McDermott, M.R. (1988a). Measuring rebelliousness: The development of the Negativism Dominance Scale. In M.J. Apter, J.H. Kerr, & M. P. Cowles (Eds.), *Progress in reversal theory* (pp.297-312). [Advances in psychology series, 51.] Amsterdam: North-Holland/Elsevier.

McDermott, M.R. (1988b). Recognising rebelliousness: The ecological validity of the Negativism Dominance Scale. In M.J. Apter, J.H. Kerr, & M.P. Cowles (Eds.), *Progress in reversal theory* (pp.313-325). [Advances in psychology series, 51.] Amsterdam: North-Holland/Elsevier.

McDermott, M R., & Apter, M.J. (1988) The Negativism Dominance Scale. In M.J. Apter, J.H. Kerr, & M.P. Cowles (Eds.), *Progress in reversal theory* (pp.373-376). [Advances in psychology series, 51.] Amsterdam: North-Holland/Elsevier.

Tacon, P., & Abner, B. (1993). Normative and other data for the Telic Dominance and Negativism Dominance Scales. In J.H. Kerr, S. Murgatroyd, & M.J. Apter (Eds.), *Advances in reversal theory* (pp.165–175). Amsterdam: Swets & Zeitlinger.

APPENDIX F

TELIC STATE MEASURE

(e.g. Svebak, S., & Murgatroyd, S., 1985)

The TSM consists of five items, each with a 6-point rating scale with defining adjectives at each end. The items include (1) serious–playful; (2) preferred planned–preferred spontaneous; (3) low felt arousal–high felt arousal; (4) preferred low arousal–preferred high arousal; (5) low effort–high effort. Item (5) the investment of effort in a task (low effort–high effort), is only completed after a task and was a later addition to earlier versions of the TSM. A sixth item, arousal discrepancy, is computed by subtracting the score for item 3 (felt arousal) from the score for item 4 (preferred arousal). Note that on items (1) and (2) low scores (1–3) are taken to indicate the telic state and high scores (4–6) the paratelic state. Subjects should be made familiar with the measure prior to its use and should be given instructions as to how to respond to the items (e.g. reporting how they feel at the time of completion). Two useful examples of how the measure has been used in research are Svebak and Murgatroyd (1985) or Svebak, Storfjell, and Dalen, (1982) (both non-sport) and Kerr and Vlaswinkel, (1993; sport/exercise).

REFERENCES

Kerr, J.H. & Vlaswinkel, L. (1993). Self-reported mood and running under natural conditions. *Work & Stress, 7*(2) 161–178.

Svebak, S., & Murgatroyd, S. (1985). Metamotivational dominance: A multimethod validation of reversal theory constructs. *Journal of Personality and Social Psychology, 48*(1), 107–116.

Svebak, S., Storfjell, O., & Dalen, K. (1982). The effect of a threatening context upon motivation and task-induced physiological arousal. *British Journal of Psychology, 73*, 505–512.

Name: *Gender: M/F*   *Age:*

INSTRUCTIONS:

Please rate your feelings at this moment in terms of the four following rating scales. Do this by circling a number.

1. Estimate here how playful or serious you feel.

2. Estimate here how far you would prefer to plan ahead or to be spontaneous.

3. Estimate here how aroused ("worked up") you actually feel.

4. Estimate here the level of arousal how "worked up" you would like to feel.

5. Estimate here how much effort you invested in the task.

1. By *"serious"* here is meant the feeling that you are pursuing (or at least thinking about) some essential goal. For example, the goal may be to achieve something in the future which you believe to be important, or it may be to overcome some real danger or threat in the present.
   By *"playful"* is meant the feeling that you are doing what you are doing for its own sake. In this case your activity is felt to be enjoyable in itself and not to require any further justification. Any goal which there might be is really an excuse for the behaviour.
2. By *"planning ahead"* is meant trying to organise your behaviour in such a way that it leads effectively to some goal in the (perhaps distant) future, and being aware of the future consequences of your present actions.
   By *"spontaneous"* is meant that your actions are undertaken on impulse, with little regard for future consequences. Note that this scale asks for your *preference* at the time in question, rather than your ability to plan or be spontaneous.
3. By *"arousal"* here is meant how "worked up" you feel. You might experience high arousal in one of a variety of ways, for example as excitement or anxiety or anger. Low arousal might also be experienced by you in one of a number of different ways, for example as relaxation or boredom or calmness.
4. *"Arousal"* has the same meaning for this scale as for the previous one, but now the emphasis is on the level of arousal you *want* rather than the level of arousal which you are actually experiencing.

APPENDIX G

TENSION AND EFFORT STRESS INVENTORY (TESI)—STATE VERSION

Svebak, S. (1993)

The state version of the Tension and Effort Stress Inventory (TESI) instrument has 20 individual response items separated into three sections. Section A (two items) requires subjects to estimate "the degree of pressure, stress, challenge or demand" that they are exposed to with respect to (1) situational factors and (2) their own bodies (i.e. internal factors). Section B (two items) is concerned with the degree of effort invested by respondents in trying to cope with the pressure, etc. from (1) external factors and (2) internal factors associated with their own bodies. The third section contains a list of 16 different emotions. Subjects respond by circling the appropriate figure on a scale of 1–7, ranging from 'not at all' to 'very much', which is placed alongside each item. Each individual emotion item can be considered in its own right, but groupings of emotions based on reversal theory concepts can be computed. These include pleasant and unpleasant somatic emotions (four items each; pleasant–*relaxation, excitement, placidity, provocativeness*; unpleasant–*anxiety, anger, boredom, sullenness*) and pleasant and unpleasant transactional emotions (four items each; pleasant–*pride, gratitude, modesty, virtue*; unpleasant–*humiliation, resentment, shame, guilt*). Also, combinations of somatic and transactional emotion groupings allow overall scores for total pleasant emotions (eight items; *relaxation, excitement, placidity, provocativeness, pride, gratitude, modesty, virtue*) and total unpleasant emotions (eight items; *anxiety, anger, boredom, sullenness, humiliation, resentment, shame, guilt*) to be computed. In addition to the state version of the TESI, a 30-day version has been developed (see Svebak, 1993). The TESI has been used by Svebak with his co-workers in a

212

study of psychological factors in the aetiology of back pain (Svebak et al., 1991). Kerr and Svebak (1994) and Males and Kerr (1996) have also used the state version of the TESI in sport research. Although reversal theory suggests that pleasant and unpleasant emotions share only pleasant or unpleasant hedonic tone rather than draw on an underlying stable trait, the internal reliability of these composite scores were calculated in the Males and Kerr (1996) study. Coefficient alpha scores of .88 were found for total pleasant emotion and .75 for total unpleasant emotion (see Cronbach, 1951).

REFERENCES

Cronbach, L.T. (1951). Coefficient alpha and the internal structure of tests. *Psychometrica, 16,* 197–334.

Kerr, J.H., & Svebak, S. (1994). The acute effects of participation in sports on mood. *Personality and Individual Differences, 16(1),* 159–166.

Males, J.R., & Kerr, J.H. (1996). Stress, emotion and performance in elite slalom canoeists. *The Sport Psychologist, 10(1),* 17–37.

Svebak, S. (1993). The development of the Tension and Effort Stress Inventory (TESI). In J.H. Kerr, S. Murgatroyd, & M.J. Apter, (Eds.), *Advances in reversal theory* (pp.189–204). Amsterdam: Swets & Zeitlinger.

Svebak, S., Ursin, H., Endresen, I., Hjelmen, A.M., & Apter, M.J. (1991). Psychological factors in the aetiology of back pain. *Psychology and Health, 5,* 307–314.

NOTE

A reversal theory archive containing almost all reversal theory publications and other material is maintained by Mary Gerkovich in the US. Those having difficulty finding references, etc. from other sources should contact her at the Midwest Research Institute, 425 Volker Blvd., Kansas City, Missouri 64110. Fax (int) + 1 816 753 7380, e-mail: mgerkovich@mriresearch.org

Subject code: *Sex*   *Age*

Please give your answers by circling the appropriate figures.

A. Estimate the degree of *pressure*, stress, challenge, or demand that you are exposed to in the current situation as due to:

	No pressure						Very much
External factors:	1 –	2 –	3 –	4 –	5 –	6 –	7
your own body:	1 –	2 –	3 –	4 –	5 –	6 –	7

B. Estimate the degree of effort that you put up in the current situation to cope with pressure etc.   from:

	No effort						Very much
External factors:	1 –	2 –	3 –	4 –	5 –	6 –	7
your own body:	1 –	2 –	3 –	4 –	5 –	6 –	7

C. Estimate here the degree to which you experience the following *moods or emotions* in the current situation:

	Not at all						Very much
Relaxation:	1 –	2 –	3 –	4 –	5 –	6 –	7
Anxiety:	1 –	2 –	3 –	4 –	5 –	6 –	7
Excitement:	1 –	2 –	3 –	4 –	5 –	6 –	7
Boredom:	1 –	2 –	3 –	4 –	5 –	6 –	7
Placidity:	1 –	2 –	3 –	4 –	5 –	6 –	7
Anger:	1 –	2 –	3 –	4 –	5 –	6 –	7
Provocativeness:	1 –	2 –	3 –	4 –	5 –	6 –	7
Sullenness:	1 –	2 –	3 –	4 –	5 –	6 –	7
Pride:	1 –	2 –	3 –	4 –	5 –	6 –	7
Humiliation:	1 –	2 –	3 –	4 –	5 –	6 –	7
Modesty:	1 –	2 –	3 –	4 –	5 –	6 –	7
Shame:	1 –	2 –	3 –	4 –	5 –	6 –	7
Gratitude:	1 –	2 –	3 –	4 –	5 –	6 –	7
Resentment:	1 –	2 –	3 –	4 –	5 –	6 –	7
Virtue:	1 –	2 –	3 –	4 –	5 –	6 –	7
Guilt:	1 –	2 –	3 –	4 –	5 –	6 –	7

Thankyou!

Designed 1987 by Sven Svebak, School of Medicine, Norwegian University of Science Technology, Trondheim N–7006, Norway.

214

Author Index

215

Subject Index